THE ANNUAL OF
THE AMERICAN SCHOOLS OF ORIENTAL RESEARCH

Volume 64

Series Editor
Joseph A. Greene

REFLECTIONS OF EMPIRE:

ARCHAEOLOGICAL AND ETHNOGRAPHIC STUDIES ON THE POTTERY OF THE OTTOMAN LEVANT

edited by
Bethany J. Walker

American Schools of Oriental Research • Boston, MA

ANNUAL OF THE AMERICAN SCHOOLS OF ORIENTAL RESEARCH
VOLUME 64

ISBN: 978-0-89757-081-7

Library of Congress Cataloging-in-Publication Data

Reflections of empire : archaeological and ethnographic studies on the pottery of the Ottoman Levant / edited by Bethany J. Walker.
      p. cm. -- (The annual of the American Schools of Oriental Research ; v. 64)
   Includes bibliographical references and index.
   ISBN 978-0-89757-081-7 (alk. paper)
   1. Middle East--Antiquities. 2. Turkey--Antiquities. 3. Pottery, Ottoman--Middle East--History. 4. Turkey--History--Ottoman Empire, 1288-1918. 5. Imperialism--Social aspects--Middle East--History. 6. Imperialism--Social aspects--Turkey--History. 7. Excavations (Archaeology)--Middle East. 8. Ethnoarchaeology--Middle East. 9. Archaeology and history--Middle East. I. Walker, Bethany J.
   DS56.R44 2009
   956'.015--dc22

                           2009036891

Printed in the United States of America on acid-free paper

Contents

Illustrations

Preface

The world-wide popularization of Ottoman culture has its roots in the picturesque descriptions of the peoples and places of the Ottoman world that filled Orientalist travelers' accounts of the 19th century. The fascination with such visual images has continued into modern times. The Ottoman era has been recreated in the graphic arts, inspired by Ottoman art displayed in exhibits like "The Age of Suleyman the Magnificent" (Atil 1987) and in literary and academic circles, which frequently evoke its material culture.

A fond remembrance of Ottoman culture is a new motif in modern Turkish literature, best illustrated by the works of Elif Shafak and the Nobel Prize-winning novelist Orhan Pamuk, who are circumventing the Atatürk cultural revolution to re-establish the connections between Ottoman and contemporary Turkish cultures. In *Istanbul: Memories and the City,* Pamuk shows that this theme is not just fiction but also a personal *leitmotif.* He describes the passing of Ottoman heritage as the main catastrophe of his childhood: "The melancholy of this dying culture was all around us. … The effect on culture was reductive and stunting, leading families like mine, otherwise glad of republican progress, to furnish their houses like museums" (Pamuk 2004: 29).

There is also a growing nostalgia, on many levels, for the internationalism and cross-border cohesiveness of Levantine Ottoman culture, especially in light of the ruptures and persistent volatile fissures that have resulted from the post-WW I carving-up of the Empire. While for some this may resonate on the religious level, a dream of a return of the Caliphate, for academics who began careers in the twilight of the Empire it is regret over the loss of easy mobility and interchange between intellectual centers arrayed between Cairo and Istanbul, and between Beirut and Baghdad.

Such a memory of Empire, of the borderless connectedness that embraced much of the eastern Mediterranean and Middle East, permeates modern academia. One need only cite in this regard the work of historians and geographers in regional universities, such as Kamal Abdulfattah (Birzeit University) and Muhammad Adnan al-Bakhit (University of Jordan), whose research on southern Syria pushed scholarly inquiry on the Ottoman era to new heights, challenging the image of the isolated "dark ages" that has hampered scholarship on Early Modern Bilad al-Sham. In recent years, historians of Ottoman Syria have broken the traditional mode of working in textual sources in isolation from other sources of data: Bethany Walker's integration of archival sources and archaeological field work exemplifies well such cross-disciplinary trends in Ottoman studies.

Archaeologists, on the other hand, have had to overcome the hurdle of their discipline's traditional Orientalist focus on the biblical and classical eras. By the mid-20th century, archaeologists were developing an appreciation for the Arabic-Islamic periods, largely through analysis of their ceramic remains. This interest gradually progressed from the discovery of pre-Islamic Arabs and the continuity of Byzantine and Umayyad cultures to the Ayyubid and Mamluk periods as the Arab cultures of the Crusades. A concern for understanding the immediate roots of modern Arabic culture in Bilad al-Sham has led to a focus on Ottoman archaeology as the means to understanding the material foundations for still-living traditions.

These advances notwithstanding, when the archaeology of the Ottoman Levant is compared to that of nearly all other historical eras in the region, a short three-letter word pretty well says it all, and that is the word "gap"! It is, indeed, quite shocking and even disturbing to have to admit that, where

Levantine archaeology is concerned, we have less to show and tell about the four centuries that span 1516 to 1918 CE than is the case with any comparable span since the beginning of the Early Bronze Age. How can this be? How is it that concerning the four centuries that are nearest to our own times, archaeology has had practically nothing to contribute, other than the most unhelpful notion of a "gap"?

The "gap" seems to be ubiquitous when it comes to the Ottoman centuries in the Levant. It is there in the stratigraphy of nearly all multi-millennial tell sites; it is there in the assemblages collected by surface surveys; it is there in specialized studies of various types of artifacts and bio-facts; and it is there in the journal articles, encyclopedia entries, and scholarly books dealing with the archaeology of the region. The archaeology of the Ottoman Levant, it would appear, is thus the archaeology of "gap".

The reasons for this sad state of affairs have just recently begun to come to light, and although it is not possible in this preface to be exhaustive in discussing these, a few are noteworthy in the context of introducing this important volume on Ottoman ceramics. Surely an important factor is the status of the Ottoman Empire in the eyes of Europeans as the demonized "other" – the evil empire, the "sick man of Europe." Thus, when the terms of reference for the newly established Department of Antiquities of Palestine were laid down during the British Mandate period, buildings and material objects dating to the Ottoman period were not included as "antiquities" to be studied and curated by the department. In other words, the official mandate of the Department of Antiquities explicitly excluded Ottoman archaeology from its scope of administration and research.

To this prejudicial European stance must be added the traditional antipathy of the Arab and Jewish inhabitants of the Levant toward their Ottoman past. In their eyes, the Ottomans and their local agents in the Levant were predatory masters whose sole concern was to collect taxes from anyone deemed capable of paying them. Their cultural heritage was, thus, not something worth preserving. Instead it was something to be forgotten!

A more subtle reason for the undeveloped state of Ottoman archaeology in the Levant is, no doubt, also the legacy of classical archaeology, which has for well over a century been biased in favor of the art, architecture, and crafts of the elite classes of antiquity, thus privileging the past of those who could afford to build great monuments, live in extravagant estates and palaces, and who had the leisure and the opportunity to learn to read and write. Such elites were, by and large, the carriers of the "great traditions" of the imperial realm. However, as Ottoman scholars now have begun to realize, theirs was only a very small part of the story, for throughout most of the Levant the footprints of powerful elites have been modest, at best, during most historical periods, and they have tended to be concentrated in urban centers.

By contrast, the much lighter footprints of the material culture of the common illiterate classes of the rural hinterlands and city slums – the carriers of the "little traditions" – have been less glamorous to track by archaeologists, as they are usually less impressive as finds to showcase in museums and lectures. Yet, it is these remains that scholars need to search for and study in order to understand what has sustained and nourished the vast majority of the inhabitants of the Levant throughout past millennia. This is especially so in the case of "gap" periods such at the Ottoman centuries when, for the most part, the attention of the imperial center was not focused primarily on this region. To uncover and learn about the "little traditions" that sustained the daily lives of the vast majority of the populations of past centuries, archaeologists have to rely less on texts and elite cultural remains and more on what has been preserved of daily life in pottery, animal bones, carbonized seeds, and many other ordinary everyday objects brought to light by archaeological study of rural sites and urban domestic neighborhoods. The present volume, focusing as it does on Ottoman ceramics, goes a long way toward remedying this situation.

However, it would be a mistake to assume that just because there was little imperial investment in the Levant throughout most of the Ottoman centuries, the region was a total economic and cultural backwater without any impressive buildings or towns. Thus, as has recently been documented by Israeli, Jordanian and Palestinian archaeologists and historians (including contributors to this volume), decentralized local market towns or "throne villages" headed by leading families, each with their own local strongman, could be found in the Levant throughout the entire Ottoman period. During the latter half of the period, the number of such villages rose steadily as economic conditions improved, the result, in part, of growing commerce with Europe. Such local leading families acquired sufficient economic and political power and fortunes to build large family mansions in their hometowns and fortified farmsteads, or *qasrs*, in the surrounding hinterlands. Into these homes they incorporated many distinctive elements from the elite building traditions of the Ottoman epicenters as a means to communicate an aura of power and prestige. Unfortunately, their existence has been a well-kept secret, at least until recently. As is suggested by several of the chapters in this volume, some of these leading families also possessed exquisite ceramic wares imported from elsewhere throughout the Ottoman world and beyond.

The vast majority of the population did not live in such relative luxury, however, but instead had to make do in smaller quarters, ranging from the typical barrel-vaulted Palestinian house to cave dwellings and, of course, tents. The town of Salt in Jordan, for example, included the large mansions of its leading families, a clustering of stone house around these mansions, and a scatter of cave residences among them. More typical of the rural hinterland during Ottoman times are Hisban and Yadoudeh, two sites which consisted of a fortified *qasr* or farmstead surrounded by rude stone dwellings and numerous residential caves. Black tents can also be seen in rows and clusters in photographs of these villages from the turn of the 19th century. In addition, there were countless seasonal cave villages and camping areas throughout the southern Levant which, to European eyes, were too primitive to be counted as villages, and their residents were judged too transient to be reckoned with as legitimate occupants of the land. The challenge such settlements present to ceramicists is that they produced and used comparatively very

little pottery. Yet, as we can see from case studies in Jordan, Syria, Gaza, and Iraq in this volume, even such relatively humble settlements were not without pottery.

To a large extent, what we have learned about the historical landscape of the Ottoman centuries is due to the keen observations and drawings of travelers to the region and biblical scholars interested in parallels that could illuminate biblical stories. Early photographs of villages and daily life also contribute to our picture, as they provide visual detail on agricultural and domestic customs and material culture. It is only very recently that archaeologists have deliberately focused on this period. Among the pioneers in this regard was the American archaeologist Albert Glock, who initiated ethnoarchaeological research on village life in Palestine during his years as director of the Albright Institute of Archaeological Research and, later, the Institute of Archaeology that he helped establish at Birzeit University. Despite Glock's untimely death in 1992, his colleagues and students at Birzeit have taken up where he left off, thanks in part to the Lower Jordan River Basin Program and the Global Moments in Levant Project – both of which are capacity-building initiatives funded by the Norwegian government in order to strengthen Palestinian and Norwegian scholarship focusing on Palestinian anthropology, archaeology, geography, and history at Birzeit University and at the University of Bergen in Norway. Although more modest in scope and funding, a similar partnership has also been pursued by Calvin College with faculty and students at Birzeit.

A further sign that the archaeology of the Ottoman period has come of age among Syro-Palestinian archaeologists is the organization of a new series of sessions at the Annual Meetings of the American Schools of Oriental Research devoted specifically to the presentation of papers dealing with the material culture and history of the Ottoman period. The initial organizers of these sessions were Uzi Baram and Lynda Carroll, who later went on to edit *A Historical Archaeology of the Ottoman Empire* (Baram and Carroll 2000). The current co-chairs are Bert deVries, Øystein S. LaBianca, and Bethany Walker. The themes for the sessions organized by this latter team have included tribal and super-tribal polities of Ottoman Syro-Palestine (2003), the role of local notables and throne villages in the decentralized socio-political conditions in southwest Bilad al-Sham during the 18th and 19th centuries (2004), Ottoman-period ceramics (2005), which spawned the idea for this present volume, textiles and embroidery in the Ottoman empire (2006), the Ottoman Empire as it shaped society and culture in the Levant (2007), and cities as links between the imperial center and the Syro-Palestinian countryside (2008).

The publication of this volume of papers surely is an important milestone in the nascent field of Levantine Ottoman archaeology because now, for the first time, archaeologists will have access to a single work devoted to the typology, distribution and production of Ottoman wares in the eastern Mediterranean. The volume, thus, provides a sort of culmination of efforts underway since the early 1970s to develop a comprehensive ceramic typology spanning the fourteen centuries from the beginning of the Caliphate to the end of the Ottoman period. Complementing the work that has already been undertaken by the contributors to this book and many others to classify Umayyad, Abbasid, and Ayyubid-Mamluk pottery, the current work fills a long troublesome gap, namely that of the Ottoman era. Not only does the book simply fill in this 400-year gap, it offers proposals for distinguishing Early, Middle and Late Ottoman ceramics. As co-organizers of the sessions that have produced this wonderful fruit, we feel well-rewarded by being able to write this preface and thank the editor for her efforts in compiling this monograph.

Bert DeVries (Calvin College)
Øystein S. LaBianca (Andrews University)

Chapter 1

Defining the Levant

by Bethany J. Walker

INTRODUCTION

It was the consensus that too many specialists of Ottoman ceramics were working in isolation from one another, and that too few archaeologists knew the work of these specialists, that led the chairs of the session on Material Culture in Ottoman Syro-Palestine at the Annual Meeting of the American Schools of Oriental Research to devote their 2005 panel to Ottoman pottery from archaeological contexts. The decision was made early on to include the work of scholars doing fieldwork in the cultural, political, and economic orbit of the larger Levant, defined loosely as the coastal regions of the eastern Mediterranean and Greater Syria. Cyprus and Jordan were included in the original panel, along with Israel and the Palestinian Authority.

Though rarely considered together in regional studies, these areas represent the political and geographic periphery of the Ottoman Empire and, as such, share a common heritage in their administrative structures, regional and international trade, and in some aspects of their material culture (fig. 1.1). They were late acquisitions – Mamluk Greater Syria being absorbed in 1516 and Cyprus lost by the Venetians in 1571 – with

the Ottoman state conquering them as a result of a shift in foreign policy, for a variety of economic and strategic reasons, to facilitate expansion into the eastern Mediterranean. Absorption into the Ottoman Empire simply strengthened what had been centuries of shared political and economic fortunes. Most recently these included Venetian monopolies on maritime trade. Even earlier, the regional dominance of the Crusader and Mamluk states, the cane sugar industry, and the rise and subsequent decline of Mediterranean trade as a whole swept these regions into a common current.

What became the Provinces (*eyalets*) of Damascus, Jerusalem, and Cyprus remained for three hundred years the political hinterland of the Ottoman Empire.[1] Their primary importance to the Ottoman state was strategic: Transjordan was a buffer zone against the Safavid state until the acquisition of Mesopotamia; the *hajj* route from Damascus to Mecca, moreover, ran through the Transjordanian interior; caravan routes connecting Anatolia, Persia, and the Syrian coast met in Aleppo; and Cypriot ports had long been the middlemen of international maritime trade in the eastern Mediterranean. An inconsistent investment by the Ottoman state in local infrastructure, and

particularly the road systems, exacerbated historical trends towards regionalism reflected in the industries of the period. Village markets and fairs, local production of agricultural and non-agricultural
goods, and intra-regional trade, as was generally
true for much of the Ottoman Empire, were by far
more important in the "greater Levant" than relations with Istanbul. The region was agriculturally
self-sufficient, and market towns established their
own credit system (the early modern equivalent
of banks) through local financiers and religious
endowments (*awqaf/evkaf*). The region as a whole
remained largely autonomous politically and ad-
ministratively, benefitting in many ways from the
millet system of local self-governance of minority
communities and was controlled by local elites
until the Tanzimat reforms of the mid-nineteenth
century, when the Sublime Porte attempted to
reclaim tax revenues, settle Bedouin, centralize administration of religious endowments, and pacify
local religious and ethnic minorities.

While isolated in many ways from the imperial
heartland, the provinces of the Ottomans' eastern
frontier were tied to one another by overlapping
economic and social networks and developed
along parallel lines from the 16th through the 19th
centuries.[2] This was, of course, a consequence of
the application of similar Ottoman administrative
practices across the region but also reflects comparable social and economic configurations and
shared political histories.[3] The populations of Syria,
in particular, rebounded over the course of the 16th
century with renewed, although temporary, invest-
ments in security and infrastructure by the imperial state and the gradual resettlement of villages.[4]
The cultural orientation of the region, as a whole,
towards Syria reflected the growing importance
of Aleppo and its port as centers of caravan and
maritime trade and as the third economic center of
the Empire (Inalçik and Quataert 2004: 479). Syria
and Cyprus continued to share a common fate over
the course of the 17th century. Frequent wars with
the Safavids weakened the Ottoman state, leading
to a delegation of imperial administrative authority to local elites, the largest tax farmers in the
region. In a state of affairs recently described by one
Ottoman historian as "economic disengagement",

intra-regional trade accounted for most economic
exchanges, as fewer revenues were sent to Istanbul
and trade with Europe was minimal (Inalçik and
Quataert 2004: 525). Population generally declined
in the countryside, with the relocation of peasants
to the hills and coasts.

This period of provincialism was transformed
in the 18th century to a fuller engagement with
the West, as the region was pulled, rather force-
fully, into the emerging world economy. European
goods flooded local markets; traditional handicrafts declined in quantity and quality. The period
witnessed the rise of Damascus as a center of
international trade, and segments of the southern
Syrian economy prospered. Inter-provincial trade
intensified with the regional exchange of silks and
foodstuffs. Coffee exported through Egyptian
ports, for example, transformed consumption and
entertaining throughout the region, and coffee
houses could be found in the most remote villages.[5]
Administrative reforms and the centralization of
the state under the Tanzimat, the boom in exports
from Damascus, Jerusalem, and Cyprus in the first
half of the century as well as subsequent decline
in the latter half, and the gradual economic and
political loss of control of the region to foreign
powers are characteristic of the 19th century in the
eastern Mediterranean.

Many of these factors – political distance from
the imperial center, the importance of intra-
regional trade, the cultural and economic central-
ity of Syria, and the gradual intrusion of Europe
into regional commerce and consumption – had
important consequences for the development of
Levantine material culture in the Ottoman period.
Analysis of local ceramics can identify patterns of
production, trade, consumption, imitation, and
revival that reflect the historical trends described
above. The following work aims at describing and
accounting for changes in the ceramic culture of
the Ottoman Levant and its immediate hinterland
in light of such socio-political-economic developments. The goals of this book are two-fold: 1.) to
create a typology and chronology of Ottoman
wares for some regions of the Levant, and 2.) to
contribute to a growing body of scholarship on
the social and economic history of the Ottoman

provinces, using ceramic analysis. The authors of the articles in this volume have aimed at abstraction for theory-building, while maintaining rigor in technical analysis, in an effort to begin to define "the Levant" in ceramic terms for the Ottoman period. We consider this a first step towards this goal and look to our colleagues working in Syria and Lebanon to build on our efforts.

Defining the Levant ceramically

While Greater Syria and Cyprus in many ways share a common administrative and political heritage after the 16th century, there are differences in their cultural orientations, which are starkly illustrated by local ceramic production. Outside of commonly traded wares (such as coffee cups and tobacco pipes, or *chibouks*, that dominate the scholarly literature), it is regionalism, or more accurately, a local particularism that defines, in ceramic terms, the Levant and its neighbors. For this reason, there has been a tendency by archaeologists and ceramicists to focus on single-site assemblages, obliterating parallel developments, commonalities in assemblage, and intra-regional exchanges that were the backbone of the Ottoman economy. One of the greatest challenges of creating a social history out of Ottoman pottery is to evaluate local assemblages in ever larger regional contexts.

This is far from easy. The challenges to producing even site-specific chrono-typologies are overwhelming. Little excavated Ottoman pottery has been published, and when it has it has been insufficiently illustrated. Ottoman sites and strata are poorly preserved, due to continued occupation until today, their frequent reuse as burial sites and the unfortunate and widespread practice in the past of removing "modern" overburden from sites without fully recording them. Pottery of the post-Mamluk period is not readily identifiable, particularly in southern Syria, where a decline in permanent settlement coincides with a more homogenous and smaller ceramic assemblage, if there is one at all, and sites are more ephemeral in nature (campsites as opposed to domestic structures). Many medieval and post-medieval sites are poorly preserved and do not facilitate a stratigraphic separation of Late

Byzantine or Mamluk levels from Ottoman ones, and, finally, rural sites yield far fewer recognizable and datable imports, which have been the key to dating Ottoman strata, than more unfamiliar locally produced wares.

Because rural sites are difficult to date on their own, there has been a tendency to rely on urban and port sites to identify and date local Ottoman pottery. No work has been more influential in this regard than John Hayes' publication of the pottery from the Saraçhane excavations in Istanbul (Hayes 1992). This volume of the final excavation series set high standards for ceramic analysis and publication, and his Chapters 13–24 were the first systematic presentations of a full assemblage of glazed and common wares that spanned the entire Ottoman period (the 15th through the early 20th centuries). In terms of presentation, his inclusions of copious illustrations (clear profile drawings, photographs of restored vessels, charts of assemblage composition), descriptions of stratigraphic contexts, and detailed fabric descriptions have made this volume an invaluable and user-friendly reference. Chapter 20 was, moreover, one of the earliest detailed studies of Ottoman coarse wares published at the time. In addition to superb analysis and presentation, one of the strengths of this volume was the archaeological context of the pottery itself.[6] At this carefully excavated site, nearly all of the Early Ottoman (15th to 17th century) pottery came from closed deposits (pits and wells), preserving a large percentage of restorable vessels. There was, as well, clear stratigraphic separation from Late Ottoman (17th to early 20th century) material, which came primarily from modern and surface fills (Hayes 1992: 233). The widest range of Ottoman wares available in the capital was represented at this site, which makes the volume very useful for the study of imports at sites throughout the Empire.

Subsequent publications of Ottoman pottery from archaeological contexts have built on Hayes' work, pursuing many of the lines of inquiry that emerged in the Saraçhane monograph: the separation of Late Byzantine or Middle Islamic/Mamluk from Ottoman wares (Gregory 1993; François 1995; Hayes 1995; Ziadeh 1995; Avissar 2005; Avissar and Stern 2005; Vroom 2003 and 2005; Walker 2005),[7] analysis of "assemblage" composition (Milwright 2000; von Wartburg 2001; François 2001 and 2005), typologies of coffee cups and tobacco pipes (Baram 1995; Simpson 2002),[8] the meaning of the introduction of new forms (the ubiquitous *ibriq*, two-handled high-necked jars, high-stemmed bowls, and new shapes of cooking pots) and the importance of fabric in establishing a typology of coarse wares (Gabrieli 2006), the implications of the dominance of glazed wares in at least urban assemblages in the 18th and 19th centuries, and the development of turn-of-the-century "cottage industries" from Late Ottoman wares.[9]

Development of these themes has proceeded with the introduction of new methods of data collection and analysis, utilizing a growing interest in petrography, ethnography, and fabric analysis. Increasingly, more specialists of Ottoman pottery are paying closer attention to coarse wares and doing comparative analysis of assemblages on a regional scale (Vroom 2003 and 2005; François 1997). Such work runs parallel to new trends in Ottoman historiography, which are emphasizing regional and provincial studies, particularly in the fields of economic and social history.

The contributors to this volume have explored each of these themes, while developing typologies of pottery from specific excavated and surveyed sites. Chronologically the wares discussed here span the entirety of the Ottoman period in the Levant (16th through the early 20th centuries), and the authors consider the myriad connections between Greater Syria and Cyprus along with the larger Ottoman world that are reflected ceramically throughout this period. The first contribution by Miriam Avissar systematically examines glazed and unglazed wares from four sites excavated by the Israel Antiquities Authority. Analysis includes a detailed discussion of stratigraphic contexts and patterns of importation and local production in an effort to define more fully the 18th and 19th centuries. Marwan Abu Khalaf's article surveys published data on the Ottoman pottery of historical Palestine, producing a concise typology of forms and their function. The third study by Hamed Salem is a historical, ethnographic, and technological investigation of Gaza Gray Ware,

one of the most characteristic wares of southern Bilad al-Sham in this period. Through an exhaustive analysis of published and unpublished data, Salem suggests ways in which fabric and stylistic analysis can be used to identify patterns of ceramic parentage and development and offers compelling evidence for the Early Ottoman emergence of the ware. Bethany Walker's contribution in Chapter 5 is a comparative analysis of Ottoman pottery recovered from recent excavations and surveys of three rural sites in northern and central Jordan. Her essay formulates a preliminary, chrono-typology for Ottoman pottery in the country, highlighting the Mamluk-Ottoman and Ottoman-Mandate transitions. The final contribution, by Smadar Gabrieli, is a socio-archaeological study of Ottoman coarse wares from Paphos, where she has developed a typology of table and kitchen wares. In this study, Gabrieli theorizes about changes in foodways that are suggested by the typological changes in the ceramic record and raises, in the process, important questions about the impact of imperial culinary culture on rural Cypriot society. For ease of access and to facilitate visual comparison of forms among sites, all profile drawings and other figures have been placed together in the Illustrations section at the end of the volume.

ACKNOWLEDGMENTS

The concept of a "greater Levant" identified in this monograph grew out of a fortunate collusion of several professional collaborations involving this editor, as well as widespread frustration with the state of publication of Ottoman pottery. The second factor is well known to publishers, as many works are written to address obstacles to one's own research: to put it simply, if there are no books on Ottoman pottery in the Levant, write one. As for the first factor, it is an important reminder that no project is completed in a vacuum. While this volume grew directly out of the Ottoman Pottery panel at the 2005 ASOR Annual Meeting, the geographical emphasis on the Levant and its neighbors and the theoretical orientations of the volume are the natural outgrowth of research I have done related to the Norwegian Global Moments in the

Levant project,[10] my own excavations in northern and central Jordan,[11] the Levantine sub-theme of the French-American Exercising Power in the Age of the Sultanates project,[12] and my own research on Mamluk and Ottoman provincial history.

What all of these projects have in common is their geographic focus: the Levant as an imperial frontier, which constitutes the political hinterland but exudes a particular vitality as a distinctive cultural unit. They also represent the efforts of scholars who have been working together for several years. I would like to recognize, in this regard, Sten LaBianca (Andrews University and Senior Director of Tall Hisban excavations), Bert DeVries (Calvin College), Pierre Bikai (former Director, American Center of Oriental Research in Amman), Jean-François Salles (Acting Director, Institut Français de Proche Orient, Amman), Sylvie Denoix (Director, Institut Français d'Archéologie Orientale, Cairo), Irene Bierman (UCLA), Jere Bacharach (University of Washington, emeritus), and Leif Manger (University of Bergen) for organizing these various collaborations and opening my mind to larger research questions and the potentials of interdisciplinary research.

The job of editing is an enormous one, and in this effort I want to recognize my assistants April Chernoby and Mariya Adams – graduate students at Grand Valley and Missouri State Universities, respectively – who helped me edit and organize the volume, as well as the staff of the Digital Studio at Grand Valley State University and Chris Conner, of Evolving Perspectives in Springfield, Missouri, for their professional touch in cleaning drawings and preparing them for publication. Funding for this work was generously provided by Missouri State University, through a Dean's Incentive Grant. I would like to especially thank the contributors to this monograph, who wrote around hectic dig schedules and whose diligence and careful work are defining more clearly the Ottoman pottery of the region. All of the contributors are, finally, grateful to the three anonymous readers of the original manuscript, whose detailed and thoughtful comments were invaluable, and to Nancy Serwint, the editor of the AASOR series at the time of completing the manuscript, whose encouragement in submitting the manuscript for publication will always be appreciated and remembered.

On a final note, although transliterations of Arabic place names vary considerably within the region covered in this volume, the editor has made every effort to standardize spellings, adapting the system used by the American journal *Mamluk Studies Review*. For the sake of simplicity and clearer reading for non-specialists, diacriticals have not been used in the English transliterations of Arabic and Turkish terms in this work.

Notes

1 The structure of Ottoman administration in the eastern provinces was fluid, however, as the administrative status of Cyprus, for example, changed from that of a province (*eyalet*) to a district (*sanjak*) within the province of the Aegean islands and back again in the 17th and 18th centuries (Pitcher 1972: 127, 137).

2 The Ottomans lost control of Cyprus in 1878 (handing it over to British administration) and Greater Syria in 1918 (with the dissolution of the Ottoman Empire at the conclusion of the First World War and the subsequent establishment of the French and British Mandates in the region).

3 The administrations of the Syrian and Cypriot provinces were similar in their incorporation of pre-Ottoman structures and their reliance on tax farming. Inalçik and Quataert 2004 and McCarthy 2001 provide good comparative summaries of the whole region. For Greater Syria specifically, see Shaqirat 1992 and Ze'evi 1996, and for Cyprus consult Inalçik 1978, Dionyssiou 1994, Gazioglu 1990, and Jennings 1993.

4 *Tapu defters* of the 16th century affirm these settlement cycles for southern Syria (al-Bakhit 1989a and 1989b; al-Bakhit and Hmoud 1989a, 1989b, and 1991; Hütteroth and Abdulfattah 1977).

5 By the end of the 16th century, villages in the Anatolian interior had coffee houses (Suraiya Faroqhi in Inalçik and Quataert 1997: 507). The Egyptian coffee trade peaked, however, in the late 17th and early 18th centuries, as the recovery of coffee cups from excavations throughout the eastern Mediterranean indicate.

6 Hayes acknowledges, however, that the absence of coins from any of these deposits and the poor stratigraphy of the later strata hampered creating a tighter chronology (Hayes 1992: 235).

7 The 1980s produced early studies that identified Ottoman pottery as distinct from Late Byzantine. Charalambis Bakirtzis' work in Thrace was an early, and often cited, study of a post-Byzantine ware (Bakirtzis 1980). For Cyprus, see Timothy Gregory's work on survey material from Palaepaphos (Gregory 1987).

8 Seriation of tobacco pipes began in earnest in the 1980s (Robinson 1983 and 1985).

9 Some of the earliest studies of Ottoman pottery in Palestine and Transjordan used ethnographic methods (see Crowfoot 1932 and Mershen 1985).

10 This project is funded by the Research Council of Norway and is described in detail on its website: www.globalmoments.uib.no.

11 Project websites for the Northern Jordan Project and Tall Hisban can be found at the Missouri State University History Department website and the Hesban website at: http://clio.missouristate.edu/bwalker/Projects.htm and www.hesban.org.

12 The project, as it was developed for a workshop in Amman, is described here at the Council of American Overseas Research Centers website: http://caorc.org/highlights/acor/acor-2005-05-16b.htm.

Chapter 2

Ottoman Pottery Assemblages
from Excavations in Israel

by Miriam Avissar

Until recently, Ottoman pottery has not received much attention, and relatively little has been published. In the past, most of the finds from the Ottoman period were not even treated as archaeological artifacts, since only pre-1700 material is, by law, considered an "antiquity." In recent years, however, this attitude has been gradually changing, and Ottoman material is being treated in the same way as the finds from earlier periods. The artifacts of some sites, excavated on behalf of the Israel Antiquities Authority, will be treated here. Those sites are Tell Yoqne'am-al Qaymun, Habonim-Kafr Lam, Qula, and al-Qubab. The Ottoman assemblages from Tell Yoqne'am (Avissar 2005) and al-Qubab (Ein Gedy 2006) have already been published, while Habonim-Kafr Lam and Qula are still in preparation.

TELL YOQNE'AM

Tell Yoqne'am is a steep hill situated at the foot of the plateau of Manasseh, dominating the eastern exit of the Milh pass, which connects the coastal region with the Jezreel Valley (Ben-Tor, Avissar and Portugali 1996: 1–2). Extensive excavations were carried out at Tell Yoqne'am on behalf of the Hebrew University, Jerusalem, from 1977 to 1988. These excavations revealed large sections of the Crusader settlement of Caymont, but did not reveal any architectural remains that could be attributed to the Ottoman period. Several tobacco pipes, however, were retrieved from the top soil (Avissar 1996). Uriel Heyd suggested that the monumental structures on the acropolis of Tell Yoqne'am (al-Qaymun) should be identified with the fortress of Zahir al-'Umar, built on the site in the mid-18th century (Heyd 1976: 89–96). This fortress was already in ruins when Bonaparte's army passed by the tell in 1799 (Avissar 2005: VII), although the square outline of the fortress is clearly visible in aerial photographs of the site (Ben-Tor, Avissar and Portugali 1996: photo 3.1). The excavation on the acropolis revealed that this fortress was surrounded by a double wall. Poorly preserved partition walls, which consisted of one row of dressed stones, created small casemate-like spaces in the area between the two encircling walls (Avissar 2005: plan 1.4). The eastern enclosure wall was traced to a length of 25 m, and several rooms built against this enclosure have been excavated (Avissar 2005: 16–18). Extensive stone robbing prevailed on the site after it was abandoned, and most

7

of the walls were reduced to one course only. Very little pottery could be retrieved from these rooms, but the small assemblage can be safely dated to the second half of the 18th century.

THE OTTOMAN POTTERY ASSEMBLAGE FROM TELL YOQNE'AM

Glazed Bowls (fig. 2.1)

There were a number of glazed bowls, those of local production as well as imported material. The monochrome-glazed bowls with sloping ledge rim and up-turned lip (fig. 2.1: 1–2) are a typical and long-lived Ottoman shape, well attested in different wares at Saraçhane, where they are dated from the 16th to the 19th centuries (Hayes 1992: 271–80). Most of these bowls are imported vessels, but there are local imitations (fig. 2.1: 2). While the imported bowls usually have a well-adhering smooth glaze, the glaze quality of the local wares is usually rather poor and the bowls are often crude and thick-walled. A characteristic feature, not encountered in earlier glazed wares, is the stepped ring base that often has a thumb-indented outer edge (fig. 2.1: 3–4). Actually there are only two groups of locally produced glazed wares: monochrome bowls and slip-painted bowls. The latter, so common during the Mamluk period, continue throughout the Ottoman period. The slip-painted patterns of the local ware lack the well executed patterns of the previous period. Now the slip is only sparsely and carelessly applied, and the glaze is usually yellow (fig. 2.1: 6–7).

The imported vessels of this group are always decorated with vertical stripes, often executed in a brown slip on a light background (fig. 2.1: 5, 8). Slip-painted bowls – local as well as imported, were produced during the Ottoman period until the 19th century (François 1995). The bowls with a pointed rim and curved or slightly carinated walls (fig. 2.1: 9–10) are common shapes in Ottoman glazed wares (Hayes 1992: 283, fig. 111 forms b 10–20). These bowls have a bright colored glaze, often decorated with monochrome or polychrome spots (Avissar 2005: color plate 2: 15; Edelstein and Avissar 1997: color plate 3: 2–4). At Akko this shape occurs also in slip-painted ware (Edelstein and Avissar

1997: fig. 1: 8). There are Italian sgraffito wares (fig. 2.1: 11–12) as well as coffee cups of Kütahya ware, which should be dated to the 18th century (fig. 2.1: 13–14). Coffee cups are a common vessel in all Ottoman assemblages and besides the cups made of fritware, are true porcelain cups. At Akko, cups of Meissen porcelain, decorated in the Chinese manner, were retrieved (Edelstein and Avissar 1997: 133, color plate 5: 5a–5b). The crossed swords mark with star identifies the piece from Akko as produced during the Marcolini period (1774–1814) (Cushion 1996: 99). Towards the end of the 18th century, the Meissen factory revived the export of coffee cups for the Turkish market (Honey 1946: 133, 164–69). An imitation of the crossed swords mark is sometimes found on stoneware Kütahya cups. Local glazed utilitarian pottery is exemplified by the large glazed bowl with out-folded rim (fig. 2.1: 15). These large bowls are usually only partly covered with a thin, purple-brown glaze, and a similar vessel was also found in Akko (Edelstein and Avissar 1997: fig. 1:14). The shape also appears in plain unglazed ware.

Cooking Vessels (fig. 2.2)

Most of the Ottoman cooking ware in the Tell Yoqne'am assemblage was handmade. The handmade cooking pots of the Mamluk period had a low, out-turned neck and often a well burnished red slip. The Ottoman pots are hole-mouth pots with a slightly thickened (fig. 2.2: 1–2) or inward-sloping rim (fig. 2.2: 3). The red slip has disappeared, and now a light brown well-burnished slip was preferred. The horizontal ear handles and the pulled-up loop handles continue (fig. 2.2: 1–3). The handmade cooking bowl with triangular ledge handles and a thumb-indented depression (fig. 2.2: 4, 5) is a new type not found in Mamluk assemblages. Glazed cooking pots (fig. 2.2: 6) are rare; curiously all pots are of more or less the same form, whether from Yoqne'am or Jerusalem (see fig. 2.11: 15), and it seems they all originate from one and the same workshop. Since the clay of these cooking pots contains mica, they are obviously imported vessels. It seems that these pots flourished during the 18th and 19th centuries.

Jars and Jugs (fig. 2.3)

Storage jars with broad, flat handles springing from the base of the neck (fig. 2.3: 1) are a popular Ottoman shape in the so-called "Gaza Ware," as well as in reddish wares. The appearance of the gray "Gaza Ware" is safely attested at about 1700 (Rosen and Goodfried 1993). However, at Ti'innik it seems to be already present in Stratum 6, dated to the late 15th and 16th centuries (Ziadeh 1995: 220, 238, fig. 13: 8–9). A similar date has also been suggested for the finds from Sataf, near Jerusalem (Gibson, Ibbs and Kloner 1991: 45–47). A light grayish ware also appeared in Late Mamluk–Early Ottoman levels, dated to the 15th and 16th centuries, from the recent excavations in the Old City of Jerusalem. It seems that during this period experiments were made to change the appearance of vessels, mainly jugs and jars. The same vessel forms appear in buff, greenish, or grayish fabric. Some of those Gray Ware vessels, however, were definitely misfired products or even kiln wasters. It might well be that these misfired pieces inspired the potters to produce gray wares. These early Gray Wares are still quite far from the true dark gray "Gaza Wares," in form as well as in fabric color.

Only a few pieces of the so-called "Rashaya al-Fakhkhar Ware" were detected (fig. 2.3: 2–4). It is made of fine orange-brown clay and decorated with red-painted patterns and occasional patches of green glaze. The pottery workshop at Rashaya al-Fakhkhar, situated at the foot of Mount Hermon, already flourished at the beginning of the 19th century (Burckhardt 1822: 35–36). The origins of the ware, however, are much earlier. In recent, and as yet unpublished, excavations at Safet[1] and at various unpublished sites on the Golan Heights, a sort of early Rashaya al-Fakhkhar Ware appeared already in late Mamluk assemblages.[2] Rashaya al-Fakhkhar Ware was widely distributed in northern Palestine and safely dated at Yoqne'am to the 18th century (Zevulun 1978; Olenik 1983). Later pieces are often decorated with a broad band of red stripes painted with a multiple brush.

The table jar (fig. 2.3: 5) with biconical body and sieve at the base of the neck is the Ottoman development of an earlier, medieval shape. Noteworthy are the "false" ring base and the pinched base of the handles, both characteristic Ottoman features, although pinched handle bases can already be observed on some Ayyubid vessels (Tushingham 1985: assemblage from Cistern E). A common Ottoman vessel is the *ibriq* (fig. 2.3: 6–8), a spouted drinking jug, made in gray "Gaza Ware" as well as in reddish fabrics. Characteristic of the earlier types are the inward beveled or simple rim, while later jugs usually have out-folded rims. Similar jugs are reported from Akko and dated to the end of the 18th and the beginning of the 19th centuries (Stern 1997: 67, fig. 18: 129–31).

Tobacco Pipes (fig. 2.4)

The excavation also yielded a large number of tobacco pipes. The majority were pipes with a rounded bowl, high straight rim, and a short shank, whose end has a stepped-ring termination. The wreath is a simple, undecorated ring, triangular in section. They are made of gray clay; the slip is frequently deep purple-red, and the surface is usually well burnished (fig. 2.4: 1–5). The majority of these pipes have a seal impression on the right side of the shank, and the impression is nearly always in the form of a crescent with several dots (fig. 2.4: 2). One of these pipes (fig. 2.4: 5) was found in a layer of small stones below the foundations of the Ottoman structures. This type of tobacco pipe can, therefore, securely be dated to the second half of the 18th century, when Zahir al-'Umar's Ottoman fortress was established on the acropolis. The production center of these pipes seems to be located somewhere in the north of the country, probably at Nazareth. Similar pipes were also found at Akko (Edelstein and Avissar 1997: fig. 2: 3a–3c; Stern 1997: fig. 19: 136) and at Habonim (in preparation), while they are nearly absent in the Jerusalem area.

HABONIM-KAFR LAM

The Umayyad fortress at Habonim-Kafr Lam was probably built by Hisham ibn 'Abd al-Malik (Khalidi 1992: 170). It is located on the coastal plain between Dor and Athlit, about 1 km from the seashore and about 20 km west of Yoqne'am.

In 1999, extensive excavations were carried out on behalf of the Israel Antiquities Authority. The excavation results show that the fortress was continually inhabited throughout the early Islamic and Crusader periods. The Ottoman settlement of Kafr Lam, probably called thus after the Crusader name Cafarlet, was first attested in documents dated to 1596, when a farm paying taxes to the government is mentioned (Khalidi 1992: 170). It is unclear whether this Early Ottoman settlement was situated inside the fortress. No architectural remains could be identified as pre-dating the 18th century; however, some pottery items as well as early tobacco pipes made of fine, light gray clay, and pre-dating the 18th century, were retrieved from inside the fortress, thus attesting some earlier activity. The earliest architectural remains inside the fortress were a paved courtyard and surrounding rooms, with a likely 18th-century date. A cistern, used as a dump and sealed by a 19th-century floor, as well as the fill below the Ottoman floors, yielded a good 18th-century pottery assemblage (figs. 2.5–2.6). The main vessel types correspond to those from Tell Yoqne'am.

Pre-19th Century

Bowls and Craters (fig. 2.5)

Recovered were imported glazed bowls, decorated with colored dots (fig. 2.5: 1–2), as well as slip-painted ware (fig. 2.5: 3). The bowl decorated with sgraffito (fig. 2.5: 4) might be slightly earlier and probably not later than the middle of the 17th century; this form of decoration was abandoned during the later Ottoman period (Hayes 1992: 272–75, Ware E). Local glazed bowls are of rather poor quality (fig. 2.5: 5–8). Often they show only patches of slip or no slip at all, and the glaze color is almost always green. The bowls had either out-folded or plain rims. A characteristic element in local glazed bowls is the stepped ring base (fig. 2.5: 8), a feature also observed on imported wares (Hayes 1992: fig. 102, Ware E) and probably copied from those wares. The base from Kafr Lam (fig. 2.5: 8) resembles that from Tell Yoqne'am-al Qaymun (see above fig. 2.1: 3) in form and material, and both probably originate from the same workshop. Often rather crude tripod marks are found on the inside of the bowls.

Unglazed bowls were fashioned in gray "Gaza Ware" (fig. 2.5: 9–10) as well as in plain reddish fabric (fig. 2.5: 11). All show more or less conical walls and a thickened rim, often with a pronounced ridge on the exterior. Handmade bowls of rather poor quality were also present (fig. 2.5: 12–13). The large handmade bowl with thumb-indented ridge is paralleled at Sataf, where the Ottoman assemblage is dated from the late 16th to the 18th century (Gibson, Ibbs, Kloner 1991: 44–47). Large basins with a thumb-indented ridge on the exterior have already been found in a Mamluk assemblage from Jerusalem (Tushingham 1985: assemblage from Cistern E). The crater (fig. 2.5: 14–15) is a new form. Most of the craters, though, are hole-mouth vessels and could also be termed hole-mouth jars. There were wheelmade craters (fig. 2.5: 14), as well as large, crude handmade vessels (fig. 2.5: 15). According to their fabric, these vessels did not function as cooking pots.

Cooking Vessels (fig. 2.6: 1–3)

The handmade cooking vessels (fig. 2.6: 1–3) found in the cistern assemblage resemble those already encountered at Tell Yoqne'am-al Qaymun: closed cooking pots with thickened, inward sloping rim (fig. 2.6: 1–2), as well as cooking bowls (fig.2. 6: 3) with thumb-indented depression. Glazed cooking pots, however, were absent.

Storage Jars and Jugs (fig. 2.6: 4–10)

The storage jar with slightly incurved neck and handles springing from the base of the neck (fig. 2.6: 4) is paralleled at Yoqne'am-al Qaymun (see fig. 2.3: 1). While at Yoqne'am-al Qaymun storage jars were made of the gray "Gaza Ware," at Kafr Lam the jar is fashioned in brown ware. The jars with a thick ridge under the rim (fig. 2.6: 5–7) seem to belong to an Early Ottoman storage jar type that continues a form current during the late Mamluk period (Avissar and Stern 2005: 102, fig. 42: 5–6) but probably was already residual during the 18th century. In recent excavations in the Old City of

Jerusalem, similar jars occurred in Early Ottoman levels that did not yield any tobacco pipes and can, therefore, securely be dated to the 16th century.[3] No complete rim profile of a jug could be retrieved from the cistern (fig. 2.6: 8–10). The partly glazed spout (fig. 2.6: 8) originates from the pottery workshop at Rashaya al-Fakhkhar. This piece in the cistern assemblage again confirms that this ware was already made before the beginning of the 19th century. All forms attested in reddish fabric were also made in gray "Gaza Ware." Here only a fragment of a flask (fig. 2.6: 9) and a base of a jug (fig. 2.6: 10) could be retrieved. Since most of the vessel types retrieved from the cistern correspond to the material from Tell Yoqneʿam-al Qaymun, it seems secure to date the early assemblage from Kafr Lam to the late 18th to early 19th centuries.

19th Century

During the 19th century most of the area inside the fortress was built up. A row of rooms also abutted the southern wall of the fortress. One building complex yielded a pottery assemblage that could safely be dated to the first half of the 19th century. There were imported glazed bowls (fig. 2.7: 1–7), plain bowls in gray "Gaza Ware" (fig. 2.8: 1–3), cooking wares, handmade (fig. 2.8: 4–5) and glazed jars (fig. 2.8: 6), as well as jars in gray "Gaza Ware" (fig. 2.8: 7–9), local closed containers (fig. 2.9: 1–2), and one imported Dutch genièvre bottle made of stoneware with the engraved company name (fig. 2.9: 3).

Glazed Bowls (fig. 2.7)

A new type of glazed bowl appears in this assemblage: bowls with a sharply out-folded rim. These bowls are decorated with vertical trails of slip under yellow or green glaze, a type that can be found in all late Ottoman assemblages. The production centers were in the environs of Istanbul, such as Ganos and Didymoteichon, from where these bowls were widely exported throughout the Ottoman Empire (François 1995: 203–17, pls. 1–5; Hayes 1992: 276–77, fig. 144). Most bowls are yellow-glazed (fig. 2.7: 2); green-glazed bowls of this ware (fig. 2.7: 1) are less common. A green-glazed bowl of this form was

reported from Ganos (Armstrong and Günsenin 1995: cat. 77). Another typical Ottoman bowl form, already found in the 18th-century assemblages, are bowls with a ledge rim, which usually have an up-turned lip (fig. 2.7: 3–6). This very form is represented by a slip-painted bowl (fig. 2.7: 3), a monochrome-glazed bowl (fig. 2.7: 5), and a bowl in Çanakkale Ware (fig. 2.7: 4). The ware is dated from 1740 or earlier to the First World War (Hayes 1992: 268–70, pl. 44: 4). The bowls with ledge rim, covered with a light brown slip under colorless transparent glaze and decorated with a stylized floral design in dark purple are assigned to the 19th century and termed by Hayes as Çanakkale II (Hayes 1992: fig. 101: 1). The monochrome green-glazed bowl with a notched ledge rim (fig. 2.7: 6) is probably a product of the Ganos kilns (Armstrong and Günsenin 1995: cat. 29, fig. 6: 29). The externally painted coffee cup (fig. 2.7: 7) in a hard white fritware is a product of the Kütahya kilns.

Plain Bowls (fig. 2.8: 1–3)

Plain bowls in gray "Gaza Ware" (fig. 2.8: 1–3) occurred in different forms and sizes. There were small bowls with slightly rounded side walls and a plain rim (fig. 2.8: 1) and sharply carinated bowls (fig. 2.8: 2), a form that probably did not appear in "Gaza Ware" before the 19th century but continued into the 20th-century Mandate period (Ustinova and Nahshoni 1994: fig. 14: 5–6). Large bowls with a thickened rim (fig. 2.8: 3) occurred already in the 18th-century assemblage (see fig. 2.5: 9–10).

Cooking Vessels (fig. 2.8: 4–5)

Handmade cooking ware prevails (fig. 2.8: 4–5), and the forms are still the same as in the earlier assemblages. Glazed cooking ware (fig. 2.8: 6) was not found in the earlier assemblage, but was present in the Tell Yoqneʿam-al Qaymun assemblage (see fig. 2.2: 6).

Storage Jars (fig. 2.8: 7–9)

The storage jars have hollowed necks, are of medium height with a slight carination at the base of the neck, and have a thickened rim. Often there is a plain or thumb-indented ridge under the rim (fig. 2.8: 8–9).

Closed Containers (fig. 2.9)

A new shape is the bottle with a long neck (fig. 2.9: 1). The jug (*ibriq*) fashioned in gray "Gaza Ware" (fig. 2.9: 2) with out-folded rim, ribbed neck, and pronounced omphalos base is a characteristic late Ottoman shape still produced in recent days. A unique find is the glazed alcohol bottle (fig. 2.9: 3). These bottles were produced in Germany and filled with genièvre (Dutch gin) in the Netherlands. The name of the distillery, attested in 19th-century sources, was incised before firing. A coin dated to 1830 was found in connection with this bottle. The pipes associated with this level are 19th-century types with a long shank and a wide shank opening. According to these finds, it seems that the whole assemblage can be dated to the first half of the 19th century, since later, probably during the second half of the 19th century, the whole area was built up. Some of these late buildings still exist.

QULA AND AL-QUBAB

Qula is situated on a limestone hill on the western slope of the Ramallah Mountains, about 10 km north of Ramla. At Qula, the pottery was retrieved from the deep fills under the destroyed Mandate houses and yielded mainly 18th- and 19th-century vessels as well as earlier types – a mixed assemblage that spans the whole of the Ottoman period.[4]

Al-Qubab is situated near Latrun, about 10 km southeast of Ramla. Both sites are mentioned in 16th-century documents. Regrettably, no Early Ottoman levels were revealed, since the excavations touched only the fringes of the villages (Ein Gedy 2006: 55*–67*). The architectural remains at al-Qubab were found immediately below the surface without any later remains above. The assemblage from this site should be assigned to the late 19th century, according to the tobacco pipes.

When comparing the 19th-century pottery assemblage of Kafr Lam with that of Qula and al-Qubab, regional differences in some utilitarian types can be observed that also seem to indicate a difference in date. Glazed and plain bowls are more or less of the same forms at all sites; the bulk of the imported glazed bowls (not illustrated here) originated in Turkish workshops, and Italian marbled wares are also found. Plain bowls were fashioned either in a reddish-brownish fabric or in gray "Gaza Ware."

Bowls (fig. 2.10)

The bowls fashioned in reddish or brownish fabric appeared with a variety of rim forms (fig. 2.10: 1–7). Bowls in "Gaza Ware" (fig. 2.10: 8–10), however, were of a very different profile: carinated walls, usually with a heavy ridge on the exterior. The ridge and even the rim are often thumb-indented and there is pronounced ribbing above the ridge. This form made its appearance already during the first half of the 19th century (see fig. 2.8: 2) and continued to be produced even during the Mandate period.

Craters (fig. 2.11: 1–9)

The wheelmade hole-mouth craters (fig. 2.11: 1–8) were very common at Qula and al-Qubab, but this form was absent in the Kafr Lam assemblage. Some necked craters with broad strap handles springing from under the rim also made their appearance (fig. 2.11: 9).

Cooking Vessels (fig. 2.11: 10–15)

The handmade cooking pots (fig. 2.11: 10–12) from Qula and al-Qubab were of a completely different type and material – they were hole-mouth pots with a thickened rim, made of brown clay with many grits and feldspar. The pots were only slightly smoothed and decorated with pin-pricked lines around the rim and the horizontal handles. Similar pots were also found in Jerusalem.[5] Wheelmade cooking pots, one in "Gaza Ware" (fig. 2.11: 13–14), came to light in al-Qubab. The glazed cooking pot from Jerusalem (fig. 2.11: 15) can be identified as an imported vessel, as it is made of well-levigated orange clay with mica.

Storage Jars (fig. 2.12: 1–7)

Many storage jars were retrieved, some nearly complete. They are sack-shaped with steeply sloping shoulders. Combed decoration on the body of the jar is common, and broad, flat strap handles spring from the base of the neck. The necks are high and hollowed; the rims are usually out-folded or thickened on the inside. The same jar types were still produced during the Mandate period.

Jugs (fig. 2.12: 8–12)

The jug forms are the same as in the early 19th-century assemblage at Kafr Lam. Jugs fashioned in gray "Gaza Ware" often show traces of irregular painted patterns in white or bright orange.

Conclusions

The material presented here is chronologically rather limited and focuses mainly on the 18th- and 19th-century forms, owing to the lack of more and properly excavated assemblages. The excavations in the Old City of Jerusalem, however, promise to fill some of the gaps in our knowledge, especially about the pottery of the enigmatic 16th and 17th centuries.[6] The assemblages presented here, nonetheless, are suggestive of patterns in distribution and consumption that warrant further inquiry. The pottery of all the sites pulls from local and regional products as well as imports, primarily from Turkey but also from Europe. Locally made glazed bowls that imitate in form and surface treatment Ottoman imports, a common corpus of handmade jars and bowls, and "Gaza Ware" fashioned in gray fabric are found in all assemblages. Pipes appear to be regional products, rather than Ottoman Turkish imports. A site such as Yoqne'am-al Qaymun, while having access to international markets, was as reliant on local products as any village. An urban center like Akko, though, had a richer assemblage, including Chinese and German porcelains

(Edelstein and Avissar 1997: color plate 4), while the four sites surveyed here reflect assemblages typical of rural settlements. It is noteworthy that Rashayya al-Fakhkhar Ware occurred already in the late 18th century deposits at both Yoqne'am-al-Qaymun and Habonim-Kafr Lam and was widely distributed all over the north of the country. The ware was first mentioned by Burckhardt at the beginning of the 19th century (Burckhardt 1822: 35–36). However, the finds from al-Qaymun and Kafr Lam indicate that the production of the Rashayya al-Fakhkhar ware started much earlier. It was probably already a well established industry by the time Zahir al-'Umar and his descendants controlled much of northern Palestine and Lebanon and invested in the port towns and international and regional trade (see Ch. 5 in this volume).

If there is any major difference among the assemblages, it is in the extent and diversity of the imports, which span a narrow time period. The assemblages are associated with different settlement types: Akko is an urban center, while al-Qaymun, Kafr Lam, Qula, and al-Qubab are rural settlements, and this seems to be reflected in the pottery itself. Both the Zaydanid citadel at Yoqne'am and the reoccupied fortress at Habonim-Kafr Lam, located on the coastal plain, should have benefited from the intensified trade that circulated goods throughout the Mediterranean. The range of imports identified at al-Qaymun, Kafr-Lam, and Qula – from Turkey (Kütahya cups, a variety of glazed and slip-painted bowls, Çanakkale Ware), Thrace (Didymoteichon Ware) and Europe (Italian sgraffitos, Dutch stoneware) – bear witness to deliberate ceramic exchanges beyond the Arab provinces. It should be noted that imported glazed ware even reached a poor rural settlement like al-Qubab (Avissar 2006: fig. 7: 1–2). Certainly, no sweeping conclusions can be made about production, exchange, and consumption on the basis of four roughly contemporary sites, but future analyses of Ottoman assemblages should consider these factors.

Notes

1   I want to thank the excavator H. Barbé for this information.

2   The publication of these sites is in preparation by the author.

3   The pottery of these excavations will be published by the author.

4   Avissar and Melavski, *The Excavations at Qula*, forthcoming.

5   See M. Avissar, "The Pottery Finds" in *Jewish Quarter Excavations in the Old City of Jerusalem,* Vol. IV, ed. O. Gutfeld, forthcoming.

6   [Editor's note] Kay Prag's very recent publication of Kathleen Kenyon's excavations at Jerusalem was not available at the time of writing this chapter. For Ottoman ceramics from this project, see Prag 2008.

Chapter 3

The Ottoman Pottery of Palestine

by Marwan Abu Khalaf

Ceramic assemblages can be very informative about site function, chronology of settlement, and socio-economic networks. Moreover, as little Ottoman-era pottery from well-stratified contexts has been published for Palestine, examining the assemblage as a whole is useful in constructing site-specific typo-chronologies. Noteworthy in this regard is a handful of publications of excavations that describe such assemblages by vessel type, techniques of manufacture, and range of wares.

One of the best-dated is the 18th-century assemblage from the summit of the tell at Yoqneʿam, discussed in the previous chapter of this volume (and partially published in Avissar 2005: 75–78, 83–93), and supplemented by Ottoman-era tobacco pipes from the Crusader complex published in earlier volumes (Avissar 1996). The first preliminary report of the site (Ben-Tor and Rosenthal 1978: 62) mentioned a caravanserai constructed by Zahir al-ʿUmar during the mid-18th century, and it is this structure that yielded a diverse and securely-dated assemblage, consisting of a variety of both imported and locally produced wares. Imports include a range of Turkish (monochrome-glazed, Kütahya coffee cups) and Italian glazed wares, as well as regional products (Rashaya al-Fakhkhar Ware, "Gaza Ware" jars and *ibriqs*, and tobacco pipes). Local production was impressive: monochrome-glazed and slip-painted wares (largely in imitation of imports), HMGP (Handmade Geometric-Painted Ware) jugs, glazed cooking pots, and plain wheelmade jars.

It is now becoming possible to define the Ottoman-era assemblages of Palestine from this and other sites. Excavations at Khirbat Birzeit near Ramallah have yielded a corpus of Late Mamluk/Early Ottoman cooking pots and frying pans from post-occupation fill (Area B, Stratum 2, Phase 2) of a ground-floor room of the medieval building excavated in 1996 and 1998 (Nashef and Abd Rabu 2000: 9–10; Abd Rabu 2000). The form of the cooking pots – rounded, with horizontal loop handles – is replicated at other sites (such as Tiʿinnik and Emmaus Qubayba), as is the frying pan with vertical handles. While only surface finds, the diversity of Ottoman-Mandate era wares recovered from the Zirʿin village (Tell Jezreel) excavations is suggestive of the wide networks of exchange in which Palestinian villages participated in the later Ottoman period. Surface finds included sherds of possible Didymoteichon and "Gaza" Wares,

Kütahya coffee cups, imported porcelains, and tobacco pipes, as well as more common cooking and table wares, such as cooking pots, combed handmade bowls and basins, and incised wheelmade jugs (Grey 1994: 60–61). A similar corpus was noted at Red Tower (Burj al-Ahmar), 9 km east of the Nathanya coastal road on the Sharon Plain. The Phase E deposits, a deep fill associated with post-destruction levelling of debris and domestic refuse and dated to ca. 1390– ca. 1920, could not be stratigraphically separated. Nonetheless, a few conclusions could be raised about the later Islamic pottery: handmade wares increase substantially during the Ottoman period; glazed cooking pots disappear; fine wares include "Gaza Ware" jars, whiteware *ibriqs*, Kütahya coffee cups, monochrome-glazed (and slipped) bowls, and tobacco pipes, in addition to various coarse HMGP vessels (Pringle 1986: 108–14, 128–30, 136).

These assemblages, while suggestive of a range of contacts and descriptive of consumer patterns, consist largely of sherds. Only at the site of Ti'innik, located in northern Palestine, several kilometers south of Megiddo, were complete vessels (or profiles of vessels, rim to base) reconstructed in enough quantities to offer a typology of form and function within an Ottoman assemblage, based on shape, size, and fabric (Ziadeh 1995). The floors, pits, and stratified fill of Strata 6–10 were attributed by the excavators to the Ottoman period, with stratigraphic separation of earlier Ottoman (16th–18th centuries) from later (19th and early 20th) centuries. Earlier Ottoman pottery at Ti'innik includes HMGP bowls and jars of both local manufacture (distinguished by their yellow slip and thick painted designs) and imports (pink slip and fine, red-painted designs), glazed cooking pots, tobacco pipes, monochrome-glazed bowls and dishes, small, plain wheelmade jars, "Gaza Ware" jars, and porcelain and stoneware cups. In the Late Ottoman assemblages, the large storage jars are replaced by *zirs*, *ibriqs* replace pitchers, and "Turkish" (Kütahya Ware) coffee cups make their appearance.

Chronological separation of Ottoman pottery within a site and within the 400-year period of Ottoman sovereignty in Palestine has been diffi-

cult to accomplish outside of Ti'innik. A few sites, however, have the potential to distinguish among various Ottoman phases. Coin-dated terrace fills at Sataf, in the Judean hills west of Jerusalem, have made possible a limited separation of 16th–20th-century pottery (Gibson et al. 1991: 44–47). The proposed chronologies are also supported by associated finds, such as tobacco pipes (which can be dated now with more confidence) and glass bracelets (a category of small finds for which the chronology is at an early stage of development). Earlier Ottoman pottery (16th–18th centuries) here includes a variety of HMGP and "Gaza" Wares, tobacco pipes, and plain wheelmade jars. The Late Ottoman/modern corpus (19th–early 20th centuries) includes modern porcelain and a greater quantity of associated glass and metal. Likewise, at nearby Abu Gosh (the village of Qaryat al-'Inab), located 13 km from Jerusalem, collapse from a ruined medieval caravanserai allows for separation of post-medieval HMGP vessels from their medieval counterparts. According to historical records, the structure was in ruins at the end of the 15th century. Handmade, painted sherds from the post-ruin debris on top of the ruined structure are distinguished from earlier deposits under the structural collapse by a coarser fabric with thick, awkwardly painted lines in reddish-purple and poorly executed compositions and an underlying pink slip.

Finally, we have the Ain Karem material, which was stratigraphically assigned to the 18th and 19th centuries. It is composed of handmade forms and unglazed wheel-thrown vessels (Saller 1946: 178–80). Of the Ottoman-period handmade ware, the painted ceramics are differentiated from those of medieval occupation by a coating of reddish or pink slip and sealing-wax-red painted decoration. The assemblage is typical of 19th-century Palestine. If the proposed chronology is correct, then this assemblage shows both handmade and wheel-thrown forms during the 18th-century occupation.

The following is a survey of the Ottoman pottery of Palestine, building on the assemblages described by the previously mentioned published reports. The survey will focus on the most common forms of the period and the techniques of manufacture.

TYPICAL FORMS OF THE OTTOMAN PERIOD

Typological classification[1] of Ottoman pottery is based mostly on technique or mode of production (handmade, wheel-thrown, glazed, etc.). Categorization based on closed and open forms is also sometimes indicated. The only two wares which are classified according to their forms are cooking pots and tobacco pipes. However, this chapter will focus on the shape of the vessels, based on whether they were handmade or wheel-thrown, painted or glazed, and open or closed. The techniques used to create the vessels will be discussed within this framework.

Tobacco Pipes

Tobacco pipes (*chibouks*; fig. 3.1) are a hallmark of the Ottoman period and frequently are relied on as "fossil types" of the later Ottoman centuries. Tobacco pipes were introduced to the region at the beginning of the 17th century and continued to be used through the Ottoman and Mandate eras. Their chronological development has been based on a variety of characteristics: fabric and surface colors; diameters of the bowl, stem ("shank"), and their openings; general shape of the bowl and stem; surface treatment, with pipes getting generally larger and darker over time. We are aided by the many published scholarly studies that have surveyed the general development of pipes over the course of the Ottoman centuries, creating typo-chronologies that are largely site- or region-specific (Robinson 1983 and 1985; Hayes 1992: 391–95; Baram 1995 and 1999; Simpson 2000 and 2002; Graf 2001; Avissar 1996 and 2005: 83–93). One of the biggest challenges today is not in dating the tobacco pipes but in determining their provenance.

Examples of tobacco pipes were discovered at the following sites in Palestine: at Yoqneʿam a pipe was dated to the 18th and the 19th centuries by Avissar (1996: 198–201); at Tell Tiʿinnik, the tobacco pipes were found in strata 7, 8, and 11, dating from the first half of the 17th century to the middle of the 19th (Ziadeh 1995: fig. 1); at Khirbat Birzeit one tobacco pipe was discovered on a floor, stratum I phase II, dated to the 18th and 19th centuries. A number of pipes were also found at the Damascus Gate excavations in Jerusalem in Ottoman-period contexts (Wightman 1989: 73–74, pl. 63), and in the Red Tower excavation in post-Mamluk strata (Pringle 1986: 172, fig. 43: 11–12). The pipes illustrated here tend to have a short stem, rounded or straight-sided bowls, a simple stem and stem ends, and have a grayish fabric, placing them in the later Ottoman centuries. They are generally believed to be of regional (Palestinian or southern Syrian) manufacture.

Jars

Several forms of jars (figs. 3.2–3.3) characteristic of this period were found during archaeological excavations at different sites. Some of them are handmade with slipped and burnished surfaces, painted with geometric designs. Others are wheel-thrown with plain surfaces. They are of various uses and include storage jars, water jars, and food jars, distinguished as such by size and shape.

FIG. 3.2: 1–6 The first form of jar has a rounded body with bowed rim; flat or concave disc base; and two (occasionally four) wide, strap handles attached to the shoulders. Examples were found at Tiʿinnik (Ziadeh 1995: fig. 6: 1–2 and fig. 12: 5). Parallels were also identified at Zirʿin (Grey 1994: fig.10: 3–4), Pella (Smith 1989, fig. 63: 2, 8. 10), Tell al-Qaymun (Yoqneʿam; Avissar 1996: fig. 13, 154, type 28; 6), and Jerusalem's Damascus Gate (Wightman 1989: pl. 58: 7).

FIG. 3.2: 7–11 The second form is a large storage jar. Although no complete form was found, its size can be judged from the opening diameter, which probably exceeds 50–60 cm. It has a short, straight or everted neck with four handles on the shoulders. Examples were found at Tiʿinnik (Ziadeh 1995: fig 6: 6) and Abu Gosh (de Vaux and Stève 1950: pl. F: 10).

FIG. 3.3: 1-2 The third form is a pear-shaped jar with a straight, short neck, thickened rim, two loop handles attached from the bottom of the neck to the shoulders, and a rounded base with a button at the center. It has a plain body, although a combed decoration is sometimes found on its upper part. Examples are found at Ti'innik (Ziadeh 1995: fig. 10: 6). Similar examples can be found in Jerusalem's Armenian Garden (Tushingham 1985: fig. 43: 13).

FIG 3.3: 3–6　The fourth form is also pear-shaped with a concave neck and a thickened rim. Two loop handles are attached from the middle of the neck to the upper shoulders. The base is slightly rounded with a button in the center. Similar examples were found during the Damascus Gate excavation (Wightman 1989: pl. 57: 11), in Jerusalem's Armenian Garden (Tushingham 1985: fig. 42: 5–6), and at Abu Gosh (de Vaux and Stève 1950: pl. G: 25).

FIG. 3.3: 7–8　The last form of jar is known locally as a *zir*, or water storage container. The body is of ovoid shape with a very short neck and concave base. Two loop handles are attached to its shoulders. It has a whitish, plain surface and sometimes appears with combed decoration (Ziadeh 1995: fig. 11: 5). Similar examples are probably found at the Armenian Garden in Jerusalem (Tushingham 1985: fig. 43: 14).

Cooking Vessels

FIG. 3.4　Cooking vessels include cooking pots, casseroles, and pans. The cooking pots are of two categories: handmade or wheel-thrown. They are characterized by a globular body, with thickened walls, and necks varying from everted to concave, rising to a simple vertical or everted rim. Two horizontal handles are usually attached at the shoulders, rising at a steep angle, sometimes vertically attached from the rim to the body. The clay is coarse, mixed with many white grits and straw, and poorly fired to light brown or gray. The pots are covered with heavy slip. Examples of this type were found at the following sites: Ti'innik, Stratum 6–8, dated between the 16th and 19th centuries (Ziadeh 1995: figs. 10: 1–3; 15: 1–2; 14: 5–6, 8); Jerusalem at the Damascus Gate (Wightman 1989: pl. 54); Khirbat Birzeit (Abd Rabu 2000: fig. 5); Jerusalem's Armenian Garden (Tushingham

1985: fig. 45: 16, 17); Pella, Group E (Smith, 1973: pls. 76–77); Abu Gosh (de Vaux and Stève 1950: pl. G: 38). The casseroles, or open-form cooking pots, are a type characterized by a hemispherical body and rounded, inverted rims. They usually have two horizontal loop handles attached to the rim. They are made of brown or gray clay containing a large amount of calcite. The ware is coarse, burnished, and poorly fired. This type of vessel was found at Khirbat Birzeit (Abd Rabu 2000: fig. 5: 29) and Ti'innik (Ziadeh 1995: fig. 10: 4–5).

FIG. 3.5　Pans are cooking vessels with flaring walls, joined with two vertical handles at the top of a flattened rim and a flat base. One was found at Khirbat Birzeit within the late Mamluk and Ottoman layers (Abd Rabu 2000: fig. 5: 30–31) and one at Ti'innik (Ziadeh 1995: fig. 15: 3–4), dated to the late 15th–18th centuries.

Jugs

FIG. 3.6　Jugs of this period appeared in diagnostic forms. They are of a rounded body attached to a wide, bowed neck. One or two long strap handles reach the middle of the neck and the shoulders. The bases are predominantly concave disks, although flat and high footed bases were also found. The exterior surface is covered with a cream to white slip, burnished and painted with geometric designs in red brown and black. Examples of this form were found at the following sites: Ti'innik (Ziadeh 1995, figs. 6: 4–5; 7: 1), which had forms mostly dated to late 15th–16th centuries; Pella (Smith 1973: pl. 73: 24); Tell al-Qaymun (Ben-Tor, Avissar, Portugali 1996: fig. 13–154. type 28); Abu Gosh (de Vaux and Stève 1950: pl. F: 1–3); Zir'in (Grey 1994: fig. 10: 3–4); Jerusalem's Armenian Garden (Tushingham 1985: fig. 42: 18).

FIG. 3.7　Another type of jug has a carinated body at the center, a bowed neck and simple everted rim, a single handle attached from the top of the neck to the shoulders, and a concave disk base. It is painted in geometric designs and is similar to a modern *ibriq*. The kind of jug was identified at Ti'innik (Zaideh 1995, fig. 7: 4–3) and Jerusalem's Armenian

Gardens (Tushingham 1985, fig 43: 9). Other forms of jugs have a globular body and funnel-shaped necks with a handle attached to the shoulders just below the rim (Ziadeh 1995: fig 7: 4–5, 7–8).

Basins or Craters, Bowls, Dishes, and Trays

FIGS. 3.8: 1–6 AND 3.10: 3 Basins or craters are large, deep, open-form vessels of thick, rounded or curved walls. They are built on flat or large disk bases and sometimes have two horizontal or vertical handles on the upper part of the body. Rope decoration, incisions, or paint are sometimes applied below the rim. The interior walls of almost all the vessels are slipped and burnished. The clay is light brown, buff, orange, and gray. The basins contain much straw and other organic material. Examples were found at Ti'innik (Ziadeh 1995: figs. 8: 6–10; 9: 7, 9), Khirbat Birzeit (Abd Rabu 2000: fig: 3: 1–5), Jerusalem (Tushingham 1985: fig; 45: 11, 13), Pella (Smith 1973: pl. 75: 950, 935), Jerusalem's Damascus Gate (Wightman 1989: pls. 55: 11; 56: 5), the Red Tower (Pringle 1986: fig. 41: 4), and Abu Gosh (de Vaux and Stève 1950: pl. F: 14).

FIGS. 3.8: 7–8, 3.9: 1–7 AND 3.10: 4 Bowls are handmade and wheelmade. Most are plain, although some are painted with geometric designs while others are glazed (in green or yellow-brown with or without a white slip). They are usually made of clay that has been low or medium-fired to a brown or gray. It contains a large amount of temper. The bowls are characterized by thickened, rounded and sometimes carinated walls, ending with thickened rims. They are built on ring or flat bases. Examples were found at Ti'innik (Ziadeh, 1995: fig. 16: 2, 4), Khirbat Birzeit (Abd Rabu 2000: fig: 2: 6), Damascus Gate (Wightman 1989: pls. 50–51; 55; 64: 9–10), and Jerusalem's Armenian Gardens (Tushingham 1985: fig. 41: 31).

FIG. 3.9: 8–15 Dishes can be handmade or wheelmade. The form is of slightly curved walls, which end with slightly thickened triangular flat-top rims. They sit on a concave disk base, and sometimes have a horseshoe handle attached to the body just below the rim. The vessel is slipped and painted with red, brown or black lines. Examples were found at Ti'innik (Ziadeh 1995: figs. 8: 2–3; 16: 5, 9, 11–12).

FIG. 3.10: 1–2 Trays are handmade, large platters with short curved walls. Very few were found in Ti'innik (Ziadeh 1995: Fig. 9: 1–2).

TECHNIQUES OF MANUFACTURE AND DECORATION

The vessels described above were constructed and decorated using a range of techniques, which are surveyed below.

Handmade Techniques

In this technique the potter usually worked the dry clay by hand until it achieved an even consistency, later crushing and soaking the clay in water to allow the non-plastic material to settle. In order to obtain clay of suitable plasticity, he then added a sort of temper (sifted, crushed sherds [grog], crushed calcite, or limestone, in addition to a vegetable matter, such as straw) to the mixture. Temper was added to facilitate particular vessel functions, such as cooking.

The material remains indicate that the handmade technique consisted primarily of coil-building and cloth sack-building. Coil building was mostly used for basins and other open vessels. For the largest basins, the coils were added along the edge of a rounded flat base, which was usually a rounded straw mat that was used to rotate the vessel. Traces of these mats on the bottom of many flat basins are frequently noted in published reports (Ziadeh 1995: 217–18). At the top of each coil there was a groove to receive the next, until the vessel reached the height needed. Many of the Early Ottoman handmade sherds show break-lines along coil grooves.

Cloth sack-building was a technique for constructing handmade vessels of closed form, such as small jars, juglets, and table amphoras. The technique involved filling a cloth sack with wet sand until it achieved approximately the form needed. Then a flattened sheet of clay was roughly pressed around the sack of sand and left to dry until it was leather-hard. Another layer of clay was then added to this first layer. This made the wall of the vessel twice as thick; sometimes three layers were used. This technique, therefore, produced rather thick-walled vessels. Finally the sand in the sack was emptied. The surface of these vessels was usually treated by slipping and burnishing (Avissar 1996: 168; Smith 1973: 240).

Wheelmade Technique

The wheelmade technique was used to construct a small number of Ottoman vessels of largely closed form and generally large size, such as water and olive oil containers used for storage and shipping. In Palestine, wheel-thrown plain wares, as well as the handmade vessels associated with village households of the 13th–15th centuries, continued to be produced in the Ottoman period but in lesser volume than before. The Palestinian olive oil industry, with its requirements for containers, may have been sufficient in itself to sustain some wheel-thrown ceramic production during this period. According to Ottoman court records from Jerusalem dated to the third quarter of the 16th century, olive oil was an important commodity and was stored and shipped in various ceramic vessels. Camels delivering oil to Jerusalem from the northern villages carried the loads of jars, which certainly consisted of wheel-thrown products (Brown 1992: 310–11).

Molding Techniques

Molds were used to produce dishes and spouted jug (*ibriq*) necks, but mostly for tobacco pipes. Hundreds of mold-made tobacco pipe fragments were discovered at sites such as Jerusalem, Yoqne'am, and Ti'innik, as well as numerous other sites (Wightman 1989: 73–74).

Painting Techniques

One important characteristic of the decoration of handmade, closed forms, and a few of the open forms, was painting with geometric designs. The paint originally came in the form of small red stones, which easily dissolved in water, and was applied with a small wooden stick. When applied heavily on the body of the pot, the paint looked almost black; when applied thinly, it looked brown. The painted designs on some pots covered the entire body, which was divided into zones, and each zone was outlined by thick horizontal lines. These zones were then subdivided by slightly narrower lines into diagonal and triangular shapes or other combinations of basic geometric patterns and filled in with plant designs.

Glazed Techniques

Glazed pottery production deteriorated in the Ottoman period, and very few glazed vessels have been published from inland Palestinian sites, although this scenario is slowly changing. The most common glazed forms were bowls, pans, and cooking pots. The glaze is mainly a green color, sometimes integrated with yellow or brown (Wightman 1989: 75–78, pl. 64: 9–13; Abd Rabu 2000: fig: 6).

Carving Techniques

This technique appears mostly on tobacco pipes. As they were manufactured by molds, decorative elements covering these pipes were carved on the mold itself. Each section of the pipes had its own, characteristic designs, which included grooves, rows of dots, wavy lines, and petals. Most of the pipes were covered with a highly polished, reddish-brown slip.

Conclusions

This survey of Ottoman ceramic forms and assemblages in Palestine suggests that the majority of Ottoman pottery was handmade, with some quantity of wheel production. It was mostly geometrically painted; glazed pottery was rare, particularly so at inland sites. The study also concludes that while some forms from the Mamluk era continued to be produced, many others unique to this period can also be identified. These include tobacco pipes, bowed rim jars, *zirs* (water containers), open cooking pots, and certain kinds of casseroles.

Although most Ottoman-era vessels are coarse and plain, some are slipped and burnished. While the quantity of glazed wares had certainly diminished in the first centuries of Ottoman rule, they never completely disappeared. Importation, even if only on a regional scale, continued, demonstrating that Palestinian villages remained part of local and regional exchange networks throughout the Ottoman period, all the while maintaining an active cottage industry of ceramic production. Future studies on vessel form should address the issue of function, in this way contributing to a better understanding of consumption, specialization of vessel types, and changing patterns in diet and kitchen culture.

Note

1   Scales in the figures vary throughout. Only general forms, not sizes, are indicated.

Chapter 4

An Ethno-Archaeological Approach to Ottoman Pottery

The Case of "Gaza Gray Ware"

by Hamed Salem

INTRODUCTION

Archaeological and historical sources suggest that many Palestinian ceramic traditions rooted in the Ottoman era continue until modern times. Although William Duncan Strong called for the use of a historical approach in analyzing archaeological remains about a century ago, it was rarely applied to Palestinian archaeology, specifically in the study of Islamic pottery. More recently, however, archaeologists around the globe have conducted analytical studies of traditional pottery in an attempt to reconstruct cultural continuity and change (Kramer 1985; Stark 2003). The following study of Gaza Gray Ware (hereafter "GGW") is an effort in this direction.

The study of the Gaza ceramic industry has been previously hampered by the paucity of published data on Ottoman pottery in general. For too long, little attention was given to the archaeology of the Ottoman period; consequently, little data was collected to facilitate a comprehensive analysis of Ottoman material culture. One reason for this is that various antiquity legislations did not provide protection for remains post-dating 1700 CE. Certain Ottoman remains were, and still are,

being removed without the need to obtain official permits from the antiquities authorities. The effects of these laws on the archaeological fieldwork are noticeable. Archaeological surveys have ignored Ottoman settlement systems as an archaeological resource with which to reconstruct the cultural traditions of a region. In many cases the surveyors have simply excluded the Ottoman remains from their reports. Moreover, few archaeological excavations were conducted with the primary objective of reconstructing Ottoman material culture; when Ottoman remains were encountered, they were merely reported as "recent," without a full analysis of the context. The upper strata were often deemed irrelevant by many excavators, who sought answers to questions related to much earlier periods than the one under discussion. In other instances, Ottoman material was reported from "mixed" deposits without describing in any detail their specific stratigraphic contexts. Consequently, the typological and chronological framework of Ottoman pottery was entirely neglected.

The second problem blocking an assessment of Ottoman deposits and sites is related to the specific nature of the Ottoman remains. Many extant Palestinian villages occupy the same living space as the Ottoman villages. Modern inhabitants have simply built on top of, or adjacent to, the Ottoman deposits. New villages have been built over abandoned Ottoman ones, and residents often reuse the ancient structures for their own purposes. As a result, recent building activities have caused severe damage to Ottoman sites, and the physical remains of these settlements are rapidly disappearing.

Finally, textual data sources fall short in fully documenting the pottery craft. Historical and travellers' accounts of the late Ottoman period took little notice of ceramic production, while at times recording other industries. It is not immediately clear why this is so, except that perhaps the craft was traditionally less prestigious on a social level and was not as worthy of documentation. In short, such written sources are more useful as chronological indicators than as detailed descriptions of the craft.

"Ottoman archaeology" as a specific field of research has, thus, emerged only recently (Baram and Carroll 2000; Walker 1999). Thanks to the recent attention given to Ottoman remains, including pottery, a new era, aimed at building the archaeology of the period, has begun. As a result, we have gained a better understanding of Ottoman remains in terms of the stratigraphic sequence at Palestinian tells. Up to this point, Ottoman pottery has been only sporadically reported. For instance, little reference has been made to the Gaza Gray pottery, even though it is the "most diagnostic ware of the Ottoman period," comprising 58 percent of the Ottoman sherds collected form North Jordan (Walker 2005: 82).

This chapter attempts to reconstruct the origin, distribution, and production of the Gaza Gray Ware tradition (GGW). The assumption is that traditional modes of production have not changed much since the early Ottoman period and perhaps before. The significance of GGW lies in its continuity – it can be traced back at least 500 years. It will be analyzed through four methods: ethno-historical documentation of ceramic production and use; technological studies of the clay and tempering agents, combined with petrographic analysis; ethnographic fieldwork; archaeological study of selected excavated sites, specifically Tell Ti'innik and the Birzeit region.

Centers of Production

Gaza

Gaza is one of the most densely inhabited cities of the world and has a long history of occupation. The ancient site of Tell al-A'jjul was occupied in the Early Bronze Age, and modern Gaza City has roots in the Roman period. Ottoman Gaza is probably the same city described by the travellers of the 7th and 8th centuries (Le Strange 1965). Gaza gained importance in the Mamluk period, primarily as a regional market and a sea port between Egypt and Mesopotamia. It became one of the most prosperous cities in the Mediterranean (fig. 4.1). Major trade routes, the oldest of which was the Via Maris, passed the city by way of the Negev and the coast. Other routes connected Gaza to Darb Gaza, Darb al-Hajj, and Darb al-Tujjar (Robinson and Smith 1856: 175). Trade caravans stopped at the city since Byzantine times in order to exchange various goods for wheat and wine.

Gaza produced wine and exported it to Egypt and throughout the eastern Mediterranean since the Middle Bronze Age (McGovern 2003), and archaeological evidence points to wine presses in Gaza and throughout the region (Mayerson 1985). In support of this prosperous wine production was the production of Byzantine-era wine jars; archaeological and historical accounts suggest that Khalsa (Elusa) was one of these wine and jar-producing centers (Negev 1993). Darom (Deir al-Balah), which is mentioned in early Arabic sources, was also known for its wine, which it continued to produce until the town was destroyed by Salah al-Din (al-Hamawi 1955: 704). The wine of Darom was famous for its quality. The Arab poet Ismail ibn Yaser praised the town's wine in his poetry, "as I am on the day they had gone, drunk … from Darom wine."

The production of Gaza pottery should be seen within the context of the region's prosperous economy: wine and olive oil production, storage, and transport required a tremendous number of jars. Al-Maqrizi reported that the Mamluk prince Yalbugha destroyed 44,000 wine jars and several other loads of the same in the Egyptian town of

Shubra, which was known for its wine industry (al-Maqrizi 1924: 1204). Byzantine Gaza must have produced a much larger amount of pottery for handling its wine production, in addition to those jars used to store olive oil and water. This mass production required a large pottery production and distribution network. During the early Arab Islamic periods, the author did not expect wine jars in a large quantity, since wine was produced only for local consumption by the non-Muslim communities. Nonetheless, water and olive jars continued to be produced in large numbers. The author's interviews with a wine maker from A'bud/ Ramallah revealed that wine and water jars have a similar form. Both have a narrow neck and base, although olive jars have a wider mouth. A jar can be used to store either wine or water, but the same jar cannot be used for both. Water jars are porous to keep the water cool, while the wine jars are non-porous.

Many writers continued to praise Gaza as one of the most important trade centers in the region. Although Robinson did not mention pottery production specifically, he praised Gaza for its bazaars and export of items to other cities on the *hajj* road (Robinson and Smith 1856: 40). Other accounts attest to the sale of locally produced pottery in the bazaars; however, Gatt (1885) observed that Gazan potters did not make an adequate amount of money from making pottery, as opposed to pottery traders, who turned a good profit. He reported that one trader made 30,000 franks from selling pottery. Gatt also reported that certain pots were made for the local market, while others were made for external distribution. Profitability, therefore, made Gaza one of the major ceramic production centers in Palestine, throughout the Mediterranean, and in the Near East.

Other Production Centers

It is often thought that Gaza City was the only production center for Gray Ware. It was, however, manufactured in other places as well. Dabagh (1964) reported that the village of Fallujah, located 30 km north of Gaza on a well-traveled trade route, was built in the 14th century by refugees who followed the Sufi Imam al-Fallujah of the town of Fallujah in Iraq. Some families living there came from Gaza, likely bringing their pottery traditions with them. It is also possible that the families who came from Iraq did the same and then transferred their own traditions to Gaza. Fallujah was once famous for its Wednesday market, which sold items that included pottery to the Bedouins of the Negev, and it may be that some of the Negev pottery originated from this village, as was the case of published examples from Tell al-Hesi (Toombs 1985; Eakins 1993) and Sataf (Gibson et al. 1991).

Another production center was Khan Yunis, located south of Gaza. Outside Gaza, Gray Ware pottery was also produced in Hebron for a short period. The Gaza tradition was transmitted to these places either by relatives or by potters who once worked in Gaza and then were hired by potters elsewhere. However, according to Gaza potters, Gray Ware pottery that was not produced in Gaza was of lesser quality. This is one reason why it did not succeed in other places. Gazans considered the tradition their speciality, which no other potters could imitate adequately. The introduction of refrigerators and water pipes had a more negative effect on the craft than competition from other potters.

The Archaeological Context

General Remarks on the Gray Ware Tradition

It is possible that the origin of Gray Ware pottery stems from an imitation of Neolithic-era basalt grinders. However, pottery fired using the reduction method was produced by the beginning of the Early Bronze Age, in a tradition known as the Gray Burnish pottery (often called Esdraelon Ware). A later tradition was known as Khirbet Kerak Ware. The closest Early Bronze Age parallels are found outside of Palestine, such as Metallic, Kura-Araxes, and Early Trans-Caucasian Wares (D. Meyer, personal communication). The same tradition, both produced locally and imported, continued into the Middle and Bronze Ages as Tell al-Yahudiyya Ware (McGovern et al. 1994: fig. 5a), Trojan Gray pottery (Allen 1994: fig. 6), the Iron Age Black juglet, Bucchero Black pottery, and Greek Black-Glazed pottery.

The so-called Beisan Ware of the end of the Byzantine-Umayyad period is an early example of ribbed Gray Ware. Landgraff (1980: 67 ff.) provides a technological analysis of the differences between black and red amphorae and the Gaza wine amphorae. He notes that the production sequence is not different, but there are small differences in details of form, such as handle attachment and amphora shape. He further implies that the black amphorae were made in a Beisan workshop. Gray Ware amphorae have been found at many sites, including Tell Ti'innik, and as late as the Abbasid period. Such amphorae do not appear again before the early 17th century.

Technically, the early examples of the Late Byzantine/Early Umayyad gray tradition differ from the Gaza Gray Ware in the application of a slip layer, a technique that we may call Gray Slip Ware. Perhaps an imitation of the black glaze, only the exterior surface is gray, while the interior surface and the core are not (usually of brownish to reddish colours). To obtain the gray hue, the potters applied a carbon-based slip, and consequently it was better termed "Gray Slip Ware." Such vessels need not be fired in a full oxygen-reduction atmosphere (*tatwisa* method) like that applied to Gaza pottery.

Ottoman Gaza Gray Ware

The Gaza region has been known for its pottery production since the Bronze Age. Pottery kilns were discovered at many archaeological sites, including Deir al-Balah. More than likely these kilns were related to wine production. Byzantine workshops producing the elongated Gaza wine jar were found at 20 settlements around Gaza (Israel 1994: 106). Another kiln was reported at Beit Hanun and dated to the Arab Islamic period. The final word on the origins of the GGW tradition awaits a thorough scientific analysis; however, it is likely that GGW originated in southern Palestine during the Byzantine period or perhaps even earlier.

Gazan potters controlled the reduction method since the Middle Bronze Age; according to the lab results of neutron activation analysis, both the Dolphin Form and perhaps the Tell al-Yahudiyya Ware were made in the Gaza region (McGovern et al. 1999: 31). Some of the earliest evidence of such an industry is found at the Nabataean town of Khalsa (Halusa or Elusa). This site was a station on the main road connecting Gaza to Petra; therefore, it may have been influenced by outsiders as much as it influenced other places. That Elusa had a pottery workshop is documented historically and archaeologically (Negev 1993). One historical account noted the existence of "white, black, and red" pottery among the ruins of Elusa (Bonar 1857: 323). A kiln was reported in the area where it produced gray ribbed ware, similar to that found today at Gaza (S. Bucking, lecture given at Albright Institute, April 2006). This may be the earliest GGW example reported in an archaeological context. Outside of Elusa, however, the archaeological record has produced little evidence that true GGW was manufactured prior to the 16th century.

Time and Space Dimensions of the GGW: Some Basic Discussions

In general, archaeological surveys and excavations have revealed scarce remains of GGW. It is perhaps a result of the little attention given to late Ottoman remains, in particular, to the Gray Ware. For a long time, this well-defined tradition was mistakenly dated to the 19th and 20th centuries and considered a production of recent Palestinian culture. However, thanks to the growing body of information, it is more acceptable today to date the pottery to an earlier period and to place it in a wider geographic distribution.

The archaeological records agree in principle with the historical records (see below) in dating the GGW to the late 16th and early 17th centuries. Archaeological finds also confirm that the tradition had a wider geographic distribution than was previously assumed. Gaza Gray Ware has been reported from Tell Ti'innik and Qabatiyya, Tell al-Hesi to the north, and at Negev to the south, as well as sites in Jordan and the Sinai (Mason and Millwright 1998; Walker 2005; Whitcomb, personal communication). The following is a discussion of selected archaeological reports relevant to the context and chronology of GGW.

Gaza Ware from Stratified or Datable Contexts

Qabatiyya

Qabatiyya is a small town located near Jenin. In 1999, the Palestinian Department of Antiquities and Cultural Heritage began excavation after a cave was accidentally discovered during a construction project (Taha et al. 2006). Two small jars were hidden in the cave, containing a hoard of 420 silver coins dated from 1538 through 1612 AD (Taha et al. 2006: 19). The overall shape, profile, and surface finishing of the jars conform to traditional GGW; however, they differ in base shape, which is concave with an omphalos (fig. 4.2: 1, 3), compared to the more typical rounded or flat base (fig. 4.2: 5). They also have a round-sectioned handle, compared to the flat section of Gaza Ware. The jars, nonetheless, fall into the Gray Slip tradition. Therefore, they may represent a transitional stage between the Ottoman Gaza Ware and other Early Islamic wares.

Tell Ti'innik

Tell Ti'innik is located about 13 km west of Jenin. The excavations of the Early Ottoman site were conducted by Birzeit University from 1985 to 1987, under the direction of the late Albert Glock. Ti'innik is one of the rare projects that focused on the Ottoman period (Ziadeh 2000). A preliminary report of the pottery was published by Ziadeh (1995). The site is of tremendous value for its stratified sequence of Ottoman pottery.

Although the published ceramic report was based on preliminary stratigraphic analysis, it provided a tentative date relevant to the development and nature of GGW (Ziadeh 1995: 211). The Ottoman period was divided into six strata, beginning with late 15th and early 16th centuries and ending with the early 20th century. Thirty-four sherds, 11 jars, and 23 ibriqs (Ziadeh 1995: fig. 13: 8, 9) were identified as belonging to this ware. The GGW was dated on the basis of thermoluminescence and associated tobacco pipes and green

slip-glaze ware. The earliest occupational floor (L. 138) was dated to the late 15th and early 16th centuries and produced four sherds, one jar, and three ibriqs. The majority of the sherds of GGW were from the 19th (25 sherds) and 20th (19 sherds) centuries. No sherd was represented in Stratum 9 (18th century). Therefore, GGW appears in Strata 6 (16th–17th centuries) and 7 (17th century) and reached its peak in Strata 11 and 12.

According to petrographic analysis, the fabric matrix of the Ti'innik product matches the traditional GGW, composed of quartz, plagioclase, microcline, and lime. It also includes small quantities of hornblende-biotite and pyroxene. As for form, the amphora rim is not comparable to that of typical Gaza jars; the ibriqs, in the other hand, belong to the Gaza tradition.

Sataf

Sataf is located 23 km west of Jerusalem overlooking Wadi al-Sarar. Surveys and excavations at the site were conducted by S. Gibson from 1987 to 1989 and were among the earliest focusing on the development of a Palestinian cultural landscape (Gibson et al. 1991). GGW sherds were recovered from the village terraces in non-domestic contexts, where two Ottoman phases were identified (Gibson et al. 1991: 45–47). The proposed late 16th-century date is based on a coin fragment, providing one of the earliest dates for GGW. Sataf Gray Ware may have originated from the adjacent village of Fallujah, which was known as a ceramic production center during the time when Sataf was active (see below).

Tell Jemmah

Tell Jemmah, approximately 15 km south of Gaza, was excavated from 1974 to 1977 by the Smithsonian Institution in Washington, D.C. (Schaefer 1989). Excavations there revealed a small Mamluk village. Three coins were discovered in Room 1, dating it and its fill to the 13th–14th centuries (Schaefer 1989: 36-37). GGW was the second most abundant type of pottery recovered from the room fill and floor, though it represents only 8 percent of the collection (Schaefer 1989: 42-43). Schaefer proposed that the Gray Ware may have originated in North Syria and was transferred from North Palestine to the southern region. He further argued that the current GGW continued a long tradition from the Early Islamic period.

As the coins imply, GGW is dated to the late Mamluk period. As a result, the site reveals one of the earliest dates for the ware. The jar shape and rim forms resemble those found at Qabatiyya and, to a greater extent, traditional GGW (fig. 4.2: 2). They also match figure 4.2: 4, which is in the Birzeit University ethnographic collection.

Negev Sites

Rosen and Goodfriend (1993) suggest that the dating of Gaza Ware will reduce the perceived gap in the occupational history of the Negev, which was long believed to have been abandoned from the 8th–9th centuries through the end of the 18th century.[1] The dates were obtained from two GGW sherds from non-occupational layers of the wadi deposit south of Bir Es-Saba. The deposits are dated from 1640 to 1760 by amino acid epimerization analysis of land snails (Rosen and Goodfriend 1993: 146). The lower date agrees with the other dates obtained by coins and thermoluminescence. The Negev form may belong to a jug or *ibriq,* which was used to carry drinking water to the agricultural fields. It conforms in form to other published examples.

Non-Dated GGW

Several stratified sites revealed GGW that could not be dated precisely. Some sherds were, however, associated with Marseilles roof tiles dated to the mid-19th century.

Tell Qaymun (Tell Yoqneʿam)

The site is located at the southern end of Marj Ibn Amir, between Tell Tiʿinnik and Haifa. Excavations under the leadership of Hebrew University between 1977 and 1988 revealed a settlement from the Crusader through the Ottoman periods (Avissar

2005). Qaymun is a castle mentioned in medieval Arabic sources (Hamawi 1955: 1457; Ibn al-Athir 1983: 220).

GGW at Tell Yoqneʿam was recovered from different loci. The most important was locus 11019, which is described as the Ottoman dismantling of a floor.[2] It seems that it is one of the earliest floors in the area, giving a *terminus post quem* for the Ottoman occupation at the site; locus 12000, a fill deposit, provides the *terminus ante quem.* Based on the site's stratigraphy, it is possible to date the GGW sherds there to the Mamluk period. Another Gray Ware sherd was identified in a mixed locus, derived from the cleaning of "fill" outside the Crusader tower down to bedrock. The majority of the pottery from this locus was Mamluk in date and earlier, although the recovery of some tobacco pipes attest to deposition of the 17th century or later (Avissar 2005: 86, 91). No precise dates from other independent materials were available. The locus, stratigraphy, and rim typology suggest an earlier date, as a whole, for the GGW sherds.

The Tell Yoqneʿam data agrees with Ziadeh's (1995) conclusion that the Geometric Painted pottery (HMGP) continues through the Ottoman period and further supports an early date for GGW (Avissar 2005: 77). However, it is possible that the sherds may belong to another tradition similar to GGW. The inverted thickened rim does not resemble the typical out-turned, thickened rims of known GGW. The site has the ability to shed light on the spread of GGW to the North.

Tell al-Hesi

Tell al-Hesi is located at the mouth of the Negev desert, northeast of Gaza. The site was excavated for many seasons, and one of the more intensive excavations was that of the Joint Archaeological Expedition at Tell al-Hesi, directed by J. Worell, L. Toombs, and others. Tell al-Hesi presented several examples of Gaza Gray Ware from the Ottoman cemetery and the site itself. The excavators did not provide any chronological data for the jars, although, when based on comparisons with burial customs from other sites, they implied that the burial jars were in the 12th–14th- or 19th-century tradition (Blakely et al. 1980: 107). Gaza Ware from the cemetery predates living memory, since none of the potters recognized the tradition (Toombs 1985: 106–7).

Birzeit Region

Surveys in the region of Birzeit have demonstrated an abundance of Gaza Ware. The majority of the sherds are from the remains located next to the abandoned Burham village between the Byzantine/Crusader church and the Sheikh Burhami shrine. Recent excavations at Khirbet Birzeit have shown scarce remains of GGW.

Sanir, North Lod

The site is identified with Sanir, or Sebatra, located north of Lod. GGW came from Stratum III (Lazar 1999: fig. 8). Locus 1009 happened to be the earliest deposit next to Mamluk Wall 1002.

Other Sites

A few other excavated sites have revealed fragments of pottery belonging to the GGW tradition (fig. 4.4): Tirat al-Karmel (Segal 2006); Zamarin (Kletter 2005); al-Jura near Asqalan (Kogan-Zehavi 2006); Khirbat al-Saharij (Avissar 2006); Emmaus (Rapuano 2000).

Historical Context of the GGW

Ethno-Historical Context

Historical accounts of Gaza have provided supplementary information on the development and chronology of the pottery. There are four types of historical records: the official Ottoman *defters*, *Shari'a* (Islamic law) records, travellers' eyewitness accounts, and photo records. Although the historical accounts make little reference to GGW, they are useful because they indicate pottery production from the 17th through the mid-19th centuries (Hütteroth and Abdulfattah 1977; Barclay 1858; Smith et al. 1888).

The earliest Ottoman *defter*s prior to 1596/7 make no reference to pottery, indicating that pottery was not taxed or may not have existed. It is also possible that pottery was included under other items (Cohen and Lewis 1978). Although one can note that Cohen and Lewis (1978) did not record pottery, it was included in the 1596/7 *defter* by Hütteroth and Abdulfattah (1977: 91). This later record is the earliest Ottoman historical account on Gaza pottery as subject to taxation. According to the register, the tax share of Gazan *fawakhir* (potters) was 600 *akçe*, which was less than 0.5 percent of the city's entire revenue. We know that this figure is very low for a town, considering craftsmanship was a main source of income, second only to farming (Schölch 1993). The potters of Ramla, as in Gaza, contributed less than one percent of the town's taxable income. It is likely that craftsmen tended to hide some of their products from the tax collectors (K. Abdulfattah, personal communication). Thus, it is difficult to rely on the register taxes for any detailed conclusions about scale of production.

The information provided by the *defter*, however, is the earliest clear reference to the ceramic production in Gaza and Ramla during the Ottoman period. The two major production centers were paying taxes at the time, implying an active and productive industry. In an early photo, Gaza pottery is displayed on Ramla Street alongside common housewares (Graham-Brown 1980: 122, fig. 34). In later historical sources, peasants made a distinction between the Gaza and Ramla traditions. This is similar to the potter's distinction today between blue-"black" and white water jars, or *zarawiyya zerka* and *zarawiyya bayda*.

Little is known of Gaza pottery production prior to the British Survey of Western Palestine. Reports from the Survey made a clear reference to Gaza production: "There is a bazaar in the town, and soap is manufactured, as well as a peculiar black pottery. The potteries are west of the town" (Conder and Kitchener 1881: 235). This is the same location of kilns today. Although travellers provided information about the importance of Gaza in the trade network of southern Bilad al-Sham, it sounds as if pottery production itself was so common and cheap that it was not considered significant.

In 1858, Gaza had an "extensive pottery works in the suburbs" (Barclay 1858: 577). *Shari'a* (Islamic law) court records of 1857–1861 indicate that the ceramic industry flourished and its products were widely distributed. The city had more than one pottery market (Rafeq 1980: 54–56). One was called by either the name *Khan Suq al-Fukhar* (the pottery market) or *Suq al-Fuwakhiriyya* (the potters market), which is located in *Mahalat al-Burjuliyya,* one of the city's largest and oldest quarters (Cohen and Lewis 1978: 118–19). Another potters' district was known as *Mahalat al-Daraj,* which is the location of present-day workshops. This area had pottery workshops and a market known in records as *Khan al-Fawakhir* (the pottery workshop) and *Khan Suq al-Fukhar* (pottery market streets).

These legal records include the workshops' economic activity, listing the names of owners and buyers. In one instance a potter named Salman Ismail (IV) bought a total of 12 *qirat* of ceramic vessels from Ali Khaled al-Qa'awah's workshop for 1080 *qirsh*. At the time the town had more than 14 workshops; four were owned by the al-Qa'awah family. Another belonged to one Suleiman A'ttallah, the grandfather of the famous A'ttalah potters' family. A third workshop was owned by a woman, although it is difficult to know whether she inherited it or was a potter herself. We know from ethnographic accounts that Gazan women worked in the workshops but only in rare cases as potters.

It is clear that the craft was a family business. When the family expanded, they split and built more workshops. Many of the workshops contained more than one wooden wheel. Pottery was produced in mass quantities and transported to other cities by camels. The records also mention Gaza pottery being transported to Jerusalem. Coleman wrote the following observation: "The pottery kilns here at Gaza are numerous, and turn out much manufactured ware. The boys bring clay from a place south of Gaza in large quantities. But the article is brittle, the clay poorly mixed, the burning insufficient, and potsherds of Gaza pottery may be seen in piles around every village from Gaza to Damascus" (Coleman 1881: 491).

Simultaneously, Gatt's (1885) report on the Gaza industry included an account on pottery production which echoes that of the *Shari'a* records. Pottery production continued as Gaza's most famous industry; potters even had their own quarter in the upper city. Gatt counted 16 workshops, some of which contained as many as three kilns and four wheels, while others had no more than two or three. Among the forms produced were jars, basins of all kinds, small lamps, and pipes.

The potters were specialized in using camel and goat dung as fuels to produce the gray color and to make the pottery stronger and more durable. It was favored in all of Palestine and among the Bedouins. Gatt also reported on caravan boats bringing goods into Gaza and loading Gaza vessels for export. One trader gained 30,000 franks from selling pottery.

A comparison of *Shari'a* records and Gatt's account indicates that the number of workshops increased from 14 in 1860 to 16 in 1885. Based on Gatt's data, we know that at least four potters were working in each workshop – a city-wide total of 64 active potters. They may have produced more than 6,000 pieces per day (an average of 90 vessels per potter per day), which was a sufficient quantity to load six kilns (see below). We can expect that thousands of vessels were produced for local and foreign trade. Later accounts also mention Gaza pottery. In his comparison of GGW and ancient pottery, Smith claimed that "this would be a globular vessel of blue porous clay – the ordinary Gaza pottery" (Smith et al. 1888: 513).

Mid to late 19th-century travellers' photos also record the production, distribution, use, and chronology of GGW. The Gaza jar appears in images of Palestinian Bedouin and peasants, who used it to carry water from the springs (Wilson 1880: 36). The jar was also used by the Bedouin to carry milk. The photos reveal other forms, such as the *ibriq*, put to various uses in houses and courtyards.

ETHNOGRAPHIC ACCOUNTS

Rye (1976) briefly reported on Gaza pottery production as well. The report is the summary of a fieldwork project conducted among traditional Palestinian potters, directed by the late Albert Glock, under the financial support of Birzeit

University and with field records by John Landgraff and Owen Rye. Rye collected data and forms from Gaza potters shortly before the closure of many workshops. Rye counted 40 potters, which was a decrease from the 1930's census (Rye 1976: 769). The decrease was due to the political difficulties experienced in Palestinian areas after the 1948 war when many potters became refugees in neighboring countries and the West Bank (Salem 1986). Rye noted that Gaza had shown the most extensive potters' movement in and out of the region for the last 40 years (Rye 1976: 770). The effect of warfare on the disintegration of the pottery craft at the end of the Mamluk period provides an appropriate parallel (Walker 1999: 224). Gaza potters, however, provided a sophisticated model of pottery transmission by re-establishing their workshops, adapting to a new tradition, and maintaining the old one (Salem 2006).

Generally, workshops were located within the urban area. Clay was brought from 30 km away to special basins, where ash from the kiln was added at the bottom of the clay. Rye reported on the particular Gaza firing method (Rye 1976: 722 ff.). The kilns were up to 3–4 m high. He stated that firing GGW was

> … essentially the same as the red pottery, except for its treatment at the end of the firing. Then full temperature is reached, if red pottery is desired the kiln is simply allowed to cool, if black ware is desired, at full temperature the firebox and chamber of the kiln are stuffed full with organic materials. The stokehole and exit flues are then sealed and the kiln allowed to cool. Carbon incorporated in the pores of the ware by this much-reduced cooling produces the black colour. The technique is used in Gaza is similar to that used in the Nile Delta, and has considerable antiquity. It is recently introduced in some other Palestinian workshops, notably Jaba.

A decade after this account, only 24 workshops remained in operation. By the mid-1990s, only four to six workshops remained open. Currently, only ten workshops are active, a reflection of the poor economic conditions in the region today. Several factors have impacted the deterioration of this craft, mainly market limitations, competition of aluminium and plastic objects, and the negative social attitudes toward the craft. Sons of potters consider it a unprofitable and difficult job (Salem 1999, 2006).

Traditional Gaza pottery is distinguished by its techniques, firing method, surface treatment, and form. It is safe to assume that this tradition did not change much over the past four decades. The following data is a brief account of Gaza pottery production based on 1996 fieldwork conducted by the author at M. A'ttallah's and other workshops. Data was obtained through extensive personal interviews, in addition to direct observation during several visits. The interviews were recorded on tape.

The Production Sequence of the GGW

In 1996, the master potter Mustafa A'ttallah was in his early 80s. At that time he was retired, but one of his sons was still making pottery. In 1857, A'ttallah's family was mentioned in the *Shari'a* records, which makes his workshop nearly two centuries old. According to him, Gaza workshops produced white, red, and black pottery. They also produced a gray pottery called *"fakhar baladi"* in the forms of jars, cooking pots, and *ibriqs*. The potters of Gaza considered "black" pottery (*fukhara aswad*) a typical tradition of Gaza that was inherited from the older generations.

Gaza pottery is identified by the black or dark gray color of its interior and exterior surfaces; the gray color also extends to the core. The pottery is made from heavy clay rich in quartz and hematite, with sand quartz and feldspar added. Usually the clay is fired red in an oxidization atmosphere, but it turns to gray in a reduction atmosphere. The primary decoration is shallow ribbing at the shoulder and upper body; however, in certain cases ribbing may be applied to all the body.

Clay and Tempering Agents

Petrographic analysis has shown that the clay matrix is rich with feldspar and small fragments of quartz, hematite, mica, and epidote. Added non-plastics, like quartz and feldspar, represent up to 30 percent (as seen in the section), while the clay matrix includes 10–15 percent small voids. The clay matrix of the Ottoman pottery is similar to that of the current pottery made in Gaza. The petrographic example of Tell Ti'innik belongs to Fabric 5a, which contains "quartz, plagioclase, microcline and lime, and the matrix includes small hornblende-biotite and pyroxene" (Ziadeh 1995: 220).

The Gaza potters use the same clay source, known as "red clay" (*tin ahmar*). It is mined from caves 20–30 m deep, located near Jabalya village, which is about 3 km from the workshops. Jabalya is derived from *jebel*, an Aramaic word meaning clay, so it may have been one of the ancient clay sources as well. The clay is placed in baskets made of straw. It was formerly brought by donkeys, but now trucks deliver it to the workshops. The amount procured depends on the potter's need; an average car load is about 8 m³, which is sufficient for two to three months of work. A'ttallah uses about five to six car loads per year. As Jabalya is close to the seashore, the clay is heavy with sand and, thus, does not need many additives. The potters of Gaza considered their clay harder to work and "stronger" than the clays of the mountainous regions, such as Hebron.

There are two methods used for clay preparation. In the traditional method, the potter spreads the clay on the ground and crushes it with a stick. It is then cleaned of any impurities such as large stones and organic materials. The clay is occasionally picked up by hand from the pile and set aside. Finally, water is added in small quantities until the clay is wet. A'ttallah introduced another method in the early 1940s, borrowing the idea from potters in Acre (who also belong to A'ttallah's family). It is the common *taswil* method, familiar to many Palestinian potters. The potters compare the process to water and oil – the oil flows over water. In the case of the clay, the light clay particles float on top, while impurities, such as sand, settle at the bottom; this process of separating the clay from other impurities is called *qasif*. The process takes place in a small pit (*fajrah*), the clay filling 60 to 70 rubber buckets (*qufas*) or plastic buckets (*jardals*). Enough water is added to liquify the clay. The clay stays in the pit for three to five days. The potters realize that the finer and cleaner the clay, the better it is to handle and work. It was the Gaza potters who first appreciated the need to improve the clay's plasticity and workability.

The second stage is called *al-taswil*. The liquid clay is poured through a special pipe from the first basin into a second basin and left there to dry for three to four days. The potter knows the clay is ready once it starts to crack (*yeshkah*), and, according to A'ttallah, it is then worked through evenly (i.e., is well levigated). If the clay dries too much, it is referred to as *'adman* or *yabis al-tin*, which means the clay is "dead" or too dry. Before that happens, the clay is stored in a large pit (*jorah*) inside the workshop and covered with plastic sacks, remaining there from one month up to two years. Clay is usually prepared during the summer and stored for the winter season; however, in an emergency, it can be prepared during the winter.

After the clay is prepared, it is kneaded either by hand or in a special machine, which is used to work the clay and produces ready molds, about 50 cm long and 10 cm in diameter. If the machine is not working or the electricity is off, then the potter has to resort to the hand-kneading method (*al-laff*). However, the potter states that without the machine, he would never make pottery because hand-kneading is a very hard process.

Forming Techniques

There is no major difference between forming the gray pottery and other wares in their initial stages of production; in all cases it is done on the wheel in the common *tajlis* method, which Rye (1976) considered one of the most sophisticated techniques in the world. There are several stages in the preparation of the clays and vessels, and the clay at each stage of the process is known to local potters by specific Arabic terms. After the foot (or machine) kneading the clay is called *dosa*; if it has been kneaded by hand (*al-laff*), it is referred to as *shilah*. Once the clay is thoroughly kneaded, a clay lump (*'amud*) is produced, which is then cut to the intended size and shape. Open forms are thrown on the wheel in a single process; the different parts of closed vessels are formed in three stages with periods of drying (*tajfif*) in between. In the initial production stage of closed vessels, the potter forms the base (known as *tajlisah* or *kata't khit*). It is then left to dry in the shade for about two hours on a platform in the courtyard before the vessel is returned to the wheel once again. The second stage is called the opening stage (*fateh*), during which time the potter opens the thickened base by throwing it on the kick wheel, with the thrown piece named according to its intended form, i.e., *ibriq, sharba, zir*. In the case of small forms, the pot is ready for the final stage. For large forms, like a water pithos (*zir*) or a large jar (*jarra*), another coil (*qata'a*) is added to achieve height. It is then placed in the shade for a second time. The final stage, referred to as *tarwisah*, involves adding the head, neck, and rim. One potter named an additional stage for making the *ibriq* that he called *a'ra*, which means adding the handles (*wadin*) and spout (*ba'buza*). When the pot is ready, it is left to dry for about one week to 10 days, depending on the weather conditions.

An experienced potter will know the size of a pot by sight and touch; however, if the potter is to make a new form, he needs to first establish a standard measurement (*ma'yar*), and apply this to new forms, measuring by "open hand" (*shiber*). The *ma'yar* is a result of measuring the shrinkage and experimenting with different clay types. The overall shape (*haykal*) should be standardized.

Two types of decoration (*zakhrafa*) are used: painting (*tila*) and impressing (*hafir*). Often the pottery of Gaza is not painted, but when paint is used, it is done after firing using modern paint. Painting is usually applied to jars, jugs, and basins, such as the *jarra, ibriq, sharba*, or *kwar*, which are imperfect in some way. The majority of the flower pots and vases (*mazhariyya*) are painted, and the painting is done by the one who buys the pots, "the distributor," who has to be careful and accurate in applying the same motif pattern and size. Impressing (*hafir*) is done on the wheel with the tip of the fingers, resulting in shallow ribbings.

Firing in a Reduction Atmosphere (Tatwisa)

GGW is produced in a special reduction kiln in a process called *tatwisa* that requires several stages. The kiln is first loaded with pottery (*al-hashi*) by placing the pots upside down. The heavier or larger vessels are placed on the bottom and the lighter ones on top, as larger vessels need more heat to be completely fired and more fragile vessels cannot bear weight on top of them. The kiln load depends on the kiln's size. The kiln is about 2.5 m high and 3 m in diameter, and it should be completely full, as firing is an expensive process. The average load is 1,000 units (depending on the size of the kiln). The normal size *ibriq* defines the standard unit (called *rafa'a*, pl. *rafa'at*), which equals approximately 1 l of water. The pot size is estimated by the number of *rafa'at*; in other words, the pot is measured by the amount of liters of water it can hold when full. Thus, a small jar equals four *rafa'at*, or 4 l. The large water jar, or pithos (*zir*), is 12 l, the medium size water jar is about 7 l, and the *zir* is about ten *rafa'at*. The *lajjan*, a deep bowl for making yoghurt (*laban*), equals five *rafa'at* and the bowls (*zibdiyya*) are a little more than one *rafa'a*. A kiln is normally loaded with 1,000 *rafa'at*; however, a larger kiln will hold 1,800 *rafa'at*. The kiln load is decided upon during the forming stage, but it usually equals one week of work. A typical load includes all types of vessels, but the size of the load depends on the forms, with fewer large jars, for example. An average load (*hamil*) comprises 100 pitchers (*ibriqs*), 25 jars (*jaras*), 10, 12 or 15 water jars (*zirs*), according to their size, 20 deep large bowls (*lajjan abu jara*), 80 small bowls (*zabadi*), 80 small jugs (*qarariz*), and 40 cooking pots (*qidras*). Often, the closed forms are placed upside down, while the open forms are placed in the kiln facing up.

After the kiln is loaded, the first firing stage starts with the pre-heating process (*al-tahmiyya*), which normally takes between two to three hours. The success of this stage depends on the potter's skill. It is done to avoid the breakage of the pottery. The fuel used in this stage consists of straw, wood, saw wood (*njara*), and used clothing. The more time given for the pre-heating stage, the stronger the firing will be. If the process occurs faster than usual, it could damage the load. The contents of a kiln may include vessels of various colors.

Later in the firing, to make the pottery gray, it is simply smoked or carbonized (*yinakhniq*) using organic materials. In the past, potters used *qasal* (the remains of the barley that is no longer good as a straw), tree leaves or papers, wood acquired from lemon and orange trees, or any other available trees. Fuel was often exchanged for pottery jars, and today the potter mixes crude oil and saw wood, about 20–25 tins of the mixture (*tankat*).

The firing process follows several stages. First, the pottery should be well fired with the flames reaching all the pottery to the top of the kiln. Then the potter quickly feeds the kiln with the organic materials, and the two kiln openings are closed; however, the top door is closed but allows for an opening of only 15 cm in diameter, and the bottom door is also closed but is allowed to remain open approximately 10 cm. In this environment, a reduction atmosphere is produced in the kiln and the black smoke (carbon) will give the pottery the black or gray colors. The firing process takes five to twelve hours, depending on the kiln's (*tanur*) size.

Typological Analysis

It is rather likely that the techniques used by Gaza potters are a continuation from the early Ottoman period or perhaps earlier and are reflected in the forming techniques of the clay, the firing method, and the final vessel form. Vessel forms are the most important criteria in making comparisons between ceramic remains from archaeological sites and traditional pottery. The potters of Gaza make more than 25 different forms, each named after its shape, function, and size. Some forms may have Ottoman names (such as *tabakha* or *laggan*), and the most dominant forms are the *ibriq* and jar. What follows is a brief discussion of some of the more characteristic vessel shapes in the Gaza repertoire:

Jar (Jarra)

The water jar is the most common form found in archaeological and ethnographic records. Gaza potters produced two water jar forms. The first, an oval-shaped jar, the most common and traditional form, has a flaring or thickened round rim, a high narrow neck, two loop handles, flat in section, attached at the lower neck and extending to the lower shoulder, and a flattened or round base (figs. 4.2: 5, 4.4: 1). In most cases, an angular projection marks the neck where the handles are attached. Surface treatment includes shallow ribbing at the shoulder as a decorative feature.

This jar form comes in several sizes, ranging from 20 to 50 cm. One variation is a small-size jar about 29 cm high. It is called *a'salayya* and usually used for honey (as the name implies). The water jar of the same size, but of variant form, is called *farkha*; in the late Ottoman period, it carried a characteristic narrow neck. This particular water jar appears in many photos from the 19th century.

Gaza jars of oval shape may have a very long history, extending back to the Umayyad and Abbasid periods. The Tell Ti'innik example is the oldest reported Ottoman form (fig. 4.2: 1). This sack-shaped jar does not, however, occur with the typical rim form of the traditional, ovoid Gaza jar, but is more akin to jars from other production places, such as Jaba'. Another early example of the traditional form was found at Tell al-Hesi (Eakins 1993: pls. 17–18 and 29). Here, in addition to protecting infant burials, Gray Ware jars were included in graves to give purity and pleasure to the deceased (a known Muslim custom). Similar customs may be known in Jordan. Walker's (2001) report did not indicate the use of pottery among funerary objects at the "Bedouin cemetery" in the Tall Hisban citadel, but concluded that funerary objects may have been influenced by the fear of ghosts. Ethnographic examples illustrate the use of Gaza Gray Ware jars in magic rituals executed by a *dervish* against demons. "The *dervish* takes with him: seven barley-loaves containing bran, water in a dark-blue Gaza-jar, demon fears a jar of this kind … a blue jar, a dark pitcher" (Kaimio et al. 1963: 29).

The second jar form is similar in size, handle attachment, and surface treatment (fig. 4.2: 2–4); however, the jar handles are round in profile, rather than flat in section as in the form previously discussed, and the jar stands on a concave or shallow ring base. The earliest jar of this form found so far in excavations of Ottoman levels is the Qabatiyya Jar (fig. 4.2: 3). The rim is rounded, has no ridge on the neck, and the base is of a concave type. However, the dramatic difference between this second jar and the first described above is the surface finish: Qabatiyya Jars belong more to the gray-slip tradition than the GGW.

Ibriq *(Spouted Jugs)*

Gaza potters distinguish the *ibriq* from other vessel forms by an additional forming stage, which they call *a'ra*. In this stage the handles (*wadin*) and a spout (*ba'buza*) are added. The Gaza *ibriq* has an oval body, high narrow neck, a spout (*ba'buza*),[3] two flat handles (one larger than the other), and a ring base (fig. 4.4: 4). The main handle is attached at the junction of the shoulder and the neck and continues to the lower point of the shoulder. The smaller handle, located on the opposite side of the vessel, extends from a ridge in the middle of the spout to the junction of shoulder and neck. The spout is held in place with a ridge-shaped attachment, which also prevents the spout from collapsing when the clay is wet and from breaking during use. Surface treatment includes shallow ribbing on most of the body (*batin*).

The *ibriq* is a form common to the late Ottoman tradition, when it served as a drinking vessel, particularly for farmers working in the fields. Within the Muslim community, it is considered a vessel of "purity" and is used when water needs to be completely sealed to prevent it from being touched by hands before ritual washing before prayer (*wado*) or during a general bathing. This ceremony requires the use of a very cheap vessel, as Islamic tradition requires that such rituals not be performed with vessels made of gold or other metals. The *ibriq* is also used as a funerary object to pour water on the graves. This Muslim funerary custom, connected to purity and the comfort of the deceased, is usually practiced for 40 days after death, after which point it continues only as an occasional practice. The Tell al-Hesi *ibriqs* (fig. 4.3: 7) may represent a variation of this custom, because they were buried with individuals, who, as

the excavators suggest, may have sold pottery when alive (Toombs 1985: 106–7).

Jug (Sharba)

Jugs are made in various shapes and forms and named according to their intended use (fig. 4.4: 5–8). One common form is the *sharba*, which closely resembles the *ibriq*, but has two handles and is without a spout. Though the *ibriq* and the *sharba* are often difficult to differentiate, when they have been confidently identified archaeologically, it is clear that they had a wide distribution, having been documented at Tell Ti'innik, as the earliest appearance of the oldest form (fig. 4.3: 2), Qaymun, and Lod (fig. 4.3: 10). Other *sharba* forms are the *baqlusa*, for water, and the *mugthas*, for milk.

Bowl (Zibdiyya)

Bowls are also made in different forms (figs. 4.3: 12–17, 4.4: 12–13). The most common is the mortar (*ka'ada*), which is the best known of all bowl forms, but tends to be restricted to the Gaza region. It has thick walls and a thickened, high, disc base (fig. 4.4: 13). This form is used to grind garlic and tomato, which are ingredients in a popular Gazan salad dish (*doa'a*); the salad is served in the same bowl.

The serving bowl comes in small (*zibdiyya*) and larger sizes (*kashkola*; fig. 4.4: 12). It is made with a thickened, incurved rim, rounded walls, and a ring base. Usually, the form occurs with a plastic decoration of attached knobs just below the rim. Some bowls were decorated with incised lines. Early examples of these bowls were reported in the Negev, at Lod and Ti'innik. Similar serving bowls were also found in the Birzeit region, an indication that the export of Gaza pottery went beyond the water jar and *ibriq* to other common household forms.

Crater (Kwar)

The typical crater has semi-rounded walls, a concave rim, a ring base, and occasionally a decorated rope at the shoulder (fig. 4.4: 11). The crater is differentiated from the average bowl by its rim diameter, which is twice as wide as that of a bowl. Because of its size, the crater is commonly used as a flower pot. Alternatively, the *laggan*, a variant of the crater, is used for grinding dried yoghurt.

Cooking Pots, (Qidra *and* Tabakha)

The majority of Ottoman-era cooking pots are handmade. However, the Gaza wheelmade cooking pots occur in two forms. One form, known from the Roman period, is globular with two handles attached from the rim to below the neck and has a flattened and sub-rounded base (*qidra*; fig. 4.4: 9). The second form is the elongated cooking pot with flattened base (*tabakha*; fig. 4.4: 10). GGW cooking pots have not been reported in published archaeological reports and are largely known from ethnographic collections only.

CONCLUSIONS

Archaeological, historical, and ethnographic records, when combined, can effectively define GGW traditions. These resources document several important characteristics of their history and development. Among these characteristics is the longevity of the Gaza workshops: Gaza has been a well-known pottery production center since the Bronze Age, and in the Byzantine period its wine jars were a hallmark of trade between Gaza/Palestine and other sites around the Mediterranean. Furthermore, the location of Gaza on trade corridors and the activity of its bazaars had positive effects on local ceramic production. Gaza Gray Ware is a unique product of this particular location and its long history of workshop activity.

In addition to a deep history, GGW had a very wide geographic distribution, to which historical sources attest throughout the Near East. The pottery of Gaza has been reported, as well, at many archaeological sites in historic Palestine, Jordan, and the Sinai. Naturally, the most dominant region for the existence of Gaza Ware is southern Palestine, given its proximity to Gaza. Ceramic vessels, bought from Gaza or transported with caravans, were taken to major cities. The case of Qabatiyya suggests that this pottery traveled with merchants. Based on petrographic analysis, which is used to ascertain origins of clays and centers of production, there is a similarity between Kerak Gray Ware and Gaza pottery (Mason and Milwright 1998: 180, 187). The physical fabric of pottery at Tell Ti'innik and Gaza is also comparable.

On a final note, various sources of information indicate that the earliest appearance of GGW dates to the 16th century. Preliminary analysis of the stratified data, absolute dating methods, and historical records supports this early date, although careful stratigraphic excavations are still needed in order to obtain a precise date for the ware. Nevertheless, all resources agree that the Gaza Gray Ware tradition continues until today.

ACKNOWLEDGMENTS

An early version of this paper was presented at the 2005 ASOR meeting in the Ottoman session chaired by B. de Vries, Ø. LaBianca, and B. Walker. I would like to thank them for their help and encouragement. I also owe an expression of appreciation to G. London for going over the final draft, to M. Sroor for pointing out some resources on the Ottoman period, and to Birzeit University for allowing me access to its collection. My family patiently supported my absence while conducting this research, and for this I am deeply grateful.

NOTES

1   We now know, however, that occupation of the settlement extended beyond the 8th century (Avni and Magness 1998; Schaefer 1989).

2   L.111019 is situated at the same level as other floors dated to the Mamluk period (Avissar 2005: 124, fig. 1.4).

3   It is often difficult to differentiate between the *ibriq* and the *sharba* (another jug form) from sherd remains only. Many *ibriq* spouts were found during the survey of the Birzeit region.

Chapter 5

Identifying the Late Islamic Period Ceramically

Preliminary Observations on Ottoman Wares from Central and Northern Jordan

by Bethany J. Walker

By Way of Introduction – A Historiographical Excursion

The last ten to fifteen years have witnessed a growing interest in the Early Modern period among historians, archaeologists, and anthropologists based in Jordan. A wide range of intellectual and theoretical perspectives has driven scholarship on Ottoman Jordan, from modernity and the state (Rogan 1999), food systems theory (LaBianca 1990), land tenure and management (Mundy 1992 and 1996; Fischbach 2000; Mundy and Smith 2007), and political ecology and environmentalism (Walker 2004, 2005, 2007a–c; Lucke et al. 2009) to core-periphery models of settlement (Brown 1992), group memory and identity (Shryock 1997), and the social constructs behind vernacular architecture and rural space.[1] What has hampered efforts to understand more fully the Ottoman period in Jordan has been the uneven historical record directly relevant to the country, to be described below, and a very poorly documented and under-studied ceramic record.

As throughout Greater Syria, the relative paucity here of published pottery from the Ottoman period has significantly impacted the archaeology of Late Islamic sites. In many respects, research on the Ottoman pottery of Jordan suffers from the same challenges faced by scholars working in Syria, Israel, and Palestine (see also McQuitty 2001 and Milwright 2000). Ottoman strata tend towards shallow surface deposits and loci contaminated by residual sherds from earlier periods. The nature of much of the rural settlement of the region in the Ottoman era, such as the reoccupation of ancient ruins, reuse of water and storage facilities, and seasonal occupation by transhumant populations, accounts for these less than ideal stratigraphic conditions. One rarely encounters the kind of well-defined floors, trash deposits in sealed cisterns,[2] or loci associated with newly constructed walls that provide stratigraphically secure contexts for isolating, defining, and dating assemblages. Moreover, without the kind of urban "pit groups" encountered in Cyprus and Turkey that have produced chronologically homogenous deposits of Ottoman pottery (Megaw 1937–1939; Hayes 1992: 299–339; Hayes 1995), recovery of complete forms and coherent assemblages becomes difficult. Surface deposits are the most typical stratigraphic context for Ottoman pottery at archaeological sites in Bilad al-Sham. As such, they are easily contaminated by modern debris and, in the case of village sites, are normally obliterated by continued occupation of the site into the 20th century. All of these factors, compounded by the continuity of many ceramic traditions over generations, make it difficult to separate stratigraphically and stylistically Late Mamluk from Early Ottoman pottery, for example, and Late Ottoman from British Mandate. While this separation is perhaps not important in terms of developing ceramic chronologies and typologies (as people do not necessarily change their ceramic traditions during periods of political change), separations are invaluable archaeologically when ceramic material may be the only evidence for dating a site or phase of occupation.

In addition, all research on the Ottoman ceramic record of Bilad al-Sham suffers from sparse publication, particularly of village sites (where locally produced, handmade wares dominate and imports are rare), and limited excavation. When noted in preliminary excavation and survey reports, Ottoman ceramic remains are not published frequently with profile drawings and photos, sherd counts and weights, and assemblage statistics. With the development of Islamic archaeology as an independent specialization, more attention is being paid to surface remains and those in shallow deposits, with careful excavation and recording of these components of a site's more recent cultural history. Nonetheless, there remains a dearth of archaeological excavations in the region specifically designed to explore the Ottoman era outside of salvage projects.[3] One reason for this may lie in the antiquities laws of the countries in the region, which have long relegated Ottoman-era sites and objects to the realm of "ethnography." In the case of Jordan, only with the Law of 2004 did the national Department of Antiquities define an "antiquity," worthy of legal protection and proper scientific analysis, as "any movable or immovable object which was made, written, inscribed, built, discovered or modified by a human being before the year AD 1750, including pottery" (Law of Antiquities No. 23 of 2004, an amendment to Law 22 of 1988). The official identification of Early Ottoman pottery as an antiquity in Jordan is, thus, a relatively recent, and limited, legal development.[4]

The archaeology of Ottoman Jordan, and specifically the science of Ottoman ceramics in Jordan, while it shares all of the pitfalls encountered in Bilad al-Sham, is hampered by its own set of historiographical, historical, and socio-cultural challenges. There are very few written sources for the period that deal directly with Transjordan (administered by the Ottoman state as Liwa' Ajlun) and, similarly, few historically documented sites which date before the Tanzimat-inspired registration of rural land with the application of the 1858 Land Code. Written records are, of course, available for the 16th century (tax registers – *tapu defterleri* – published in al-Bakhit 1989a–b; al-Bakhit and Hamoud 1989b and 1991; and Hütteroth and Abdulfattah 1977) and the 19th and early 20th centuries (European travelers' accounts; personal memoirs and letters; land registers – unpublished Ottoman *tapu* and Mandate-era Land Settlement files); this author has made regular use of such sources in print and manuscript or ledger form (Walker 2004, 2005, 2007 b and c; Walker et al. 2007; Lucke et al. 2009). However, the Ottoman state essentially withdrew from Transjordan, with the exception of a handful of garrisons, after the end of the 16th century, leaving control of the region in the hands of semi-autonomous client tribes (Peake 1958: 84–91) and reimposing itself in the form of tax collector and police force only in the second half of the 19th century. Thus, we have no official records published from this period and precious little in the way of private documents, chronicles, Muslim or European travelers' accounts,[5] legal documents, or purchase, sales, or customs accounts as exist for Syria proper and, to a lesser extent, the more densely settled regions of Ottoman Palestine.[6]

Today in Israel, the West Bank, and Syria, archaeologists rely heavily on historical sources to date sites and document periods of construction, occupation, and abandonment, using the written record to facilitate the dating and separation of pottery from this period. This is simply not possible at this stage in Ottoman historiography in Jordan. Instead, Jordan-based scholars revert to oral tradition to reconstruct village histories for the late 19th and early 20th centuries. In short, written sources are not as readily available as chronological anchors independent of the pottery itself, at least for the historical "black hole" of the 17th through early 19th centuries. The ceramic record, then, becomes that more important in Jordan for reconstructing the socio-cultural history of the Middle Ottoman period, which has too long been described as ahistorical, aceramic, and nomadic.

Certainly, Jordan's history of settlement and its culture sets it apart from the rest of Ottoman Syria. Transjordan was less densely populated than Palestine and Syria proper, with fewer and smaller villages and a greater percentage of its territory under the control of nomadic and semi-nomadic tribes; 16th-century tax registers attest to this. This was traditionally a rural society, dominated by small villages occupied largely by subsistence farmers and pastoralists. Tax registers from the late 16th century attest to either seasonal occupation of villages or farming by semi-nomadic communities (the official implications of the term *mazra'a*, which is essentially a cultivated tract of land not directly associated with a settlement, are still disputed), as well as abandonment of many villages (registered as *khali*, or "empty," of year-round, permanently settled residents) from the late 16th century. Outside of a handful of *hajj* forts (Russell 1989: 30; Walker 1999: 214; Kareem 2000: 17; Petersen 2007) and perhaps one or two mosques (Ghawanmeh 1986a and 1986b; Shaqirat 1988; Walker and Kenney 2006), there have been very few buildings of the 17th to early 19th centuries identified and systematically recorded in Jordan by archaeologists and architectural historians. There is more archaeological evidence for reoccupation of ancient ruins during this period than construction of new buildings.

In short, the Ottoman period in Jordan is one of low ceramic visibility. The nature of settlement changed from the Mamluk to Ottoman periods from an extensive network of villages tied to intensive agriculture to a more dispersed occupation and less intensive land use. These demographic shifts are expressed ceramically in a relative scarcity of imports and glazed wares, a greater percentage of handmade wares, and a more limited range of wares and forms (and these are dominated by

multi-purpose vessels used for food preparation, serving, and small-scale storage; large storage and transport vessels are rare), mostly of local production. Wooden vessels, animal skins, and metal replaced ceramic vessels in peasant households in southern Jordan, Syria, northern Iraq, and western Iran (Oleson and 'Amr 1993: 479; Kalter et al. 1992: 136–37 and figs. 331–32). Similarly, with increased nomadism, indicated in some parts of the country by archaeological surveys, there was less need of ceramics in certain segments of the population. This is not to say that transhumant pastoralists do not use pottery, for ethnographic reports and "folk art" displays in local museums document the daily use of coarse stew pots and jars of irregular shape, along with porcelain coffee cups, in nomadic households.[7] Some of the coarsest, most friable, low-fired, and arguably quickly produced and disposable, small hand-made bowls (Fabric G), described in detail later in this chapter, may constitute the common wares known as "Bedouin pottery."

Such factors combine to present special problems in the study of the local pottery. With the exception of smoking pipes and the rare imported sherd, one does not have the benefit of using Turkish, Syrian, Palestinian, European, or Asian imports to help date the lesser known sherds of handmade, village-produced wares, which form the bulk of the local corpora. The extreme regionalism that characterizes Ottoman ceramics, in general, in Bilad al-Sham is particularly acute for the Late Ottoman period, where the assemblage of one village may contrast significantly with another nearby. The dating and seriation of pottery must often be done on a site-by-site basis, using criteria internal to that particular site with little reference to ceramic imports or written records. Other chronologically sensitive elements of the material culture of the period, such as glass vessels, bracelets, and coins, are found only in fragments and often in secondary deposition and are less helpful in dating local coarse wares than they are in Palestine and Syria.

This chapter is meant to serve two purposes: as a general introduction to the Ottoman pottery of Jordan (providing the range of wares, their chronology, and the many challenges of analysis) and as a preliminary analysis of largely unpublished material from two archaeological projects in different regions of the country. The pottery presented here comes from excavations and surveys in central and northern Jordan under the author's direction. The two archaeological projects that have generated the ceramic analysis – the Northern Jordan Project (NJP) and the Madaba Plains Project excavations at Tell Hisban – share a common research agenda: to more fully explore Islamic-period settlement in Jordan (comparing different regions), to better understand the mechanisms of imperial change on the local level (and indigenous responses to it), and to understand the nature of and factors behind the demographic shifts of the 15th and 16th centuries. The ceramic analysis is meant to fill in gaps in the historical record and to help write a history of rural life in the pre- and Early Modern eras. We begin with a review of the wares themselves and evidence for lines of ceramic continuity and discontinuity from the Mamluk era.

INTRODUCTION TO THE WARES

Continuation of Local Mamluk Wares

The Ottoman conquest of Bilad al-Sham from the Mamluk state in 1516 CE, while disruptive on many levels, did not usher in an immediate change in material culture. This is duly recognized by archaeologists, as the moniker "Late Islamic" is preferred to "Early Ottoman" in describing 16th-century deposits. What begs for special inquiry, however, is why two particular wares introduced during the Mamluk era dominate assemblages of this period and why their production, distribution, and consumption are apparently unaffected by the disruptions in communications, trade, and transport during the conquest and subsequent imposition of Ottoman rule in the region.

The long decline of the Mamluk Empire from the early 15th century onwards is a topic of debate among Mamluk historians. While reviewing the details of this debate goes well beyond the mandate of this chapter, its relevance for the analysis of Ottoman pottery in Jordan lies in the fallout from the political and economic turmoil of the day: civil war (some of the bloodiest skirmishes between Mamluk amirs and the sultan were fought on Jordanian soil) and imperial reprisals, combined with tribal incursions against both villages and the state that cut off roads, impacting long-distance trade, large markets, agricultural production (and particularly state-run enterprises, such as sugar plantations and olive oil export), and village life, in general. Archaeological and historical evidence attests that many villages were abandoned but certainly not all, as the hill country of northern Jordan provided protection to villagers from attacks by officials and nomads alike, and village life continued there without any significant interruption from the 15th through 16th centuries (Walker 2004). Nonetheless, the response of villages to these events suggests a turning inwards and a renewed self-sufficiency, as agricultural production reverted to more traditional patterns: abandoning state-led, mono-crop production for a diversified regime and subsistence farming; smaller, local markets, replacing larger, regional ones; and a revival, for a time, of private and communal tenure of land, legally safeguarded through the *waqf* system (Walker 2007d).

Superimposed on these localized processes of transformation, however, were the superstructures of continuity, the result of the way the Ottomans governed their newly acquired Arab provinces. Upon their annexation of Bilad al-Sham, the Ottomans kept many Mamluk structures and institutions in place: high-placed officials who formerly served Mamluk sultans retained their positions; most rural estates (created as *awqaf* – religious endowments) were maintained physically and fiscally; many elements of the Mamluks' administration of the region were incorporated into the new provincial and sub-provincial structure of Ottoman Syria; the tax structure initially remained unchanged. Throughout the 16th century, the Ottoman state did very little to visually impose itself on the countryside, as no new towns were built in Palestine or Transjordan and few structures of "classical" Ottoman form were built locally, with the exception of the forts on Jordan's Desert Highway (Petersen 2005: 41–44; Petersen 2007). Early Ottoman governance, in effect, kept intact the structure of Mamluk rule. This is not to say that the imperial state did not invest locally; the Ottomans initially built garrisons and cleared roads in Jordan, and the renewed security that resulted facilitated demographic and rural growth, a phenomenon documented by the tax registers described above. Nonetheless, it is doubtful that villages here had reached the number and size they had attained under Mamluk sovereignty and a general decline of the countryside is dutifully noted in the registers.

The ceramic correlate of this dualism in Jordan is a greater regionalism in material culture than before, reflected in differences between the assemblages and ceramic visibility of the northern hill country, central plains, and the south, a marked decrease in ceramic imports (but not the "disappearance" often assumed by archaeologists), and a continued production and consumption of at least two wares from the Mamluk period. The arguable dominance of later types of HMGP (Handmade Geometric Painted) Ware in 16th-century assemblages makes sense, given the degree of cultural, administrative, and economic continuity from the Mamluk era. As a cottage industry, its production would not be impacted significantly by the political events of the day. However, along with HMGP Ware, a variety of monochrome, green-glazed wares continues not only in this century but throughout the Ottoman era in southern Bilad al-Sham and is found throughout the Transjordanian countryside, in the smallest of villages and in surveys of regions no longer settled. Glazed wares did not completely disappear in the 15th and 16th centuries, as often assumed. Although their percentages relative to local assemblages significantly declined in some regions, in others they are a regular component of household equipment, developing and diversifying in form and surface treatment and reaching smaller, rural markets, all at a time when communications systems and the market economy were supposed to have broken down.[8] Our understanding of both the structural transformations of this transitional period and the production and distribution of glazed wares, in general, needs to be revised to fully appreciate the role of green-glazed wares in 16th-century Jordanian society.

Wheelmade, green-glazed bowls appear in Jordan in the 14th century, where they constitute an important part of the Mamluk assemblage at even the most rural sites. Their wide distribution throughout Bilad al-Sham, Anatolia, Greece, and the Jazira, and their striking variety in glaze and slip technology and fabric suggest localized production, a wide exchange network, or both. There has been a tendency in recent scholarship to extend the production of such wares into at least the 16th century citing evidence from Ti'innik (Stratum 6 – Ziadeh 1995: 211, 242, 243; fig. 16.4). At most sites in Bilad al-Sham, however, it has been impossible to stratigraphically isolate these wares in a way as to date them with any precision. At Khirbat Faris in Jordan, for example, they have been recovered from abandonment phases that have been dated by the excavators between the 14th and 19th centuries (Faris II, Stage 6 – McQuitty and Falkner 1993: 43 and 58–59, figs. 21.41–42). The chronology at Red Tower (al-Burj al-Ahmar) in Israel is only slightly better: here monochrome glazed bowls are largely associated with Phase E strata, which have been dated somewhere between the late Mamluk period and the end of the British Mandate, or ca. 1390–ca. 1920 (Pringle 1986: 136 and 147). Monochrome, green-glazed wares were dominant among both the Mamluk and Ottoman glazed sherds collected at Malka during the Northern Jordan Project's 2003 survey season (Walker 2005: 81), as well as during the 2006 survey of Saham and the Hubras excavation, where they comprised some 30 percent of all sherds attributed to the Ottoman period.[9] Although analysis of the pottery from the Hubras excavation is ongoing, characteristics of the Ottoman assemblage have been identified that differentiate it from the Mamluk repertoire of green-glazed pottery: changes in rim form (from the more typically Mamluk, in-turned and carinated rims to simple upright, out-turned, folded over, hooked, and T-shaped rims); changes in the form of base (to a generally "heavier" form – a lower ring foot, often with a stepped or sharp inside edge, or a cushion base); a variant glaze quality (dark and glossy without a slip, mottled or streaked, or a thin green glaze, applied on a white slip that tends to bubble and crack (Fabric J: figs. 5.3–5.4, 5.17–5.18;

also Walker 2003: 98, fig. 19.3; Walker et al. 2007: fig. 21.3). These characteristics are echoed at Dhra' al-Khan, a *khan* (caravanserai) in the northern Jordan Valley, in both green- and yellow-glazed bowls (Kareem 2000: figs. 1. 5–6, 3. 4, 4. 1, 7. 8, 8. 3, 12. 7, 16. 5, and 7)[10] and Israel (Avissar 2005: 75, fig. 2. 25. 1–2), as well as sites throughout the Eastern Mediterranean (see Hayes typology, below).[11] One should also note that many of the Mamluk and Ottoman sherds from the three villages exhibited mend and suspension holes, bearing witness to their value to households, and six sherds of green-glazed ware at Hubras were recut at a later date as stoppers, their dimensions suggesting use for water jars (*ibid.*).[12]

Monochrome, green-glazed sherds also dominate the glazed repertoire of many Ottoman sites, predominantly small villages and hamlets in today's Iraq and Turkey.[13] They have been variously attributed to the 16th, 17th/18th, and 19th centuries on stylistic and stratigraphic criteria. Green-glazed sherds from both deep and shallow bowls were recovered from Stratum 6, the only contexts where tobacco pipes were absent, at Ti'innik in the West Bank, leading to their being dated to the late 15th and 16th centuries (Ziadeh 1995: 243, figs. 16.4 and 16.6). Their association with such common Ottoman-era small finds as multi-colored glass bracelets and tobacco pipes in test trenches at the site of Gundi Shkaft (Shanidar village in northern Iraq; Solecki 1957: 166), pipes at Hatara Saghir (also in northern Iraq; Simpson 1997) and various sites in the Upper Euphrates Valley (Greater Anatolia dam Project salvage surveys; Algaze 1989: 246), and 17th-century coins, 18th-century porcelain, and pipes from stratigraphically sealed contexts at Sardis, Turkey (Hanfmann 1964: 14), has led the project directors and ceramicists to attribute them to the 18th and 19th centuries. The ware, or derivates of it, appears to have outlived the Ottoman state, as comparable green-glazed pottery is documented from the latest occupational levels of the Pactolus North site of Sardis (*ibid.*) and, according to ethnographic reports of the 1980s, in modern Turkish, Iraqi, and Iranian villages.[14] The published reports, thus, suggest changes in this ware (the color of its glaze, the use of slip, and the

form) or production of multiple, related wares over the course of the Early Modern period and the 20th century; too few of the reports, however, illustrate enough of the sherds and vessels to make this case typologically.[15] One important exception is the work of John Hayes, whose monograph on the pottery of Saraçhane (Istanbul) has become the single most important reference on Ottoman pottery in print.

In two publications, Hayes has differentiated among three general groupings of green-glazed wares that span the entirety of the Ottoman period: pottery from Troy representing the Late Byzantine– Early Ottoman transition, or the late 15th/early 16th century (Hayes 1995); a sub-group of his "Turkish coarse wares" from Saraçhane, spanning the late 15th through 17th centuries (Hayes 1992: 271–98); a sub-grouping of Iznik monochrome glazed ware, also from Saraçhane, produced from the late 16th century on (*ibid.*: 256–58). The earliest examples of his green-glazed sequence span the Byzantine–Ottoman transition and were recovered from the upper fills sealing several medieval burial pits in the Lower City of Troy. These loci produced the kind of pottery that is characteristic of the Early Ottoman period in Anatolia: "Miletus"-type, unglazed mica-coated (Hayes' Ware H) and green-glazed wares. The published vessels include bowls on a low ring foot, either square in profile or T-shaped and with an upright rim and simple lip (Hayes 1995: 77, fig. 4.61–63), forms that are also a common occurrence in late Mamluk–early Ottoman contexts in Jordan.

Fifteen pits and wells in Saraçhane produced a well-dated sequence of green-glazed vessels from 1500–1650, which included bowls, stemmed cups, two-handled jars, and spouted jugs. Hayes calls these reddish earthenwares "Turkish coarse wares" to differentiate them from the finer quartz-based "fritwares" of the same period. What is striking about this corpus is the variety in shape, glaze color and application, and associated surface decoration. Hayes suggests that while many of the wares are locally made, several appear to be imports or are known to have a wide distribution in the eastern Mediterranean (Hayes 1992: 276–77). Table 5.1 describes the green-glazed wares represented at

TABLE 5.1 Green-glazed Turkish Coarse Wares from Saraçhane (adapted from Hayes 1992: 272, fig. 4)

WARE	SHADE OF GREEN GLAZE	ADDITIONAL SURFACE TREATMENT	FORMS	DATE
B	dark		deep bowls	15th–mid-17th c.
	emerald	sgraffito		
	pale	stains		
C	emerald		deep bowls/jars	pre-1550
D	glossy, pale lime	sgraffito (floral, radial), stains	small bowls/dishes (low foot, sharp inside edge)	16th c.
E	dark lime	sgraffito (tondo circle), stains	bowls (low or high splayed foot), dishes (wide, flat rim)	16th–mid-17th c.
P	glossy	stripes of white slip, marbelling,	bowls (hooked rim, sloped side)	
	speckled	rouletting	bowls (rounded)	all 19th c.
Q	smooth, light speckled		slender necked jars, alberellos	16th–17th c.
Y	thin, speckled		spouted jugs (irregular profile)	17th–19th c.

Saraçhane and defined by Hayes from sealed contexts as well as surface deposits.

A finer green-glazed ware (Hayes' green "Iznik monochrome") was produced from the end of the 16th century and imitates many of the same forms found in other Iznik products: shallow plates with wide, horizontal rims and small cups with thin walls. Hayes estimates that 25–30 percent of the Iznik wares at Saraçhane belong to this category (*ibid.*: 235) and were an important part of the fine ware assemblage. The green glaze ranges from a bright hue to yellowish tint to sage green (he argues in imitation of celadon) and is of very high quality, not crazing as it ages. Some bowls are decorated with sgraffito under the glaze, in simplified designs based on geometric and floral patterns developed in Byzantine and Seljuk incised-slip pottery.

In summary, the Istanbul series, as a whole, suggests that the production of green-glazed wares peaked in the 16th and 17th centuries, declining in quality (with thinner glazes, prone to decay, and irregular vessel profiles) and perhaps quantity thereafter, as porcelain cups, bowls, and dishes from the Orient, as well as Europe, became more readily available. The general design of fine, green-glazed wares in the 17th century was likely inspired by the import of fine celadon and porcelain cups from China (Hayes 1992: 256), which the Ottoman wares began to resemble in form (small, thin-walled cups and bowls with a simple upright or slightly out-turned lip; bowls on a low and squarish ring foot; the occasional scalloped rim; dishes with wide and flat rims) and surface treatment (glossy glazes, varieties of shades of green; Hayes 1992: 253, figs.

96–97 and 256). The development of the coarser wares of the 16th and 17th centuries away from their 15th-century predecessors parallels these trends and may also reflect changes in diet and culinary practices (see Gabrieli in this volume) or exchange networks. There is, nonetheless, a great deal of continuity with Late Byzantine ceramics, and the Ottoman assemblage should be appreciated in this sense. The green-glazed pottery of Jordan shares many characteristics of Hayes' "Turkish coarse wares" sub-group. Petrographic analyses and related provenance studies are needed to determine to what extent the diversity in green-glazed products in Jordan was the result of importation from Syrian centers and further abroad or a broadening of localized, rural production.

Green-glazed sherds are usually found in association with what is often called a "degenerate" form of HMGP Ware in post-Mamluk strata. HMGP Ware is the hallmark of the Mamluk period in Bilad al-Sham; although found throughout the entire Levant and Jezira, it comprises the largest percentage of Mamluk assemblages in Transjordan. Its origins are generally traced to the 12th century, with continued production through the 16th century and derivatives manufactured through the Ottoman period into the 20th century. In his careful analysis of the Mamluk ware, Johns gives the most coherent presentation of its fabric, forms, methods of manufacture, and surface treatment. Johns defines Mamluk HMGP as a handmade ware of coarse fabric with large, inorganic inclusions (such as ground sherds, basalt, and quartzite) and organic temper (chaff and straw) in a poorly levigated clay. It is represented in a limited repertoire of open forms (mostly bowls and jars)[16] built with coils, slabs, and molding cloths; the vessels' rough surfaces are smoothed with a white, beige, or pink slip over which are painted geometric designs (often imitating woven patterns or designs in contemporary glazed wares) in red, brown, and black paint; the finished products are low-fired in an uneven heat, possibly in an open fire or clamp (Johns 1998: 87, fig. 2).

The stratigraphic separation of "Ottoman" HMGP from Mamluk is, unfortunately, difficult at most sites where their differentiation is typically based on stylistic analysis. There is some consensus that Early Ottoman (16th century) HMGP Ware is defined by surface decoration of less complicated geometric designs (simple, repeated linear patterns and zigzags, as opposed to complex woven patterns) executed in a broader line and in a reduced palette (variations on a reddish-brown), and production of more carelessly executed and irregular profiles, likely on a slow, foot-controlled, turntable (fig. 5.20; for parallels from the Kerak Plateau, see Brown 1991: 243 and Johns 1998: fig. 2; for Sataf, west of Jerusalem, see Gibson et al. 1991: 43–47). The fabric of Late Ottoman (19th-century) HMGP (our Fabric F), on the other hand, is extremely coarse, with a high percentage of grog and visible chaff scars and inclusions; the vessels are covered in places by a heavy slip of plaster-like consistency, used for mending the vessels and holding the friable fabric together (fig. 5.21: 10; see also Walker et al. 2007: fig. 21.4).[17] It is these latter characteristics – the heavy use of chaff to lend plasticity to the clay and the application of a "plaster"-slip to the interior – that allow us to identify 19th-century HMGP from surveys and excavations of the Northern Jordan Project (Walker 2005; Walker et al. 2007). Approximately 25 percent of the sherds collected during the 2003 survey season at Malka produced handmade wares, and of these, 25 percent were what was identified as Late Ottoman HMGP Ware (Walker 2005: 82). During the 2006 season (survey at Saham and excavation at Hubras), the Ottoman pottery was dominated by such coarse and friable jars, in addition to what appear to be transitional Late Ottoman to Mandate-period red-painted wares (in Fabric F), which are possible derivatives of Palestinian Sinjil Ware (Walker et al. 2007; see below).

The use of such characteristics to differentiate chronologically within this ceramic tradition, however, is limited, as there is much regional variety in Jordan in terms of materials, technology of production, and surface decoration and treatment (Brown 1989: 297). Nonetheless, these stylistic categories are supported by a handful of published contexts where there is some degree of stratigraphic separation of Mamluk from Ottoman HMGP Wares: Kerak (Brown 1989), Shobak (Brown 1988), and

Khirbet Faris in Jordan (McQuitty and Falkner 1993); Sataf in Israel (Gibson et al. 1991); Ti'innik in the West Bank (Ziadeh 1995; for all sites, see also the discussion in Johns 1998: 66). At Shobak, hand-made jars and jugs in Phase IV (Ottoman) deposits are more "crudely fashioned" than their Phase II/III (Ayyubid/Mamluk) counterparts, with their "heavily chaff-pocked surfaces" covered in red slip or decorated with red-painted "schematic designs," and the vessel cores thick and incompletely fired (Brown 1988: 240).[18] According to Ziadeh, HMGP Ware in Palestine becomes dominant only in Ottoman times (Ziadeh 1995: 210).[19] Although the dating of the strata at Ti'innik, a West Bank site east of Megiddo, is controversial, floor levels of abandoned houses in Stratum 6 have produced abundant evidence for food storage, preparation, and serving vessels of the HMGP fabric that share the characteristics of the Ottoman period described above, in addition to the use of calcite as temper and burnishing of the exterior slip. The excavators date Stratum 6 to the late 15th and early 16th centuries on the basis of four criteria: 1. historical data (reference to the village in 16th-century tax registers), 2. ceramic assemblage (the presence of green-glazed pottery confirms, for Ziadeh, a 16th-century date by reference to ceramic material at Khirbet Faris), 3. the absence of pipes (chibouks, which were not used in the region before the early 17th century and are present in Stratum 7), and 4. thermoluminescence (one sherd sample from Stratum 6 floor deposits dated to c. 400 BP; ibid.: 210–11). HMGP Ware sherds were found in abundance in Strata 7 and 8 as well, where they were associated with smoking pipes and unpainted handmade sherds.

There is, in summary, a bit of an anomaly in the longevity and coexistence of what appear, on first glance, to be two very different ceramic traditions: the wheelmade, green-glazed wares, and the Handmade Geometric Painted Ware. If the continuity and dominance in the Early Ottoman assemblage in Jordan of HMGP is to be attributed to the collapse of the imperially supported market economy and its supporting infrastructure in the 16th century and a "widening economic gulf" between "rich and poor" and the town and

countryside,[20] what can one make of its regular association, in all types and scales of sites in Jordan, with a glazed ware? Mamluk-era glazed wares were produced all over Bilad al-Sham and not only in large towns. This is true for the medieval Syrian "fritwares," traditionally associated with Damascus (Redford and Blackman 1997), as well as the more commonplace yellow and green-glazed bowls recovered from most sites in the southern Levant, in Jordanian literature occasionally classified with "southern Levantine wheelthrown" wares (Hayes 1992: 232, his "Turkish coarse wares;" see also Pringle 1986: 147 ff. for local, post-Crusader products).[21] There was no centralized production of such pottery. It is doubtful, moreover, that consumption of glazed wares was limited to the "elite." Although there are demonstrable differences between the ceramic assemblages of the Citadel at Kerak and the Mamluk-era town (Brown 1989 and 1991), at contemporary Tell Hisban the same kinds of pottery are found in the Citadel and the civilian settlement: as many HMGP jars were retrieved from the Citadel storeroom and kitchen as Glazed-Relief Ware and Monochrome-Glazed bowls from the nearby Wadi Majar and floor levels of the courtyard houses of the Field C medieval village (Walker and LaBianca 2003), one of which produced evidence for local production of both yellow and green-glazed ceramics (Walker and LaBianca 2004). Clearly, glazed wares were neither produced only in large towns nor only for the political or economic elite. A more localized production and exchange, responding in part to a breakdown of inter-regional communications and trade, is suggested by the agricultural history of the late 15th and early 16th centuries (Walker 2004, 2007b and 2007c). Ceramic production and consumption may follow the same pattern: both HMGP and green-glazed wares had been produced in rural, Mamluk Transjordan,[22] and their manufacture continued for local clients when the larger networks of inter-regional trade were interrupted by the political upheavals of the collapse of Mamluk imperial power and the Ottoman conquest. Both wares, in fact, were available to the end of the Ottoman period, underwent long-term developments in form and surface treatment, and have enjoyed a certain popularity in modern times.[23] One could casually suggest reasons for the longevity of these two wares and their overwhelming presence in Ottoman-era assemblages: affordability, practicality,[24] cultural associations with particular painted patterns and the color green. What is of particular significance for the ceramic history of Jordan, however, is that together they define the material culture of the 16th century.

New Ottoman Wares

While one may argue for local production of these "transitional" wares in Jordan, pottery of the "Middle Ottoman" period (17th to early 19th centuries) here appears to be largely imported. A wide range of wheelmade wares was available in the region at a time when Jordan was sparsely populated,[25] had few markets of any size (see below), and hosted few officials of the Ottoman state outside of lightly-manned *hajj* forts. Nonetheless, the ceramic repertoire of Jordan mirrors that of other regions in the Ottoman Empire, including western Anatolia, suggesting that Jordan was not as economically isolated as the published scholarship would lead us to believe. This author knows of no published pottery from this period from Jordan, outside of isolated sherds, but recent finds from Hisban and the villages of the NJP study area, while relatively few, do indicate that the glazed wares consumed in urban centers made their way to rural locations in a pattern that is emerging in ceramic studies from the Ottoman heartland.

The Ottoman conquest of the Levant revived the local economy by creating "an enormous free trade zone" with new markets and commercial links (Philipp 2004: 403–4). The demographic growth documented by 16th-century censuses can be attributed to this economic trend. However, it was not until the 17th century that such new markets and networks made an impact on the Syrian interior with the import of basic tablewares. When pottery was used, it tended to be imported. The most basic personal effects of both peasants and pastoralists in the Jordanian interior, as described earlier, included porcelain coffee cups and fine tobacco pipes (*chibouks*), which were produced at imperial or regional centers. Turkish glazed wares, for example, have been found at Hisban and Hubras at a time when the villages have no documented history of settlement.

The flow of goods from urban production centers to the countryside and on to pastoral communities requires an explanation. Regional (intra-Ottoman) trade, organized largely through caravans and village markets, contributed considerably more to the Ottoman economy than international commerce.[26] Regional trade was, likewise, the backbone of economic activity in Jordan (Walker 2007c).[27] Unlike the Levant of the Middle Islamic (Crusader and Mamluk) period, Ottoman port towns, which controlled access to imported goods, did not dominate the regional economy. That is not to say that the ports of the eastern Mediterranean did not play a role in the exchange of certain commodities. The growth of Aleppo, the origin point for several caravan routes, and Acre, which controlled the export of local cash crops to Europe, certainly facilitated the commercialization of agricultural production in this period.[28] It is likely, though, that land transport of ceramics accounts for the greatest distribution of glazed wares in the Syrian interior. In support of land transport is the growth of cottage industries, and particularly textiles (weaving, spinning, and knitting), in the 18th century (Quataert 2000a: 137). The shift from male-dominated urban guilds to rural, female labor would find its fullest expression in the 19th century, providing a meaningful context for the wide diversity of handmade wares in 19th-century ceramic corpora discussed in the section following.

A number of theories have recently been advanced to account for the apparent increase in rural consumption of glazed wares. The first focuses on the decision of the Ottoman state to collect agricultural taxes in cash, rather than in kind. One result of this fiscal policy may have been the transformation of the rural economy to a cash economy, and with greater cash flow came greater ability to purchase imports, even in the most remote regions. Alternatively, the consumerism of the 18th century may have led rural families to purchase consumer goods more frequently, as their cash incomes rose

(Quataert 2000a: 130). Either way, one assumes the availability of the same kinds of consumer goods in rural markets, although in more limited quantities, as those found in the bazaars of larger towns and cities.

If the 17th century in the Ottoman Empire was the age of the nascent bourgeoisie, the 18th century was the era of consumerism. Best illustrated by the Tulip Period (1718–1730) and the coffeehouse craze, daily customs related to the dinner table, attire, and evening entertainment were defined by trends set in the capital. The first "mass consumption commodities" in the Ottoman state – coffee (introduced in the 16th century) and tobacco (in the early 17th) – transformed popular culture not only in the cities but also in the countryside, as coffeehouses, where the two commodities were consumed together, could be found in the most remote locations (İnalcık and Quataert 1997: 507–8). The widespread use of coffee and tobacco, moreover, redefined the kind of pottery used by most households; as noted previously, porcelain coffee cups and wheelmade smoking pipes were staples of entertainment and possessed by all demographic groups. Ceramic consumption of the 17th and 18th centuries was further transformed by a marked rise in production and use of glazed wares. At Saraçhane, Hayes notes that 60–80 percent of the excavated pottery from 18th-century contexts consists of glazed wares, compared to 35–40 percent in the Early Ottoman period (Hayes 1992: 233). Similarly, at the rural site of Aphrodisias in western Anatolia, a combination of common and fine glazed wares contributed an estimated 25–45 percent of the pottery dated to the late 15th through early 17th centuries (François 2001: 154).

Jordan was not isolated from these trends. While in the 17th century much of the country was controlled by local tribes in the nominal service of the sultan and Syrian governor, for part of the 18th century, northern Jordan fell under the jurisdiction of the Zaydaniyya dynasty based in Acre.[29] Zahir al-'Umar al-Zaydani carved an autonomous amirate out of northern Palestine and parts of Syria, Lebanon, and Jordan from 1730 to 1775; his domain extended, at its height, from Sidon to Gaza and from Acre to Irbid. The region

benefited financially, politically, and socially from his active investment in roads, fortifications, ports, and religious architecture, as well as his efficient administration, which pacified restless tribes (for a time), revived international trade, and encouraged settlement by religious minorities. The region experienced a higher level of security and law and order than any other region of Syria had for years (Joudah 1987: 133). Zahir al-'Umar assigned the administration of Irbid and Ajlun to his youngest son, Ahmad, who governed northern Jordan effectively from the village of Tibneh from 1765 to 1775. Like his father, Ahmad built mosques and fortifications and encouraged agricultural development; he also established a *majlis al-hakim* (local court) at Tibneh (Shaqirat 1988: 53). The amirate can, thus, be credited with the rejuvenation of the local economy, some level of demographic growth, and the reinforcement of exchange networks between northern Jordan and the port of Acre.

Glazed wares produced in Istanbul, Thrace, southern Europe, Damascus, and possibly Cyprus made their way to villages in northern and even central Jordan during this period. It is not clear, however, what exact mechanisms of exchange brought them to villages so far inland. The annual pilgrimage (*hajj*) is one possibility, although no *hajj* stations in Jordan have been excavated to demonstrate the distribution of ceramics in this manner (McQuitty 2001: 577; Brown 2006: 384). The primary *hajj* route, which for Anatolians and Syrians began in Damascus, ran from the provincial capital through the Jordanian *badiyya* to Ma'an and on to the Hijaz. There is a single known Ottoman-era pilgrim's account that documents travel through the Jordanian interior during the *hajj* season (see note 5, this chapter). The pilgrim does not, unfortunately, describe any of the pilgrims' markets that must have existed at the time and makes no reference to the purchase or use of tablewares, ceramic or otherwise, during his travels.[30]

According to a *defter mufassal* for Liwa Ajlun in 1005 AH / 1596 CE, Kerak had both a town market and a pilgrims' market (endowed with a *khan* for that purpose), which together paid a market tax (*baj bazaar*) of 2,500 *akçe* annually to the Ottoman state. Such taxes were also collected from Kerak and Salt, which were, with Ajlun, the main market towns of this provincial sub-district, as well as from Irbid and Hubras in the Qada of Golan (al-Bakhit and Hmoud 1991: 30, 117, and 292; Hütteroth and Abdulfattah 1977: 25).[31] Household goods were an important part of the kinds of commodities typically sold in such markets, which were frequented by townsmen, villagers, and *bedu* alike. They would have been the most likely distribution point for ceramic tablewares and smoking and water pipes.

The most comprehensive catalogue of Ottoman glazed wares from this period remains Hayes' seminal study of the pottery from the Saraçhane excavations in Istanbul (Hayes 1992), and it has become the standard reference for all subsequent work on Ottoman ceramics and an invaluable resource for ceramicists and archaeologists. In his catalogue, Hayes recognized two broad categories of locally produced glazed wares, "Turkish Fine Wares" and "Turkish Coarse Wares," in addition to a range of glazed products imported from other regions of the Ottoman Empire, Europe, and the Far East. His local fine wares include material from Miletus (14th–15th centuries), Iznik (late 15th–17th centuries) and Iznik-derivative (16th–17th centuries), Kütahya (generally 18th century), and Çanakkale (18th–19th centuries). Miletus Ware, an early blue-and-white underglaze-painted earthenware developed from Seljuk pottery, had little impact on Jordan, which seems to have imported little Ottoman pottery before annexation in 1516. Iznik Ware and its monochrome-glazed variety, however, was one of the most widely distributed fine glazed wares in the Ottoman Empire, reaching Syrian markets from the later 16th century. The compact, quartz-frit body and underglaze-painted designs (in blue, white, and red by the 16th century), under a lead-soda glaze to which small amounts of tin oxide were added, generally defines the ware (Hayes 1992: 244). Vessel forms are quite standardized and include the characteristic shallow plate, with horizontal rims that turn sharply upwards at their tips and thin-walled, hemispherical bowls, with a vertical rim and thin lip or slightly out-turned rims, in likely imitation of contemporary Chinese porcelain "export cups" (*ibid.*: 256). A subcategory of this ware with a monochrome green (by far

the most widespread), blue, or turquoise glaze is equally common and imitated in local workshops throughout the region.

It was only in the 18th century that other locally produced fine wares challenged the dominance of Iznik products on the market (*ibid.*: 266–69). The underglaze-painted fritwares associated with Kütahya in the 18th century had a wider palette than Iznik wares, if of lesser quality in execution of painting and appealing polychrome floral patterns. Its products directly serviced the coffee industry, with the most common forms being small, thin-walled coffee cups, jugs (for serving juices with coffee; see Gabrieli in this volume), and coffee-pots – a fact that may explain, in part, the popularity of this ware. Çanakkale Ware dominated glazed-ware exports in the late 18th and 19th centuries. It is named after the glazed pottery sold to ships passing through the port (*çanak*, or "bowl," and *kale*, "castle," in Turkish) at the entrance to the Dardanelles (Tekkök-Biçken 2000: 94) and is usually characterized as a kind of folk art with its very thick, polychrome slip-painted designs, which featured flowers, ships, palaces, etc., yellow-green glaze, and occasional baroque-like relief ornaments (a later development). Çanakkale jars, some with appliqué, and coffee cups were widely distributed and imitated locally in the 19th century. The emergence of numerous local, painted traditions in the 19th century may be related to the popularity of this ware.

Hayes' catalogue includes many imported wares, which have been identified throughout the Empire and even in rural locations. The wares with the greatest distribution include Didymoteichon Ware (19th century; described below) and a variety of small porcelain coffee cups of European (Meissen, 18th century) and Far Eastern (Chinese, 17th century) origins. Some of the porcelains identified at archaeological sites outside of Istanbul, however, may actually be softpaste porcelains imported from a variety of European factories in the 18th through early 20th centuries.[32] In his review of the scholarly literature on Ottoman pottery in Syria, Milwright suggests that European "porcelains" generally replaced Chinese ceramics in this period (Milwright 2000: 197). Coffee cups, of both stoneware and porcelain varieties, are found in urban to pastoral contexts in Syria and beyond and do not appear to be imitated locally in less expensive materials.[33] In short, there was no "cheap" option to fine coffee cups; they were an important component of basic housewares, as coffee-drinking was an integral part of socializing by the 17th and 18th centuries. Such cups, along with smoking pipes, because of their small size and importance in daily socializing, were taken on long journeys, such as business trips and pilgrimage (François 2002: 161). Porcelain and stoneware coffee cups were the most common Ottoman-era ceramic import in the Jordanian countryside and are frequently the only glazed vessels recovered from archaeological sites. Smaller quantities of Italian sgraffitos (16th-century polychrome sgraffitos of Venice and the 17th-century painted style of Pisa) as well as Chinese porcelains from the 17th century on complement this imported assemblage at Saraçhane and abroad.

The second category of glazed wares at Saraçhane (Hayes' "Turkish Coarse Wares") is a very diverse group of pottery representing some 21 wares produced locally and regionally from the 15th through 17th centuries (Hayes 1992: 271–98). These glazed earthenwares generally share the same range of forms – simple bowls, stemmed cups, two-handled jars, and *ibriqs* – and a similar lead-glaze, usually in green in a wide variety of shades, but also in yellow. They are differentiated by the quality of their glaze (thick or thin, "glossy," speckled, streaked or "mottled"), the presence or absence of an underlying slip, additional surface decoration (through slip-painted or sgraffito designs, staining through addition of a glaze of another color, rouletted patterns), and idiosyncrasies in form (a hooked rim, extraordinary sharp inner edge on a ring foot, etc.). This is the broadest category of Ottoman pottery identified by Hayes and includes what appear to be local derivatives of Turkish wares. Outside of the few porcelains and fine-glazed wares imported from Ottoman centers, the majority of pottery from Middle Ottoman contexts in Jordan appears to be regional Syrian variations of Turkish Coarse Wares.

What is striking about the glazed wares of Saraçhane, in spite of the wide variety of decorative techniques and places of origin, is the standardization of vessel forms. Large transport jars have disappeared (Hayes 1992: 234) and are replaced by special forms for serving and eating, reflecting new dining customs connected to diet, individual place settings, and entertaining centered on smoking and drinking coffee. New forms replace old ones, as the *ibriq* (spouted jug), high-stemmed bowls (goblets), and pipes (*narghila*, water pipe, and *chibouk*, tobacco pipe) become standard fare in urban households (*ibid.*: 233). In rural areas a more restricted range of forms in glazed wares relates directly to diet, with jars (to store condiments and yoghurt), simple hemispherical bowls (to serve yoghurt), plates with horizontal rims described above (for deserts, cooked crème, rose petal sweets, salads, and lamb), stewpots, and small cups (for syrup and coffee) defining the tablewares of town and country (François 2001: 186). Their standard dimensions and forms, known by specific Turkish terms, and their wide distribution through export and local production underline a consumerism in common to households of all segments of Ottoman society.

The generally unglazed tobacco pipe (*chibouk*), found in regular association with such glazed vessels, is perhaps the most widespread ceramic form of the Middle and Late Ottoman periods and, because of its documented typological development, is one of the most dependable chronological markers of the 17th century and beyond. As standard fare in urban coffeehouses, roadside stops, and Bedouin camps alike, it was produced in workshops throughout the Empire as well as in Europe, where smoking was equally popular. Tobacco-smoking had become widespread in Ottoman lands by the end of the 17th century; therefore, the pipes can be dated to the 17th through 19th centuries. The *chibouk* is a three-part smoking apparatus, consisting of a bowl (usually ceramic), a long stem (usually wood), and a mouthpiece (the most expensive part, generally of semi-precious stones or gold). The cheapest segment, the bowl, was frequently replaced, which accounts for the relative abundance of ceramic pipe bowls at Ottoman sites (Simpson 2002: 170). Hayes' typology of pipes, based on bowl forms (Hayes 1992: 391–95), has become the standard reference; his 27 bowl types can be roughly divided chronologically into three periods. Seventeenth-century pipe bowls are generally made of a gray-firing white clay, have narrow stems, thin walls, and stepped-ring shank ends, and their surfaces are rouletted. In the 18th century, red-brown clay, with a smooth surface, is more common, along with the occasional splashed glazing. Nineteenth-century pipes have a characteristic heavily burnished red clay, are larger and thicker than the earlier bowls, have a lily-shaped or disk base, and are frequently stamped with a manufacture mark.

One of the greatest challenges in the archaeological interpretation of *chibouks*, however, is determining their place of manufacture. The claim made that at Kouklia Early Ottoman pipes were locally produced and Late Ottoman ones imported cannot be substantiated and has no relevance in the Arab realms of the Empire, where historical sources document increased activity of local workshops in the 19th century (Graf 2001: 396).[34] There is a distinct regionalism in not only *chibouk* bowl form, but also in the general assemblage. Most assessments of provenance are based on stylistic comparisons and makers' marks (when identified); only petrographic or chemical analysis of clays can determine with more certainty the original place of manufacture of excavated and surveyed pipes. Published corpora indicate that people acquired their pipes from a variety of locations, as they did glazed wares. The city of Istanbul had a quarter for pipemakers and, not surprisingly, Hayes believes most of the *chibouk* bowls found there were local products (Hayes 1992: 391–95). In Greece, excavated pipes from the Kerameikos, Corinth, and the Athenian Agora have been attributed to local workshops in Istanbul, Bulgaria, Central Europe (the former Czechoslovakia, Austria, and Hungary), and possibly France (Robinson 1983; Robinson 1985). Local manufacture has been suggested for pipes at Yoqne'am (Avissar 1996: 198) and Tell Jezreel (Simpson 2002: 165).

This general assemblage of glazed wares and pipes was not restricted to the imperial capital. As a result of intensified intra-imperial and inter-regional trade from the 17th century on, as well as consumption patterns that permeated the kitchens and parlors/*madaafas* of most town and village households, the same kinds of glazed wares used in Istanbul could be found throughout the Empire. Turkish glazed wares were both imported and imitated locally, and European, Asian, and Mediterranean porcelains, sgraffitos, and lustered wares found ready markets in town, village, and Bedouin community alike. It is useful to describe a few published assemblages from different regions of the Empire to illustrate this point.

The Ottoman pottery of Aphrodisias, in western Turkey, dates to the 15th through 19th centuries (François 2001). Glazed wares dominate the assemblage at this rural site and include imports from Turkey (Millet, Iznik, Kütahya, and Didymoteichon Wares), Europe (Meissen porcelain cups and Spanish lusterware), Asia (Chinese porcelains), and Syria (polychrome floral sgraffitos, which François suggests originated in Ephesus; *ibid.*: 181), as well as a range of Turkish Coarse Ware bowls and plates. The range of locally produced material is equally impressive; in addition to wheelmade, unglazed pots, basins, jars, jugs, and cooking pots, one could find monochrome green-glazed (and occasionally yellow-glazed) bowls, night pots, and *ibriqs*, in addition to a polychrome sgraffito ware called "Spot Painted," which has been identified only at Aphrodisias (*ibid.*: 173). The locally produced pottery, as a whole, imitates the forms of Istanbul imports and can be considered largely derivates of those glazed wares.

Kouklia, a rural site in southwestern Cyprus, offers an appropriate parallel to this assemblage from the eastern Mediterranean. The excavated material ranges in date from the 16th through 19th centuries and represents the kind of pottery available to and used in peasant households: locally produced monochrome-glazed wares (mostly green), Greek imports (Didymoteichon and Marbled Wares from Thrace), Turkish imports (Iznik, Kütahya, and Çanakkale Wares, slip-painted and monochrome-glazed Turkish Coarse Wares, and green-painted sgraffitos), European imports (Pisan marbeled ware, North Italian majolicas), Asian imports (Chinese porcelains), and imports of unknown origin (a green and brown slip-painted ware and incised water jugs of "Fine Gray Ware," arguably of North African provenance), in addition to locally-produced monochrome-glazed bowls and jars (von Wartburg 2001). Several complete vessels of Çanakkale and Didymoteichon Wares were recovered from the Manor House site; the excavators suggest that their low price was what made them so attractive to rural customers and explains their wide distribution in the 19th century (*ibid.*: 386).

Didymoteichon, in Thrace, is the type site of the "Drip-Painted Ware" mentioned above. The ware for which this site is known is a slip-painted earthenware in which broad lines in thick, white slip are carried across the interior of bowls and exterior of jars and covered in a yellow or green lead glaze. The bowls have a characteristic rim form: an "envelope" or radically overturned, externally folded rim (Bakirtzis 1980; François 2002). It is the most widely distributed Ottoman pottery of the 19th century in the Empire and widely copied on the local level in southern Syria; it is surpassed numerically only by Gaza Ware, a regional product. In addition to large numbers of Didymoteichon Ware and kiln evidence for its production, the ceramic assemblage is what one would except from a 19th-century site in the Ottoman heartland: unglazed *ibriqs*, night pots, handmade pithoi with rouletted patterns and appliqué, local glazed wares (sgraffitos, Çanakkale derivatives, monochrome olive green-glazed jars and bowls), and Marble Ware, another Didymoteichon product.

At the provincial capital of Damascus, there is also a wide range of imports but in modest quantities: Iznik, Kütahya, and Çanakkale Wares from Turkey; Didymoteichon Ware from Thrace; Meissen and Viennese porcelain, Staffordshire faience, Pisan marbled ware, Kraak and "Dead Leaf" porcelains, Ligurian faience and Tuscan majolicas from Europe; Asian celadons (François 2002 and 2005). The weaker presence of Italian wares reflects different patterns than that found at coastal sites in the Levant and is suggestive of alternative (possibly non-Mediterranean) exchange networks (François 2004: 247–49). Locally produced were a variety of Iznik and Kütahya derivatives (mostly cups), monochrome-glazed wares, HMGPs, and wheel-made but unglazed jars, *chibouks*, and *narghilas*.

Closer to Jordan, in Ottoman Palestine, one encounters a similar assemblage. Excavations of the Zaydaniyya capital of Acre produced glazed imports from Turkey (Çanakkale II Ware and Kütahya coffee cups) and Italy (Tuscan painted pottery), as well as dark green-glazed hemispherical bowls, wide-rimmed plates, and *chibouks* that might also be imports. The excavators could only identify a group of burnished, red-slipped *narghila* heads as local products (Edelstein and Avissar 1997: 135). Further inland at Yoqne'am (Zahir al-'Umar's fortress) on the Sharon Plain, relatively little imported pottery was recovered. The small number of sherds, however, repeats a pattern that is quite familiar by now: Turkish imports (green-glazed Turkish Coarse Ware bowls, Kütahya coffee cups, Didymoteichon Ware, and glazed cooking pots), and European imports (yellow-glazed pithoi and painted pottery from Italy). In addition, a range of more regional wares of the 19th century also defines this assemblage, and these were common to Jordan in this period as well: Syrian imports (painted jars and jugs named after their production center in southern Lebanon at Rashaya al-Fakhkhar, which is described in the next section), Palestinian pottery (Gaza Ware storage jars), local monochrome-glazed and slip-painted wares, and miscellanous *chibouks* and *ibriqs* of mixed provenance (Avissar 2005: 75–78).

Ottoman pottery in Jordan, and particularly that of the 17th through early 19th centuries, is largely unpublished and unknown. Only now are we capable of identifying sherds of this period during pottery readings at excavations, and these are of very low frequency. This point should be emphasized: at this stage in our exploration of Ottoman-era sites in the country, there appears to be relatively little Middle Ottoman pottery in Jordan. Nonetheless, the material identified consists of a similar range of glazed wares and *chibouks* available elsewhere in the Empire and identified at the sites described above. These wares are, moreover, critical to dating strata and sites where pottery is otherwise absent or takes the form of unfamiliar coarsewares. The sites from this author's field projects that best illustrate this period are Hubras (Northern Jordan Project; the mosque and farmhouse excavations) and Tell Hisban (excavations of the citadel and Field O farmhouses). The pottery falls into three general groups: fine glazed wares (which include Didymoteichon and Iznik Wares and their derivatives and European stonewares), common glazed wares (monochrome-glazed bowls, with or without slip, and the glaze frequently streaked and described by Hayes as Turkish Coarse Wares or regional derivatives), and unglazed wares (the ubiquitous *chibouks* and *ibriqs*, which will be treated in the following section). There is no evidence that any of the sherds of this period that appear in the catalogue below were locally produced, though many may have been regional (Palestinian or Syrian) products. Of the glazed imports, coffee cups of stoneware fabric were found with the most frequency, though their numbers are always low in relation to sites outside of Jordan. Sherds of these wares at Hubras were found in association with glass bracelets of the Ottoman period, green-glazed sherds recut as jar stoppers, and *chibouk* fragments, which range in date from the 18th to the early 20th centuries (Walker et al. 2007). Their specific stratigraphic contexts are discussed in the catalogue.

Transitional Late Ottoman–British Mandate

In many respects, the mid-19th through mid-20th centuries constitute a single unit in Jordanian socio-cultural history. This period represents an attempt by the Ottoman government to reassert its authority over the inland regions of southern Syria through policies that redefined local-imperial relations, landholding, and local production, and which were continued by the British Mandate authority that controlled Transjordan from 1920 to 1946 (Fischbach 2000; Mundy and Smith 2007; Walker 2007c). There is, as well, considerable continuity in the material culture from the Late Ottoman (1830s–1918) through the Mandate periods, making it extremely difficult, without good stratigraphic contexts, which are rare, and imports, which are limited in quantity, to differentiate the pottery of the two eras. With the recent excavation of Late Islamic sites in Jordan, the material described in this subsection has been found in relatively large quantities, but very little has been

published; it has not been securely dated anywhere and is the least well-known of all the ceramic traditions of Jordan.

The Late Ottoman period in Syria is framed by two events: the occupation of the region by the Egyptian forces of Ibrahim Pasha (1831–1840) and the implementation of three edicts for reform issued by the Sublime Porte between 1839 and 1878, known collectively as the Ottoman Tanzimat. Ibrahim Pasha invested in the Syrian economy largely through his security efforts: during the Egyptian occupation, nomads were encouraged to settle, and the protection money paid to them by villagers temporarily put an end to raids on their properties; villages were reoccupied; with safer roads came a revival in trade; schools were built; many new villages were established (particularly in the Ajlun district), as old ones were resettled (Hisban, for example; see Kareem 2000: 23). Many of these efforts were continued by the Ottoman authorities, who were primarily concerned with maximizing tax revenues and insuring rapid movement of troops through the region. The most important Tanzimat-inspired law applied in southern Syria was the Land Law of 1858, which required registration of land in the hands of a single owner for tax and conscription purposes. While the impact of this law varied from place to place and its long-term repercussions are still debated by historians, it can be credited in Jordan, directly or indirectly, with the gradual settlement of the Bedouin, rural revival (due to increased security), an improved infrastructure,[35] the restructuring of regional trade (accelerated by the "grain boom" of the mid-century and the growth of the ports of Haifa, Jaffa, and Gaza; Walker 2007c), and the emergence of new markets and market towns locally with the arrival of merchants and moneylenders from Palestine (Abu Jaber 1989; Carroll, Fenner, and LaBianca 2006).[36] Municipalities were gradually established in each district center (Irbid and Salt in 1867, Madaba in 1913, and Kerak in 1893), as Ottoman authority was re-established and taxes collected (Russell 1989: 32; Rogan 1999: 120).

Ceramic production and consumption in this period responded to these phenomena, as Jordan was pulled into the mercantile and socio-political orbits of Palestine, southern Syria, and Lebanon, and the growth of villages translated directly into the revival of cottage production and regional exchange of local handicrafts. While excavations of Late Ottoman–Mandate sites in Jordan are few, it is fortunate that many contemporary and historical ethnographic studies which record traditional potting in Jordanian and Palestinian villages are available that are rich in data on production methods, household assemblages, functions of specific forms, the identity of customers and producers, prices paid, and mechanisms of transport (Gatt 1885; Einsler 1914; Badè 1931; Grant 1931–1939; Crowfoot 1932; Dalman 1964; Matson 1974; Franken and Kalsbeek 1975; Rye 1976; Zevelon 1978; Mershen 1985; Khammash 1986; Amiry and Tamari 1989; Salem 1999; Tekkök-Biçken 2000; 'Ali 2005; Carroll, n.d.). Such reports describe essentially the same range of pottery used in peasant households: gray-firing water and storage jars; painted wares, both wheelmade and handmade; handmade bowls, cook pots, and jars of coarse, friable fabric, either covered with a white slip or left plain; handmade jars of a more sturdy fabric, combed or incised; *ibriqs*; porcelain coffee cups; *chibouks*.

The reports reflect a rather limited range of forms – namely bowls and jars of varied size. Ethnographic collections in local museums can be quite useful in reconstructing common village assemblages. The best documented collections are Palestinian but illustrate forms for which parallels are known in Jordan: the handmade cook pot (*qidra*) with two everted and pierced handles; the small, two or three-handled water jar (*jarra, habiyya*), frequently painted, burnished, or embellished with simple appliqué; the large, stationary water storage jar (*zir*), handmade through coil construction; wheelmade plain and painted spouted jugs (*ibriqs*), frequently stopped with ancient pottery sherds recut to fit the mouth; small jugs (*maghatis*) and bowls (*zabadi*) (Khammash 1986: 69–70; Amiry and Tamari 1989: 44–45; Kalter, et al. 1992: 110–15; Dalman 1964: figs. 75–78 and 97). Einsler's study of pottery and kilns in the region of Ramallah at the turn of the century documented in detail what a typical village household needed in ceramic vessels each year: two large storage jars, three medium-sized jars, five bowls,

ten small jars or jugs, four cook pot lids, five to six ovens, and a grain bin (built inside the house and made of sun-dried clay (Einsler 1914: 257).

The limited repertoire of shapes is offset by an impressive variety in fabrics and surface decoration, reflecting household production (every village likely produced some kind of pottery for its own use) and intensive inter-village exchange of wares. The ethnographic studies largely target production centers; the best-known being in in Palestine Gaza (gray-firing, wheelmade jars; Gatt 1885; Salem 1999: 77 and contribution to this volume), Hebron (a wheelmade red ware; Salem 1999: 77–78), Sinjil (handmade, red-painted bowls; Crowfoot 1932: 180; Salem 1999: 75), Haifa (wheelmade wares in a distinctive white fabric; Salem 1999: 76–77), and in southern Lebanon the village of Rashaya al-Fakhkhar (a painted wheelmade ware; Dalman 1964: 199–200; Matson 1974: 345–46). Women generally produced handmade cooking pots, water pots, and storage jars at home, using calcite (for cook pots) and crushed pottery (i.e., grog, for water storage jars) as temper, and usually firing their vessels in the open air (Rye 1976: 769). Men worked at the wheel in workshops (frequently attached to the home) and employed kilns. Both handmade and wheelmade wares were sold in local markets and sent to more distant ones through middle-men, transported overland by donkey (Salem 1999: 78) and camel with large jars being carried in bags (Gatt 1885: 71; Khammash 1986: 70). Occasionally, women potters traveled to neighboring villages to take orders (Einsler 1914: 257). Desirable clays were frequently imported,[37] and vessels made locally could be transported to the next village, markets 35 km away, or to Transjordan (*ibid.*). Such extensive travel by the potters themselves would have been unthinkable a half century earlier. The regular movement of potters and the multiplicity of production centers characterize the Late Ottoman period as the era of local ceramic traditions. Pottery-making and decorative designs (described below) were passed down in the family, lending a particular distinctiveness (or "localness") and longevity to village products.

The Late Ottoman assemblages of Jordan are not as well known as those of Palestine, as there have been fewer ethnographic studies and excavations of relevant sites, and Jordan has fewer known centers of ceramic production.[38] Nonetheless, archaeological reports, ceramic analyses, and the occasional ethnographic study have provided a glimpse into the kind of pottery used in Jordan in this period and its distribution. Pottery collected from Kerak Castle and the Plateau always consisted of handmade cook pots and jars with chaff temper, Gaza Ware was present but rare[39] and was the only recognizable Palestinian import of the assemblage, and *chibouk* fragments were recovered in small numbers (Brown 1991: 243 and 279, pl. 9; Milwright 2008: 181). The assemblage of northern Jordanian villages is quite different. It is richer and reflects a more varied range of wares, a mixture of local production and importation, and a greater evidence of the use of glazed wares. Excavations at Dhraʾ al-Khan, the caravanserai in the northern Jordan Valley discussed above, produced a combination of HMGP jars and bowls (with straw inclusions) and wheelmade jars and jugs (Kareem 2000: figs. 20, 31, 43, 47, 49–51, and 57).[40] The same handmade, coarse, poorly fired wares are also found at Umm al-Jimal near Mafraq, where they are decorated with black painted designs, combing (Parker 1998: 215), and one wheel-thrown jar betrayed traces of black glaze (*ibid.*: 216, cat. 62).

The Ajlun and Irbid regions, however, have produced the most diverse assemblages of pottery from the Late Ottoman–Mandate period. Women potters in Ajlun, Kufranja, Umm Qeis, and neighboring villages in the early 20th century made a striking variety of handmade sieves and thick-walled bowls and jars, their surfaces livened with red-painted zigzags and hatched designs or simple clay appliqués; basalt, locally available, was used as a temper. Villagers used such vessels along with wheel-thrown black water jars imported from Gaza (Mershen 1985). Thirty percent of the pottery recovered from our Saham survey and Hubras excavation in 2006 was Ottoman, and an additional 27 percent was attributed in the lab to the Mandate period. Together the Late Ottoman and Mandate-era material presented an impressive range of wares: imports from Gaza and Sinjil in Palestine and Rashaya al-Fakhkhar in Lebanon; lo-

cal versions of the same, as well as HMGPs and very coarse handmade wares; the omnipresent *chibouks* and *ibriqs* from various places of manufacture; a few fine imports from Europe.[41] There is, therefore, a distinct regionalism in Jordanian pottery in this period that reflects, on the one hand, the earlier reincorporation of the Irbid region under Ottoman suzerainty (and, in turn, into Ottoman-sponsored regional trade networks) in comparison to central and southern Jordan and, on the other, the configuration of traditional trading partners on both sides of the River Jordan (Maʿan and Gaza, Kerak and Hebron, Irbid and Haifa; Walker 2007c).

Wheel-thrown, painted pottery has a long history in Syria, one that in Islamic ceramics can be traced back to the fine-bodied, painted bowls of the Umayyad period. Rashaya al-Fakhkhar Ware represents one of the latest manifestations of this tradition in the late 19th century. The village of Rashaya al-Fakhkhar is located near the foothills of Mount Hermon in a region of southern Lebanon known for pottery production.[42] The ware has an orange-pink or white fabric, is wheel-thrown and well-fired, and is decorated in parallel lines in brown or red over a white slip or white paint; occasionally, the interior is glazed in dark green or black and the exterior splashed with glaze (personal communication, Edna Stern, Israel Antiquities Authority). Vessels range from jars (*ibriqs*, sometimes ribbed, and jars with two lug handles; Olenik 1983; Zevelon 1978: 191, 194–97) to bowls and cups, all of which share thin walls. Rashaya al-Fakhkhar Ware has been identified outside Lebanon in northern Israel (as far south as Nazareth: personal communication, Edna Stern; Kabri: Kempinski 1988: XXXI; Tel Yoqneʿam: Avissar 2005: 77, figs. 2. 26, 4–6, 78), and northern Jordan (Tibneh: Khammash 1986: 70; Hubras: Walker et al. 2007: fig. 25. 4). This kind of pottery apparently was produced for a long time. The 19th- and early 20th-century wares described in ethnographic reports (Dalman 1964: 199–200) and represented in museum collections (Olenik 1983; Zevulun 1978) continued to be manufactured in the village in the 1950s and 1960s (Matson 1974: 345–46); a 15th-century prototype has recently been identified in unpublished excavations in northern Israel (personal communication, Edna

Stern, November 2003). At Hubras in northern Jordan, sherds of this ware were recovered from stratified contexts (a plastered floor) dated to the Late Ottoman period by their association with *chibouks* of the 19th century (Walker et al. 2007: 458).

A more familiar wheel-thrown ceramic is the so-called "Gaza Ware." Described in detail in a late 19th-century ethnographic report (Gatt 1885), the gray-colored wares of Gaza kilns have become synonymous with Late Ottoman occupation at archaeological sites in Palestine and Jordan. The moniker, however, has been overused and extended to a variety of reduction-fired, wheel-thrown ceramics that may or may not have had anything to do with the many production sites of southern Palestine. The result has been an ambiguity of ceramic identification and, certainly, chronology. As one of the most important ceramic indicators of the period and one ubiquitous enough to help date most sites in the region, clarification of what the ware is and when it was produced is a necessary prerequisite to any discussion of Late Ottoman pottery in southern Syria.[43]

Gaza Ware is a class of wheelmade pottery that fires a gray color, the result of firing red clay in an oxygen-reducing kiln (Salem 1999: 77). Vessel forms are wide-ranging and include large jars and *ibriqs*, with their distinctive collared mouths, strap handles placed high on the shoulder, sharply accentuated transitions from neck to body, and omphalos bases, cook pots, bowls, basins, *tabuns* (clay ovens), lamps, and *chibouks* (Gatt 1885: 71). There is very little surface decoration other than the ribbing on jars (Rye 1976: 773) and the occasional addition of glaze in the vessel interior (Walker et al. 2007). The use of additional surface decoration, such as white painted designs, combing, and appliqué, could possibly belong to local derivatives of the ware and not the Palestinian product *per se* (see catalogue below; also Saller 1946: 180). Gaza Ware, which is produced in several Palestinian kilns, has the widest distribution of pottery of the Late Ottoman period, having been identified throughout Israel and Palestine ('Ayn Karim: Saller 1946: 180; northern Negev: Schaefer 1989: 42–43 and Rosen and Goodfriend 1993; Judean hills: Gibson

et al. 1991: 44–46; Tell Jezreel: Grey 1994: 61; Giv'at Dani: Lazar 1999: 134; Ramat Hanadiv: Boas 2000: 547–48; Salem, in this volume; south of Nazareth: personal communication, Edna Stern), in various regions of Jordan (Kerak Plateau: Brown 1991: 279, cat. 481; Tell Hisban: see below; Ajlun, Kalter, et al. 1992: 112, fig. 259; northern Jordan: Mershen 1985: 82 and Khammash 1986: 70; Malka: Walker 2005: 96, fig. 18; Saham and Hubras: Walker et al. 2007: figs. 23 and 25–26), and in Lebanon, northern Galilee, and southern Syria (Boas 2000: 548). There is no consensus on the chronology of this ware. While usually attributed to the late 19th and early 20th centuries, it has been dated as early as the 15th and 16th centuries (Schaefer 1989: 42–43; Gibson et al. 1991: 44–46; Rosen and Goodfriend 1993) and as late as the mid-20th century (Mershen 1985: 82, fig. 1). Gatt's account (1885) describes the long-distance transport of this high-quality ware, which was in demand in villages throughout the region.

It is in the handmade wares, however, that the Late Ottoman pottery of Jordan reveals its greatest diversity. Red-painted wares were likely produced in many villages throughout Palestine and Jordan in the late 19th and early 20th centuries. As cottage industries, they were made by women with the decorative patterns passed down from mother to daughter and each village having its own unique style. However, it is the products of the village of Sinjil in central Palestine, near Nablus, that have the widest distribution and may have inspired imitation in other villages. Sinjil Ware, first identified by Crowfoot, who visited the village in 1931, is a handmade ware decorated in red-painted geometric designs, generally on a yellowish or cream slip (Crowfoot 1932: 180). The patterns tend towards linear and hatched designs in wide lines along with dots; the range of forms is limited: handmade cook pots, bowls, and large two-handled water jars, with the handles hugging the waist and the neck tall and cylindrical. We know the ware was produced in Sinjil during the Mandate period and likely earlier, as it appears to have been an established tradition by the time of Crowfoot's visit. Unfortunately, there are up to now no published examples of the ware in Jordan or Palestine from excavated contexts to confirm its chronology. Sinjil Ware was sold on

Palestinian markets in the 1970s (personal communication, Robin Brown); the village continued to produce painted wares as late as the 1980s, when Salem documented the manufacture process there (Salem 1999).

The methods of producing red-painted wares were similar in each village. Groups of women worked together, led by a specialized potter. In the late spring they dug to locate appropriate clay beds, adding straw, sand, and grog (made by grinding pottery sherds acquired from local archaeological sites) for temper and to improve the porosity of the clay. Large jars were coil-made and the surface design was produced in a thin red slip applied by the womens' fingers. After two weeks of drying, the vessels were fired in the open air (Einsler 1914: 249–57; Mershen 1985; Khammash 1986: 70; Amiry and Tamari 1989: 43–46; Salem 1999: 71).

Sinjil Ware proper has been identified in stratigraphic contexts at Hubras (Walker et al. 2007), and similar pottery has been found in villages throughout Palestine (for Ramallah, see Einsler 1914: 256) and northern Jordan (Irbid and Ajlun regions: Mershen 1985; Tibneh: Khammash 1986: 70). It is not clear from published ethnographic and museum studies, however, how many of the vessels described are actual imports from Sinjil and how many are local derivatives (local versions of the same common tradition). The practice of painting red designs on handmade jars was widespread and probably belongs to a regional tradition. Without laboratory analysis of fabric, attribution of provenance cannot be confirmed. It appears, however, that this tradition in Jordan was limited to the north. No published examples from central Jordan are known to this author, and the ware has not been identified at Tell Hisban; red-painted wares (Sinjil or derivative) are unknown in the Kerak region (personal communication, Robin Brown).

The red-painted tradition may have developed out of, or be a variant of, HMGP Ware, which continued to be produced in a degenerate form in the Late Ottoman period. This later ware is differentiated from its earlier Ottoman version in its limited color scheme (painted in a monochrome red or black in dull tones, Walker 2005: 104, fig. 22.4, basin from Malka), the poor quality of its slip (a thickly and unevenly applied white slip of plaster-like consistency, which seems to hold the fabric together), the coarseness of the fabric (high percentage of quartzite, grog, and straw and often quite friable), its incomplete firing (there is often a black core), and its limited range of forms (almost entirely basins and jars, usually medium-sized and with two strap handles; see fig. 5.20).[44]

Not all handmade pottery was painted, however. Unpainted pottery in the same fabric and range of forms as Late Ottoman–Mandate HMGP is also found in Jordan, often covered in an extremely thick white plaster, perhaps to repair cracked pots (Mershen 1985: 77, 79). It is difficult at this point to determine distribution of plain, handmade wares in Jordan, as they are frequently mentioned but seldom described in any detail or illustrated in published archaeological reports. Handmade jars, including *ibriqs* and bowls in the same coarse or finer fabrics, were frequently embellished with appliqué (usually on red-slipped, burnished surfaces), combing, incision, and punctuate designs (Shatana and Kufr Hall: Mershen 1985: 83, figs. 6 and 7; 86, fig. 18 with appliqué; Ajlun: Kalter et al. 1992: 112, figs. 254 and 259 and 115, figs. 267–68 with combing and appliqué; Umm al-Jimal: Parker 1998: 217, cat. 78, with combing). Combing on both handmade and wheelmade wares is associated in a very general sense with later Ottoman occupation throughout the Mediterranean, although it is difficult to determine a more specific chronology for such wares at most sites.[45] One common combed design that consisted of parallel, vertical waves can also be found in Late Ottoman–Mandate-period wares, which supports dating many of the handmade wares with combing in Jordan, at least, to the later Ottoman era. Combing as a surface treatment has a particular longevity, and in the 1970s, combing was a specialty of Hebron and Jabba potters (Rye 1976: 773).

The kind of trade indicated by Late Ottoman–Mandate ceramic wheel- and handmade assemblages in Jordan is regional and was conducted between neighboring settlements and with villages in Palestine. Identifiable imports from outside the region are few and generally limited to European stonewares (see note 32).[46] The importation of glazed stonewares throughout Syria, primarily from England, began in the 18th century and continued with a wider range of wares, including less expensive coffee cups and English spongeware. The market for affordable porcelain coffee cups from Europe and China expanded in the 20th century; many of the *finjan* fragments in Jordan, and particularly those recovered from surface deposits, are "modern" (for examples from Kerak, see Brown 1991: 244, 279, cat. 482).

Site Catalogue

Northern Jordan

Launched in 2003 to initially explore patterns of expansion and reduction in village life in the region during the Mamluk and Ottoman periods, the Northern Jordan Project grew in 2006 into a multi-disciplinary exploration of the history of rural society, agriculture, and the physical environment of northern Jordan from Irbid to the Yarmouk River. The northern hill country has traditionally been the most densely settled region of Jordan and is, fortunately, well-documented in historical sources for much of the medieval and early modern periods. It has, however, not been the focus of systematic archaeological investigations of the later Islamic centuries. The project, which relies on the model of political ecology to frame its inquiries, is currently concerned with four objectives: to document and explain the transformations of village society here from the Middle Islamic period; to compare the settlement history of northern Jordan to other regions of the country; to identify and create a chronology for Ottoman and Mandate-period pottery (much of which was locally produced); to develop a typology of vernacular architecture, both sacred and secular, in Mamluk, Ottoman, and Mandate-period Jordan.[47] The targets of archaeological investigations each season are living villages, selected on the basis of their historically documented history of settlement in the medieval and early modern eras and their architectural remains.

The preliminary season in 2003 consisted of a surface survey of the historical village of Malka,

located 7 km east of Umm Qeis, and a preliminary architectural survey of the historical mosque(s) at Hubras, a village located 16 km north of Irbid (fig. 5.1; Walker 2005). In the 14th century, Malka was a sultanic estate and continued to be one of the largest and most affluent villages in the region. Hubras, attested in Mamluk sources, was a religious center with several mosques and shrines in its vicinity and had a history of settlement spanning the Ottoman era that was confirmed historically and architecturally. Excavation commenced in the village of Hubras in 2006 in two fields: Field A (a mosque surveyed in 2003 and a Mandate-era mosque built inside the sanctuary of a larger medieval one) and Field B (an early 20th-century farmhouse across the street from the mosques). In addition, two weeks were devoted to surface and architectural surveys in the village of Saham, located 22 km northwest of Irbid near the Syrian border, and Wadi Saham and its tributaries (Walker and Kenney 2006; Walker et al. 2007). Saham is a single-period village with its well-preserved remains of public buildings, abandoned farmhouses, and agricultural installations dating to the Late Ottoman to British Mandate eras. Research in all three villages has been supported by ethnographic interviews with local residents and research in the archives of the local Awqaf Ministry and Land Survey offices in order to more fully document local histories of settlement, land use, and architectural development.

The only fields excavated in the NJP during these two seasons were the Hubras mosque(s) and the Field B farmhouse. The stratigraphy of both fields was shallow and heavily disturbed by bulldozer activity, which was the result of road construction in the village in the 1970s that physically cut the farmhouses in the neighborhood off from the community mosque and destroyed many other buildings in the vicinity. Nonetheless, a few stratigraphically secure loci were identified that have relevance for the study of Ottoman pottery. A well-preserved flagstone pavement outside the walls of the Mamluk-era mosque provided an excellent stratigraphic reference point for excavations in A.3 (east side of mosque) and A.6 (the northern doorway).[48] Several loci associated with the pavement (pottery pails A3.5B.16) and immediately above it (pails A3.6D.29, A3.7A.10, A3.9C.32–33) contained a similar range of pottery, dominated by Ottoman-period glazed, Gaza, and post-Mamluk forms of HMGP. In the same pails were identified pipes of the 18th century (figs. 5.10 and 5.12) and late 18th-century stoneware imports that allowed dating the flagstone pavement to the late 18th or early 19th century. In A.6, wall collapse above an extension of the same pavement outside the mosque's northern entrance sealed debris containing similar wares, in addition to several pieces of a large Rashaya al-Fakhkhar Ware jar (fig. 5.2: 4–5). Excavation of the Field B farmhouse took place largely in the exterior courtyard, which produced semi-stratified kitchen refuse. The best contexts, however, came from B.3, a small probe placed inside the kitchen of the original farmhouse. The contemporaneity of "20th-Century Painted,"[49] Gaza derivatives and late HMGP Wares was confirmed by their stratigraphic association under a beaten earth floor (B3.17) and fill (B3.9) sealed by the construction of a plaster floor (B3.14).

Central Jordan

The Tell Hisban excavations are part of the larger Madaba Plains Project, a 20-year-old consortium of American and Canadian teams dedicated to exploring the ancient tell and town sites of this grain-producing, highland plateau. The project was launched by the early excavations at Tell Hisban, which were begun in 1968 by Andrews University in Michigan and came to a close in 1976. Andrews University returned to the site with a new team of Islamic specialists in 1996.[50] This second phase of fieldwork, which continues to the present, has had four seasons of excavations since its inception (1998, 2001, 2004, and 2007) and is driven by its mandate to better understand the nature and chronology of occupation of the tell and surrounding village in the Islamic periods through the lens of food systems theory. Tell Hisban has become the flagship of scholarship on Islamic ceramics in Jordan and is the archaeological project of greatest longevity in the country.

Tell Hisban is located in the village of the same name, some 25 km south of Amman, half the distance from the modern capital to the town of Madaba. With a history of occupation that spans the Paleolithic through modern times, the site is known best for its Iron Age water facilities, the Roman monumental building (frequently, but not confidently, described as a temple), three Byzantine basilicas, and the Mamluk-era military-administrative complex that dominates the fortified summit. After abandonment of the Citadel proper (Fields A, L, M, N, and Q) sometime in the 15th century, the summit was reoccupied and the surrounding village (Fields C, G, and O) revived in the Early Ottoman period. Byzantine and Mamluk-period structures were rebuilt and settled, at least on a seasonal basis, for much of the Ottoman era. Since then the history of occupation at Hisban has oscillated between temporary settlement by semi-nomadic groups and fully settled village life. Travelers' accounts of the 19th century describe only sporadic occupation of this "tent-site" until late in the century (Russell 1989: 30–32; Vyhmeister 1989).

Ottoman-era construction was concentrated in the medieval Citadel and the southwestern slopes below the tell. The ruins of the storeroom of the 14th-century "palace" on the summit of the tell (Field L) were reused for burials of a local population in the 19th century (Walker 2001). The roots of the modern village can be found in this cemetery, in addition to remains of farmhouses, stables, and a fortified agricultural complex, the Nabulsi *qasr* (Walker and LaBianca 2003; Carroll, Fenner, and LaBianca 2006; Carroll 2008). Tell Hisban has not, unfortunately, produced the stratigraphic clarity that was expected from this important Jordanian site. Erosion accelerated by the high winds of the plains and deforestation, along with millennia of reoccupation and rebuilding, have confounded the stratigraphic sequencing required for confident separation and dating of pottery. Nonetheless, the excavation of a single-period farmhouse of the 19th century in 2004 (Field O) offered promise of exploring the occupational history of the site, at least for the Late Ottoman period, with some chronological control.

The widest range of Ottoman pottery was re-trieved during the 2007 season with the excavation of a deep midden in the Citadel's northeast tower (M.6 and M.7) and occupational and erosional fill in the farmhouses of Field O. Ottoman sherds were represented in all fields this season, largely in topsoil and secondary deposition. The *chibouks* were the best chronological anchors for Ottoman contexts; unfortunately, of the five illustrated in this catalogue, three were surface finds (fig. 5.15: 1, 4–5), one was recovered from sub-topsoil (fig. 5.15: 2), and another came from a midden of mixed pottery (fig. 5.15: 3). The less than ideal stratigraphic conditions can be explained, in part, by two factors. First, excavation in the nine new squares opened in the village portion of the site (Fields C and O) did not reach floor levels this season. Additionally, the farmhouses newly excavated in Field O appear to have been originally Byzantine constructions, reoccupied and rebuilt in the Late Ottoman period, which accounted for the mixed deposits. The range of Ottoman pottery at Hisban, the stratigraphic challenges notwithstanding, offers appropriate parallels to the assemblages identified in the northern villages mentioned above where imports were more numerous and participation in Syrian exchange networks more marked. It should be noted that Rashaya al-Fakhkhar and Gaza Wares were identified in small quantities at Hisban in 2007.

Introduction to the Catalogue

The following catalogue, found in the Illustrations section under figures 5.2–5.21 (and their accompanying charts), represents the range of Ottoman pottery used by villagers in the two project areas from the 16th through the early 20th century. Included in the catalogue are some wares that span the Late Ottoman–British Mandate transition, some of which can be dated as late as the middle of the 20th century, such as the "20th-Century Painted Ware" and some HMGPs. They are included because their roots are in the Late Ottoman era. The dates assigned to each sherd in the catalogue are based largely on published parallels (as described in the charts). Fig. 5.6: 1 is one exception to this pattern.

The deposits that produced the pottery illustrated and described below were shallow, yielding only sherds; no complete (or mendable) vessels

were recovered. The inventory number of each sherd in the catalogue reflects the inventory system of the two projects. For NJP, this includes, in order: site, field, square, pottery pail number, and sherd registry number. The specific field projects include surface surveys at Malka (inventory code "KM," for Khirbat Malka), the village of Saham ("SV," architectural survey of abandoned farmhouses and interviews with their owners), and Wadi Saham ("SW"), as well as excavations in Hubras at the mosque site ("HM") and the farmhouse across the street from it ("HF," the largest and oldest standing building in Old Hubras). The inventory system at Hisban is more brief: site, field, pottery pail number, and sherd registry number. The fields in this catalogue, excavated in the 2007 season, include Q (the southern gate to the Citadel, reused in the Ottoman period), L (the storeroom of the Mamluk governors' residence in the Citadel, also reused and rebuilt during the Ottoman period), M (the area around the Citadel's northwest tower, preserving refuse and erosional contexts), C (the medieval village on the western slopes of the tell, largely erosional), and O (the Ottoman village on the southwestern slopes that reflects a primary deposition). "AN" refers to an unsystematic survey of the modern village by local residents in 2001.

Following the very useful system established by Hayes for the Saraçhane assemblages, this catalogue relies on a categorization of wares based, in part, on common fabrics that relate directly to ware classifications and places of manufacture. The fabrics and the codes used in the catalogue appear below.

FABRICS (BY WARE)

Wheelmade

Rashaya al-Fakhkhar
– *produced in southern Lebanon*

FABRIC A (MOST COMMON) hard-fired orange clay with small black and red inclusions; purple-brown painted lines and occasional glaze (applied without slip); mostly jars with handles.
Surface and core: 2.5 YR 6/8 (light red).

FABRIC B   lighter clay than above, fires nearly white on surface, same inclusions; painted lines in red-purple to dark brown; large ribbed jars.
Surface: 2.5 YR 8/2 (pinkish white).
Core: 2.5 YR 8/4 (pink).

FABRIC C   well-fired beige fabric with no visible inclusions; brown-painted, broad lines sparsely applied to surface; handled jars.
Surface and core: 7.5 YR 8/3 (pink).

20th-Century Painted Ware
– likely Jordan or Palestine (possibly inspired by Rashaya al-Fakhkhar Ware)

FABRIC D   high-fired fine clay with visible white and black inclusions and light gray core; broad red or dark brown painted lines; very large jars with handles and thin walls.
Surface: 5 YR 7/4 (pink).

Stonepastes and Soft Paste Porcelains

FABRIC E (SYRIAN "FRITWARES," POSSIBLE IZNIK DERIVATIVES)   friable quartz fabric, frequently with sand added; underglaze-painted floral and geometric designs in blue, brown, or blue-red-green combination; clear (often with greenish tint) or turquoise alkaline glaze; bowls (earlier forms on a high ring foot) and jars.
Surface and core: 5 YR 8/1 (white).

FABRIC N (EUROPEAN)   high-fired and fine light-colored clay; opaque white (tends to craze) or dark blue glaze.
Surface and core: 5 YR 8/3 (pink).

Slip-Painted

FABRIC H (LIKELY SYRIAN MANUFACTURE)   fine, well-fired red or orange fabric; wide slip-painted lines (patterns develop out of Mamluk geometric repertoire) in white under a green glaze; bowls.
Surface and core: 2.5 YR 4/8 (red).

FABRIC I (ANATOLIAN)   deep red fabric with occasional gray core; slip-painted floral designs

(a development of Seljuk patterns) and wide vertical lines ("tongues" – Didymoteichon Ware, a.k.a. "Drip-Painted Ware," and derivatives), frequently thickly applied, under a yellow or green glaze; mostly bowls (of various forms) and dishes.
Surface and core: 5 YR 5/4 (reddish brown) to 5 YR 5/6 (yellowish red).

Monochrome-Glazed

FABRIC J (LIKELY SYRIAN)   coarse, light-colored fabric covered with a glaze of yellow or green color (various shades), frequently spotted or streaked and applied either directly to body or over a slip; jars with handles, bowls (of varied forms), and specialized vessel forms (flower pots, night pots, etc.).
Surface and core range in color: 7.5 YR 7/3 (pink) to 2.5 YR 6/6 (light red) to 5 YR 7/6 (reddish-yellow).

FABRIC K (EASTERN MEDITERRANEAN, NON-SYRIAN)   sandy, light red or brown fabric with grayish hue; covered in dark glaze (without slip); occasional sgraffito design (slip applied); dishes.
Surface and core: 2.5 YR 6/6 (light red).

Gaza Ware – regional (southern Syria)

FABRIC L1 (PALESTINIAN)   a gray or gray-firing fabric, fine and well-fired, with mica and quartz inclusions; large water (*ibriqs*) and store jars, basins.
Surface: GLEY 1 6/5–6 (gray).

FABRIC L2 (PALESTINIAN)   as above, except clay is red and remains red on surface after firing; visible black and white inclusions; frequently gray core; same range of forms.
Surface: 2.5 YR 5/6 (red).

FABRIC M (DERIVATIVES OF ABOVE, MADE IN PALESTINE AND/OR JORDAN)   coarse and sandy red fabric with black and red inclusions, firing a light gray; sometimes a dark glaze added and frequently combed or with simple incised wavy design; large jars and basins.
Surface: interior 2.5 YR 5/6 (red); exterior 2.5 YR 4/2 (weak red).

Pipes (chibouks)
– largely Palestine (Jerusalem) and Syria

Fabric O fine red clay with gray core; heavily burnished, red-slipped surface; frequently stamped.
Surface: 2.5 YR 4/8 (red).

Fabric P pale brown or yellow-red clay with burnished surface of same color; stamped and incised.
Surface and core: 5 YR 7/3 (pink).

Fabric Q sandy off-white fabric with black inclusions; stamped.
Surface and core: GLEY 1 8/10Y (light greenish gray).

Handmade

HM/HMGP – mostly local production

Fabric F (common; includes Sinjil Ware and local derivatives) poorly-levigated and unevenly fired clay with a range of medium-sized inclusions (quartz, grog, and frequently chaff); surface frequently burnished or covered with a white or pink slip or a thick white slip of a plaster-like consistency; surface decoration, if any, of moldings or red-brown lines (geometric or woven patterns); mostly large bowls or basins, jugs, jars with strap handles, and cookpots.
Surface and core range in color: 5 YR 6/6 (reddish brown), 7.5 YR 7/2 (pinkish gray), 7.5 YR 8/4 (pink), 7.5 YR 5/4 (brown).

Fabric G extremely coarse and friable fabric with large inclusions (including gravel, large grog, and chaff); firing appears to be in open air; no surface decoration; mostly bowls/basins.
Irregular coloration (result of uneven firing): variations of brown.

Acknowledgments

Completion of this chapter would not have been possible without the dedicated assistance of several students and staff at Grand Valley and Missouri State Universities. The profile drawings were a joint effort by Grand Valley students April Chernoby and Cara Camp, and this author; Mariya Adams (Missouri State) assisted with copyediting; Cory Weaver and Stephen Niebauer of Grand Valley's Digital Studio electronically produced the plates. The photographed figures were produced by Lynda Carroll (SUNY-Binghamton) and the author.

Notes

1 See Shami 1987 and 1989 and Mershen 1992, as well as Walker 2005 and Walker et al. 2007 for bibliographies of numerous articles on these topics by A. McQuitty and C. J. Lenzen.

2 One notable exception in Israel is a well inside a Crusader tower at Acre, producing Late Ottoman water vessels and smoking pipes (*chibouks*) and published in Stern 1997: 65–68.

3 The Northern Jordan Project (NJP), described below, is perhaps the first of its kind to directly address Ottoman settlement in Jordan.

4 It should be noted that according to the same law, the protection of objects dating after 1750 AD is at the discretion of the Ministry and is not automatically guaranteed.

5 One Muslim pilgrim describes, in Arabic, travel through the Jordanian interior during *hajj* season in the 17th century (al-Nabulusi 1986).

6 The extant *Shari'a* court records, for example, are not readily accessible and have not been the focus of coherent study for this time period in Jordan (Kareem 2000: 20).

7 To further illustrate the point, one Angevin source, during his visit to Ottoman territory in the 17th century, describes the typical caravaneer of the time and his traveler's kit, which would include accoutrements for making and serving coffee, including porcelain coffee cups (de La Boullaye-Le-Gouz 1653: 60–61, as cited in François 2001: 187). The same kit – a leather

sack for storing coffee grounds, a metal roaster, a copper box to transport the cups, the requisite handle-less porcelain *demi-tasses* and their copper gilt chased cup-covers, along with tobacco pipes with ceramic heads (*chibouks*) – was traditionally among the personal goods of Bedouin men (Kalter et al. 1992: 113, figs. 315, 317–18; see also Quataert 2000b: 154).

8 Handmade wares, in general, do come to dominate local ceramic assemblages, relative to wheelmade wares, by the early Ottoman period in Transjordan (Brown 1988: 240; McQuitty 2001: 577). As for Palestine, Pringle emphasizes that the percentage of handmade pottery at al-Burj al-Ahmar in the Sharon Plain rose to 12.9 percent by the late Mamluk and Ottoman periods (Pringle 1986: 136). It is important to note, moreover, that a combination of both "common" (Palestinian) and "fine" (imported) glazed wares constituted only 5 percent of all pottery recovered from Phase E deposits (dated to ca. 1390–1920) at this site (*ibid.*: 138, fig. 40).

9 Glazed wares, in general, represented nearly 1/6 of all ceramic material recovered from these latter two villages (Walker et al. 2007). This is a relatively high percentage for rural Transjordanian sites. The high recovery of glazed sherds from the survey may be, in part, a factor of their easy visibility to my student surveyors, but their presence in the excavation – where we sifted 100 percent of all guffas of dirt and collected 100 percent of the sherds – is a meaningful representation of the importance and availability of glazed wares in the Mamluk and Ottoman village.

10 According to Kareem, the bulk of this material came from stratified contexts dating to the 13th through 15th centuries (Kareem 2000: 86). However, the stratigraphy of the site is far from secure, and the *khan* was in use well into the Ottoman period.

11 François notes the important developments in form in many wares from the Mamluk to Ottoman periods, based on her analysis of the later Islamic wares from the citadel of Damascus (François 2005: 291–93). The problematic of the continuity of green-glazed bowls, however, has not been settled.

12 The sherds came primarily from the A.3 "Eastern Building" attached to the eastern wall of the medieval mosque at Hubras, which has been tentatively identified as a structure connected with a *sabil* (a fountain), with a single stopper retrieved from the northern doorway (in A.6) in sub-topsoil. All of the stoppers in A.3, however, come from bulldozer debris and are in a secondary context. Therefore, they cannot be dated with any more precision than "Ottoman era."

13 Seventy percent of the glazed sherds were collected during the surface survey at Hatara Saghir, a village north of Mosul (Simpson 1997: 91); the glazes of sherds from the GAP (Güneydoğu Anadolu Projesi – "Southeastern Anatolia Project") salvage project in southeastern Turkey were "almost exclusively greenish in color" (Algaze 1989: 246).

14 The modern equivalents are storage jars for *leben*, pickled foods, olive oil, sheep-tail fat, salted cheese, and butter (Simpson 1997: 94–95).

15 Simpson notes, however, some important characteristics of the 18th/19th-century assemblage at Hatar Saghir and illustrates others: an uneven, dark green glaze applied directly to the vessel body (without the intermediary of a slip – his "Glaze Type 2"); limited range of vessel forms (primarily bowls and jars); low ring bases and T-shaped or simple, upright rims (Simpson 1997: 95 ff. and 121, fig. 1).

16 For a range of published forms, see Franken and Kalsbeek 1975.

17 This kind of "cement" continued to be used as late as the 1980s in villages in northern Jordan to repair handmade storejars (*habiyes*; Mershen 1985: 77). This kind of slip is also known from Sataf in the Judean hills (Gibson et al. 1991: 44, fig. 21.9, "Late Ottoman/Modern" context in Trench 2, L2). It, therefore, has a very long tradition in Jordanian cottage production.

18 The jars at Shobak illustrated in fig. 5.14 (of Brown 1988: 241 cat. 47, 48, and 51) come from a pit and loci associated with a low rubble wall built in secondary use of the "Ayyubid Palace" Reception Hall.

19 Handmade wares, both painted and plain, represented 60.4 percent of the ceramic assemblage from Strata 6–8 at Ti'innik (Ziadeh 1995: 217).

20 This scenario has been coherently argued in Johns 1998: 83–84 and Brown 1991: 243–44 and 1992: 310–24.

21 A firing tripod with traces of green and yellow glaze retrieved from the fill of a Middle Islamic farmhouse (Field C) at Tell Hisban in 2004 and petrographic analysis of this tripod and a monochrome, yellow-glazed bowl from a potential 16th-century locus in a Field M house/stable (Murphy, n.d.) suggest local production of such wares in the Madaba Plains. For evidence of the same in the Ottoman heartland, see Hayes 1992: 271–98 (Saraçhane) and François 2001: 164–73 (Aphrodisias).

22 Certainly a more systematic approach to determining provenance by petrographic or chemical analyses of comparative collections, tripods, and clay sources than has been attempted to this point is needed in order to determine places of manufacture and distribution networks. Such work has only begun with sherds from a variety of sites in the Irbid District (in the NJP study area) and the Madaba Plains (Tell Hisban) (Walker 2005: 81; Murphy, n.d; Holzweg, n.d.).

23 The potential Mandate-era derivatives of HMGP Ware are described later in this chapter.

24 The range of vessel forms in both wares is relatively limited and reflects the kind of ceramic shapes most suited to self-sufficient, mixed farming communities, e.g., glazed, utilitarian two-handled jugs for carrying water from wells and storing milk by-products and quickly produced, hand-made bowls and jars for everyday use.

25 A late 16th-century census and tax survey documents only 140 villages in Liwa Ajlun (Hütteroth and Abdulfattah 1977: 19).

26 For analyses of the Ottoman economy in this period, see Quataert 2000a and b; İnalçık and Quataert 2004; Philipp 2004.

27 The three-way trade among farmers, pastoralists, and merchants and artisans created a network of economic and political alliances among these segments of the local population. Peasants, for example, would exchange olive oil for butter and wool from "Bedouin," and both might sell their goods to purchase housewares, textiles, and imported goods in town markets.

28 The rise of the coastal towns of Palestine in the 17th century was a result of imperial plans to re-open the doors of trade with Europe and revive the economy of the coastal areas (Ze'evi 1996: 161). Such efforts paid off: by the end of the 18th century, one quarter of the Empire's maritime trade passed through the ports of Greater Syria (İnalçık and Quataert 1997: 734).

29 For a general history on Zahir al-'Umar, see Joudah 1987. An in-depth historical and architectural analysis of the rule of his son, Ahmad, in Tibneh can be found in Shaqirat 1988. Peake 1958 is the most commonly cited work on the tribal history of Jordan in this period.

30 In only one instance does al-Nabulusi describe a local endowment in the village (qarya) of Ramtha that provided fatirs (pastries), eggs, and bread for pilgrims (al-Nabulusi 1986: 487).

31 Although the 1596 tax register likely reflects census and tax data collected from an earlier part of the century, the reference to market taxes demonstrates the existence of market centers in Jordan in the Ottoman period, contradicting the claims of modern scholarship (Schick 1998: 567).

32 Staffordshire potters in England, for example, produced fine, white stoneware teapots, cups, and bowls in the 18th century for a fraction of the price of Chinese porcelain (Hildyard 1999: 73). Opaque, cobalt blue glazes were added later in the century on jars and bowls (ibid.: 74–75, fig. 100).

33 In their study of modern "Bedouin" burials in northeastern Jordan, the Lancasters describe the custom of placing the deceased's personal belongings, which always included coffee cups and pipes, on top of the grave (Lancaster and Lancaster 1993: 153 ff.). Additionally, the structure of the stone tomb markers included schematic replicas of hearths with coffee-making and serving equipment. Clearly, coffee, as a symbol of hospitality, was and is as widespread among pastoral communities as it was in the formal coffee houses of towns and villages.

34 In 19th-century Syria, there were documented pipemakers' workshops in Damascus, Jerusalem, Jaffa, and Nazareth (Simpson 2002: 169).

35 Abu Sha'r's masterful study of the Irbid District in the late 19th century, based on Ottoman yearbooks (*salnahmehs*), local land registers (the *tapu defters*), and contemporary newspapers in Syria, provides an important window into the development of the road system during the Tanzimat era (Abu Sha'r 1995: 426–30). According to her sources, there were no paved roads in Syria outside of the route between Damascus and Beirut before 1876; travelers in Jordan still generally used the old Roman roads. After the withdrawal of Egyptian forces in 1840, the Ottoman authorities made plans to create a network of paved roads throughout Syria to ensure effective troop movements should such an offensive occur again. Through corvée labor (20 days per able-bodied man every five years) and the commandeering of draft animals and wagons from local farmers, the state was able to clear and pave roads and build bridges in the region from the 1880s on. The roads between Dar'a and Irbid was completed in 1911 and soon after extended to Ajlun. Travel time between nearby villages was reduced in this manner to an hour or two, and Jordan was tied directly to Mediterranean markets and ports.

36 For links to an ongoing research collaboration on these early merchants in Jordan, see the work of Anders Bjørkelo and Kamal Abdulfattah, Global Moments in the Levant project, University of Bergen (www.globalmoments.uib.no).

37 It was learned during the NJP survey of Saham in 2006 that water pots were made in local households from imported yellow clay. They were used in the family and sold to other families (Carroll, n.d.). On the basis of studies he conducted in West Bank in the 1980s and 1990s, Salem has documented the acquisition of clay by potters in the village of 'Aqabet Jaber from 50 km away (Salem 1999: 73).

38 Contemporary workshops specializing in wheel-made wares include Karama, Marsa, Zarka, Zizya, and Rusafa (Brown 1991: 244). The centers of production for the late 19th and early 20th centuries are, until now, not known with certainty.

39 Only five or six sherds from a collection of 50,000 were identified as Gaza Ware (personal communication, Robin Brown, Nov. 10, 2005).

40 One of the objectives of this excavation was to separate Mamluk from Ottoman ceramics (Kareem 2000: 28); however, only two stratigraphic contexts could be dated with confidence to the "post-16th century:" the surface and a single trench (C-Tr2/07; p. 81). It is likely that some of the loci dated to the 13th–15th centuries did contain Ottoman material (see note 11 above.)

41 One informant, during oral interviews in Saham, claimed that pottery was once imported from Iraq (Carroll, n.d.).

42 Many neighboring villages, such as Aytha al-Fakhkhar, made their own pottery in the early–mid-20th century (personal communication, Prof. James Goode, Grand Valley State University, September 2007, based on interviews with émigrés from the village in Grand Rapids, Michigan). Rashaya al-Fakhkhar is proud of its ceramic heritage, which the village displays prominently in its website: www.rachaya-al-foukhar.com (thanks to Prof. Goode for this address).

43 See Salem's chapter in this volume for an in-depth study of this ware.

44 For good illustrations of sherds from stratigraphic contexts from northern Jordanian sites, see Parker 1998: 217–18 (Umm al-Jimal) and Kareem 2000: figs. 31, 43, 47 and 49–51 (Dhra' al-Khan).

45 For such decoration in Ottoman Coarse Wares on Cyprus, see Gregory 1993: pls. 30 and 33; Gabrieli 2004: 295, fig. 5 (18th–19th centuries.); Gabrieli's contribution to this volume, fig. 6.6. For combing on late 18th- and early 19th-century Gray Ware jars, see von Wartburg 2001: 381, figs. 8.70–71 (Kouklia, Cyprus) and François 2002: 163, fig. 1.1–3 (Damascus).

46 The *chibouks* discussed earlier in this chapter and illustrated in the catalogue appear to be largely Palestinian and Syrian products. One cannot eliminate the possibility, however, that

some are imports from Turkey or the larger Mediterranean.

47 The NJP is under the direction of this author and has received financial support from the Oklahoma Humanities Council and Oklahoma State and Grand Valley State Universities. More information about the project can be found shortly at the author's current website at Missouri State University: http://clio.missouristate.edu/bwalker/Projects.htm (under development).

48 In accordance with agreements with both the Jordanian Department of Antiquities and the Ministry of Endowments, pavements were not removed for further exploration beneath.

49 This ware, described under "fabrics" below, was first identified by the excavation team in Hubras in 2006. Found in large quantities in the latest deposits of the abandoned farmhouse, as well as in similar contexts at Hisban, it has been tentatively dated to the first half of the 20th century.

50 Senior staff of the Phase II project includes Senior Director Prof. Øystein S. LaBianca of Andrews University and this author, who serves as Co-Director and Chief Archaeologist. For a list of field reports and publications, see the project website (www.hesban.org), as well as the Missouri State website described in note 47 above. The project is primarily funded by the students and staff of Andrews University and its consortium schools and has received additional support from the communities of Oklahoma State and Grand Valley State Universities.

Chapter 6

Stability and Change
in Ottoman Coarse Ware in Cyprus

by Ruth Smadar Gabrieli

INTRODUCTION

From its early history, Cyprus has been subject to successive waves of immigration and to cycles of foreign control. The Greek colonization of the 15th century BCE had a decisive effect in determining the perceived cultural identity that persists to the present day, and by the 8th century BCE, Greek was the predominant language (Metcalf 2002: 3). This identity survived the period of Roman control (mid-1st century BCE to mid-7th century CE) and the Byzantine-Arab co-regency, and was reinforced by the Byzantine takeover in 965. When Richard the Lion Heart took control of Cyprus in 1191, Cypriot identity was Greek-Byzantine, and the persistence of the strong cultural ties is evident, for example, in the church art, in which European influence never became dominant. As the Ottoman conquest of 1571 followed nearly four centuries of Frankish and Venetian control, the foreign cultures seem to have been integrated into an ever changing, yet always strongly local, culture.

Historical and archaeological studies of medieval and post-medieval Cyprus often emphasize its role within the eastern Mediterranean or between Europe and the East, its place in the international trade networks, and its political and strategic position in the Crusades – in short, Cyprus' role in other peoples' history. The life of the local population, though, has hardly been studied, and what information we have is largely limited to the aristocracy. The occasional glimpse can be found, for example, in oblique references within travel diaries (Cobham 1908; Grivaud 1990). Such reports present a dismal picture of the peasant's life, used and abused by foreign government and local aristocracy alike, poverty-stricken and overtaxed. The following statement, an observation of a 16th-century visitor to the island, is a typical example:

> Besides all the inhabitants of Cyprus are slaves to the Venetians, being obliged to pay to the state a third part of all their increase or income, whether the product of their ground, or corn, wine, oil, or of their cattle, or any other thing. Besides every man of them is bound to work for the state two days of the week wherever they shall please to appoint him: and if any shall fail, by reason of some other business of their own, or for indisposition of body, then they are made to pay a fine for as many days as they are

absent from their work. And which is more, there is yearly some tax or other imposed on them, with which the poor common people are so flayed and pillaged, that they hardly have wherewithal to keep soul and body together (Baumgarten, 1704, in: Cobham, 1908: 55).

Even passages like this one reveal little about the daily life and the cultural perception of peasants or of the artisans and lower classes of the cities and towns. Yet the lives of the non-elite, the local networks of economy, regional trade and manufacture, form the basis of the larger systems of economy and trade. The time has come for an in-depth study of these local and regional aspects of life and, given the scarcity of documentary evidence, it is necessary to make the material culture speak.[1]

A natural point of reference for daily life is the utilitarian tools used to perform mundane chores – vessels that are invested with the identity of their makers and users. Coarse ware, the pottery of food preparation and storage, touches on the very basic aspect of survival and is an intimate signifier of culture and identity. Initially a theme pursued by anthropologists (Mintz and du Bois 2002: 109–10), and possibly best known through the works of Levi-Strauss (1965) and Goody (1984), archaeological research has since taken up the relation between food and culture and food and social organisation. Among the seminal works in this regard are Bats (1988) and Garnsey (1999), in addition to the more site-specific interpretation of Berlin at Tell Anafa (1997) and Wright (2000), who widened the scope to include the spatial organization of food-processing and storage installations as indicators of work distribution and social organization. In the periods under discussion, mention should be made of the recent work of Vroom (2000, 2003), but the subject is a fast expanding one.

The traditional attitude to Cypriot coarse ware of the medieval and post-medieval period is that it shows extreme conservatism. Not 15 years ago, Gregory (1993: 157), analysing survey material from western Cyprus, said that there was little or no development from the 13th century to recent times. Gregory has since modified this position

somewhat (Given and Gregory 2003: 286), suggesting that there are differences in the fabric of the pottery that are chronologically significant. Unfortunately, detailed descriptions that would allow his work to be assessed or continued by others are missing. The potential of changes in fabric to chart chronological development of coarse wares should be further explored.

This chapter attempts to trace the development of form, decoration, and manufacture of coarse ware from the medieval to the Ottoman periods. The assemblage as a whole is considered with special concentration on local production and imports, and finally, some possibilities of the socio-economic context of change and stability are posited.

This study revolves around Paphos (fig. 6.1), where the University of Sydney has been excavating the site of the ancient theater of Nea Paphos since 1995. The theater was built against the side of a hill known today as Fabrika (fig. 6.2) and was in use from the end of the 4th century or early 3rd century BCE to the 4th century CE. Following the final destruction of the theater, the site was extensively quarried and robbed, and by the time it was finally abandoned in the 7th or possibly early 8th century, it was probably unrecognizable as a theater. There followed five centuries of desertion, and then in the 13th century, the area was resettled when a ceramics workshop, part of the famous Paphos-Lemba glazed ceramics industry, was built on the area of the former orchestra. The name of the hill, Fabrika, probably dates to this period. This workshop was destroyed in the early 14th century, possibly in an earthquake. The subsequent gap was short, and sometime during the late 14th or early 15th century occupation was renewed to continue until modern times. Though occupation was continuous, there were shifts and changes, including possible breaks in tenancy. The preservation of the walls of the Venetian/Ottoman period of more than a meter in height and covered by the garden of recent buildings provides fairly good evidence for this (fig. 6.3).

Paphos is a good place to look at local identity and foreign influence. Though its days of prosperity and cultural florescence were waning by the end of the medieval period, it remained the center of administration of western Cyprus. Being a provincial center, it did not have the intensive international trade of Nicosia and Famagusta and, therefore, was less exposed to outside influence. Paphos, however, was the point from which goods were widely exported and where imports were received, and the tax lists of the Ottoman period show that more than a third of the taxes for Paphos came from the customs of the port (Jennings 1993: 258–59). Paphos was not really urban, yet not entirely rural. As a port, it was a place where one would expect reasonable economic activity and, therefore, development of material culture impacted by other centers, yet its provincial status would guarantee that local material culture would not be obscured by the foreign.

The archaeology of medieval Paphos includes the large sites of Saranda Kolones – the castle near the harbor (Megaw 1971, 1972; Megaw and Rosser 2001), the Chrysopolitissa basilica – located midway between Fabrika and Saranda Kolones – and the sugar plant at Kouklia – sited about 13 km east of Paphos (von Wartburg 1997). In addition, there are small sites, such as the medieval structure at the Garrison Camp (Giudice et al. 1993, 1996; Giudice and Giudice 2004), Leptos walls (von Wartburg 2003) and Odos Ikarou (Raptou 2006). Though not a very large corpus, the situation in the Paphos region is better than it is in most parts of Cyprus and varied enough to be considered representative, even if the material leans strongly towards the 12th–14th centuries. If this sample seems small, Ottoman archaeology presents an even worse case. The only publication from the Paphos region known to this author is from Kouklia (von Wartburg 2001). Within this corpus, Fabrika provides an unusual profile of continuous, long-term occupation.

From the Medieval to the Ottoman – An Overview

A short overview of the coarse ware from the 13th to the 19th centuries is necessary in order to examine the question of stability and development from the Medieval to the Ottoman periods, but first the boundaries of the assemblage, which is the subject of this paper, should be defined. Coarse Ware is a term that is variously used to encompass all utilitarian vessels or specific categories of domestic pottery. The term refers, in the first instance, to vessels used for food preparation and storage, but the multi-functionality of many shapes means that the assemblage also contains serving vessels, such as jugs and plates. The assemblage is further defined by reference to fabric. The production of unglazed domestic pottery in Cyprus can be roughly divided into two fabrics: the first is a light fabric, ranging from very light brown or very light red to nearly white, while the second is a dark, reddish-brown fabric. Although cooking ware seems to be manufactured only in the reddish-brown fabric, food processing and storage vessels are manufactured in both. The division between the fabrics is also one of manufacturing technique: the vessels produced in the light fabric are thrown on the fast wheel, while the reddish-brown ones are exclusively hand-formed or shaped on a turntable until around the 16th century; from that time onwards, some, but not all, vessels are thrown on the wheel. This chapter concentrates on the reddish-brown pottery, referring only briefly to the light-fabric vessels. Mainly this decision stems from the fact that the light-fabric industry is in a minority in the Fabrika assemblages, and following its development or even outlining a typology is not possible. Hopefully, as the pottery from the excavations of the major sites that have been excavated by the Department of Antiquities in Nicosia in recent years are published, this situation will be redressed. At the moment, the most pertinent publication for the study of the light-fabric vessels is that of the coarse ware from Saraçhane in Istanbul (Hayes 1992: 271–98), and the parallels with Paphos are restricted to jugs.

Figures 6.4–6.7 document the common shapes of the coarse wares of the medieval and post-medieval periods that will be discussed here. This study of their development is based on as yet unpublished Ph.D. research (Gabrieli 2006). A detailed description of the study that led to the following overview is outside the scope of this chapter, but it is important to stress that the conclusions are not based solely on the Paphos excavations but on results of an examination of numerous assemblages, both published and unpublished, from the regions of Paphos, Limassol, and Nicosia. Among them are assemblages published by Flourentzos (1994), Megaw (1937–1939, 1971, 1972), Prokopiou (1997) and von Wartburg (1997).

The continuity throughout the period is obvious. In manufacturing techniques there is an uninterrupted use of the slow turntable or hand-forming, and the reddish-brown fabric contains the same quantity of inclusions and shows the same quality of firing across all shapes, cooking and storage alike. There is no mistaking the similarities between, for example, the jugs produced by the present-day potters of Phini and Kornos (fig. 6.8) and the 13th-century ones (fig. 6.4: 9). Nevertheless, the differences on close examination, in the section of the handles or the shape of the spout, are obvious. The nearly exclusive shape of cooking pots in the early stage of the 13th–14th centuries is that of globular pots (figs. 6.4: 2–3; 5: 2), a shape that largely gave place, probably in the 15th century, to hole-mouth pots and bowls (figs. 6.5: 1, 5–6) – which, in turn, led to the *tavas* (baking pans) and *tianistra* (frying pans) of modern times. The only shape of liquid containers until the end of the 14th century is that of jugs and jars with a pinched spout (figs. 6.4: 1, 8; 6.6: 1), and although these continue to the present day, there is a startling appearance of elaborately decorated jugs with a sharply carinated body in the 15th–16th centuries (fig. 6.6: 3–4). These vessels, however, seem not to have survived into the Ottoman assemblages where, in turn, we find a new form with a spout on the shoulder (fig. 6.6: 8). It is not only change in existing forms that marks the progress of time, but also diversification and the increasing variation in shapes that starts in the 15th and 16th centuries and continues into the 16th and 17th centuries. This diversification is particularly noticeable in the assemblage related to drinking, such as jugs (compare fig. 6.4 and fig. 6.6), but is also apparent in cooking pots and in overall decorative patterns.

Cooking vessels from the 15th century onwards are mostly crafted with an in-turned lip (fig. 6.5), and the most common is a deep hole-mouth pot (fig. 6.5: 1, 6). Later, the in-turned lip series begins to develop in two directions. In one direction, the lip becomes shorter until it is finally hardly more than a flattened form with slight in-turned edge (fig. 6.7: 1, 3). The second direction is for the lip to lose the thickened base and become a simple in-turned lip (fig. 6.7: 4). These derivative shapes are fully developed in the Ottoman period, although development probably started prior to the conquest. The new shapes do not supplant the medieval ones but supplement them. An assemblage from the church of Panayia Galactotrophousa in the area of Limassol demonstrates this continuity. Found under a floor that could be dated by an inscription to a renovation of 1780 (Prokopiou, personal communication), this assemblage shows homogeneity of manufacture and similarity in details that indicate a group manufactured within a short period. Among the vessels recovered were bowls with in-turned lip, along with wheel-made wares and those with plastic decoration and Kornos-style designs, all ceramic developments of a much later period (see below).

Development is apparent not only in the introduction of new shapes but also in details of manufacture and decoration. This has significance for the possible dating of jars and jugs with a pinched spout, which often constitute the largest part of assemblages and are the most conservative and longest-lived shapes. The earlier vessels, dating from the 12th and 13th centuries and until the end of the 14th century or the early part of the 15th, have flat, thin handles with squared edges, often slightly concave on the upper face. This typical section of the handles is found in all vessels of the period (fig. 6.4). In the later period, vertical handles of jugs, jars, and pots have rounded edges or even a flattened oval section (figs. 6.5: 2; 6.6: 1). The pinched spout is level with the rim and usually is well rounded in the early phase, but later is elongated and pulled forward, often slightly downwards.

The same uniformity that is evident in the morphological details of the vessels dated to the 13th and 14th centuries extends to the decoration, which is limited to four motifs: horizontal multi-line bands that are either straight, wavy, or interrupted, and parallel multi-line oblique strokes, often ending in straight or wavy bands (fig. 6.6: 11).

Figure 6.6: 3–4 and 6–10, by comparison, shows a considerable increase in creativity in decoration, both incised and plastic, from the 15th century onwards. So far, all but one of the decorative motifs and styles that post-date the Early Phase are found on the carinated jugs of the Middle Phase.[2] The one exception is the design of interconnected arches, usually with a dot-rosette at the center of each arch (fig. 6.6: 10), which is known today as the mark of Kornos pottery (London 1989: 72). The earliest secure deposit in which this decoration has so far been found is the late 18th-century one from the church of Panayia Galactotrophousa. At Fabrika, Kornos-style decoration is only found in deposits containing 18th- and 19th-century pottery. The decoration also has strong associations with tobacco pipes.

Not only local production but also imported coarse wares demonstrate developments through time. During the 12th to 13th centuries and until the fall of the Crusader Levant in 1291, foreign coarse wares are limited to glazed cooking pots and pans from the Levantine coast (fig. 6.4: 4–6). Imports seem to be completely absent from the 13th century until the 16th, when jugs first from the Levant (fig. 6.9: 1–2) and later from North Africa (fig. 6.9: 3) and casseroles from Siphnos (fig. 6.7: 6–7) appear. Pottery may have also arrived from Europe, notably France, but the evidence is still uncertain. Ottoman-era imports will be discussed in more detail below.

Against the background of a strong, uninterrupted coarse ware tradition of reddish-brown fabric, incised patterns, and pinched spouts spanning the medieval period until today, are ceramic innovations of the Ottoman era, which are the focus of the following section.

Ottoman Coarse Ware

In addition to development in vessel form and decorative motifs, assemblages dating to the 16th century and later are distinct from earlier ones in three ways:

(1) Introduction of the fast wheel for the manufacture of the reddish-brown coarse ware.
(2) An overall increase in the quantity of jugs.

(3) A significant increase in imports, most of them jugs.

Production

Already during the 7th century, hand-forming of coarse ware was introduced into the Cypriot ceramic industry (Rautman 1998). How long it took before it became the predominant, and later the only, manufacturing technique is not clear, but by the time Cyprus emerged from the "dark age" of the 8th–11th centuries – a period during which little of the material culture is known – the fast wheel was abandoned for the production of red-fabric coarse wares. This change to hand-forming, though extreme, is not unusual within the fragmented post-Roman eastern Mediterranean (Hodges and Patterson 1986), but the persistent use of hand formation as the overwhelmingly dominant technique is curious in view of the central place that ceramic production had in the Cypriot economy. The continuous hand-forming of reddish-brown coarse wares contrasts not only with the thriving glazed-pottery export industry of the 13th century onwards but also with the production of light-fabric utilitarian vessels by means of the fast wheel. This situation remained unchanged from the 12th century through the late 15th and 16th centuries.

In the 16th century, the fast-wheel was reinstated as a means to produce vessels in reddish-brown fabric, but it did not supplant hand-formation. From the 16th century onwards, the two manufacturing techniques existed side-by-side, quite likely representing two distinct industries producing the same shapes and using the same decorative patterns. If one turns to the model of production formulated by Peacock (1982: 8–9), the two industries would roughly correlate with household industries and individual or nucleated workshops. Some of the characteristics of the hand-formed pottery suggest, however, that Peacock's model requires modification. Only a small part of the coarse wares have a thick gray core that indicates a short firing time, possibly without a kiln. The majority of hand-formed vessels and sherds (Peacock's household industry) have a quality of firing that indicates the use of a kiln, and the uniformity of manufacturing details suggest that production was on a scale that would render it a vital source of income (Peacock's individual workshops). Perhaps a more accurate model for the manufacture of hand-formed vessels in medieval and post-medieval Cyprus would be the production mode described by Longacre at San Juan Bautista in the Philippines, where potters hand-formed vessels throughout the year and sold them in the local markets. In the right weather condition, during the dry months, each potter could produce about two hundred pots in a week (Longacre et al. 2000: 274–76). The Philippine study, thus, presents a case of a household industry based on hand-forming, with access to kilns and the ability to produce on a relatively large (and marketable) scale.

An urban–rural dichotomy is a possible explanation for the variable distribution of the wheelmade, light-fabric pottery and the hand-formed reddish-brown vessels, and may extend to the division between the wheel- and hand-formed reddish-brown pottery. Such a dichotomy has been documented for the 19th- to early 20th-century industries (Ionas 2000: 28–29), but it is not known when the simultaneous use of the wheel and hand-forming started, and the urban–rural model leaves some unresolved issues. One issue relates to the production of cooking vessels: none have been conclusively identified as having been produced on the wheel in any medieval assemblage in Cyprus, although some cooking pots have ridges on the upper body that indicate the use of a turntable. If the distinction between wheel-manufacture and hand-forming, indeed, reflects urban–rural production, it would imply that only rural workshops produced cooking pots. A related question is why urban workshops should start manufacturing coarse wares using the reddish-brown fabric. It is possible that increasing demand triggered this change or that some rural workshops, perhaps those closer to urban centers, changed their mode of production and assumed the fast-wheel, while others did not. The assumption of a rural–urban dichotomy should, however, be considered only tentative. It cannot be assumed that the 19th-century model of production fits the 13th–15th centuries, in spite of the continuity in production. Production sites of reddish-brown coarse ware that would help resolve these questions have not yet been found.

The interaction between the two local industries is interesting. The wheelmade production obviously has its origin in the handmade one, as can be recognized by the shapes, decoration style, and fabric, yet there seems to be a predilection to concentrate on jugs. At the same time, hand-formed manufactured vessels take on some of the features that are better associated with wheel-manufacture, such as the ring-base, which occasionally appears in handmade vessels. The relation between the industries can only be conjectural at the moment and might be investigated in future study.

Composition of Assemblages

During the 16th century, there is a shift in the composition of the assemblages of coarse wares, and jugs become considerably more prominent. The following discussion refers to the assemblages from Fabrika, but preliminary survey of other sites of the period, although so far not properly quantified, seems to indicate that this is a general phenomenon.

Figure 6.10 shows the composition of the assemblages at Fabrika in the various chronological phases according to functional groups: for storage (in a range of sizes) or for cooking (as closed shapes, semi-closed, and open).[3] Figure 6.10(a) illustrates vessels that are dated to the 13th–14th or early 15th century (Early Phase). This is the only chart that includes material from outside of Fabrika itself – an assemblage of a deserted household that was found in a vaulted Roman tomb about 100 m from Fabrika.[4] Figure 6.10(b–e) concerns those vessels that could be dated to the 15th century or later. The overall change between (a) and (b–e) is striking, with a shift in the dominant type from cooking pots to light storage vessels, which were a minor type in the Early Phase. Figure 6.10(b) includes all the vessels that have been independently dated, outside of stylistic criteria, to the Middle Phase (mostly small jugs with carinated body, which are known from secure deposits in Nicosia; fig. 6.6: 3–4). Figure 6.10(d) includes the vessels that are exclusive to the Late Phase (e.g., the North African jugs; see below). In Figure 6.10(c) are the shapes that are known to be in use during the Late Phase but may have been introduced earlier, and vessels from deposits that can be dated to the Middle Phase and early part of the Late Phase ("Late (a):" 15th–17th century) or were predominantly of the 16th century. Figure 6.10(e) includes the vessels from both the Middle and Late Phases.

There are some problems with this division, but it serves to present the uncertainties of the assemblages at this stage of study. Most problematic for the present purpose is the fact that the quantity of undatable vessels is by far the largest group and that the dating of specific vessels is largely confined to jugs (e.g., the small jugs of the 15th–16th centuries and the imports of the 16th century onwards; see details below). Consequently, types other than jugs will be underrepresented in (b–d) and over-represented in (e). There is a general trend towards light storage vessels (jugs) from the Early Phase. More specifically, it is the jugs with a long narrow neck, a newly introduced type, that become dominant.

In order to better understand the role of these jugs within the storage assemblage, figure 6.11 presents a more focused view and plots the quantities of storage/transport jars and jugs of the same assemblages as figure 6.10(b-e). Jugs with a long narrow neck form 32 percent of the Middle Phase storage assemblage (fig. 6.11[a]), 74 percent of the Middle/Late (a) Phase storage assemblages (fig. 6.11[b]), and 53 percent of the Late assemblage (fig. 11[c]). The long-necked jug, on the other hand, constitutes only 19 percent of the non-datable vessels, as illustrated in figure 6.11(d). This low number is not surprising, however, given the fact that a large proportion of this type is datable, including two types of imported jugs, which are included in figure 6.11(b) and (c), and the small carinated jugs of the 15th–16th century, as documented in figure 6.11(a).

It is still possible that the increase in the quantity of jugs between the Middle and Late Phases is false, because there is no way of assessing what proportions of the jugs that cannot be dated are, in fact, of the Middle Phase. In order to test the possibility that the increase is mainly due to lo-

cal jugs not being dated properly, all the undated jugs with a long narrow neck (fig. 11[d]), were added to the Middle Phase. The result is figure 11(e), which demonstrates that even with this artificial bias in favor of the Middle Phase, jugs with a long neck constitute no more than 51 percent of the assemblage (compared with 74 percent and 53 percent in the later assemblages). Even when shoulder fragments, which may or may not belong to long-necked jugs, are included in the count, cumulative results for this full assemblage of light storage/drinking containers constitute 71 percent of the Middle Phase assemblage, 87 percent of the Middle / early Late (a) one, and 86 percent of the Late Phase. The increase in popularity of jugs with a long narrow neck between their first appearance in the late 14th century and the Late Phase, at least until the 17th century, seems, therefore, convincing. The increased use of light storage/drinking containers is not in doubt.

Imports

Around the same time that production underwent a change, a new corpus of imports becomes visible at Fabrika. Four types of imports, three of them jugs (jugs with rouletted decoration, fig. 6.9: 1–2; North African jugs with thin walls and incised decoration, fig. 6.9: 4; jugs with white slip and flowing incised decoration, fig. 6.9: 5) and the fourth a casserole (Fig. 6.7: 6–7), were securely identified, because their fabric is visually distinctive. The imports come from different sources, and their contemporaneity can neither be proven nor disproven at this point. It is very unlikely that the situation at one site in Paphos is representative of the trade in coarse wares into Cyprus during the Ottoman period, but the situation is clearly indicative of a change in pattern of exchange and consumption.

Most of the jugs with rouletted decoration date to the 16th century, although evidence from shipwrecks indicates their survival into the 18th century (Amouric et al. 1999: 175, fig. 341). Rouletted jugs at Fabrika have a wide diversity in shape but are united by a distinct fabric, manufacture, and decoration style, and clearly represent imports from a single source or location. The fabric is gray, as a result of a reduced firing atmosphere, with a brown/gray or orange/gray outside surface. It is very hard, breaks with conchoidal section, and usually contains lime inclusions. The decoration reflects rows of tight rouletted zig-zag patterns on the neck and shoulder and close to the base; the same zones can also be partially glazed. Four different shapes are represented in the eight vessels found so far at Fabrika. Two have a wide mouth, one with a concave lip and a sloping shoulder (fig. 6.9: 1), and the other, of which the lip and short neck are preserved, with a convex lip. The third shape (fig. 6.9: 2), with a spout on the shoulder, has a narrow neck and cup-shape lip and is partially covered in light green glaze. Only the lower body of the fourth shape is preserved. The rounded shoulder is similar to that of fig. 6.9: 2, but it has no spout; the body is tall and tapering towards the base, which is missing.

A parallel found in mid-16th-century deposits at Saraçhane was published by Hayes who suggests a Levantine origin (Hayes 1992: 311, Unidentified 76.21, fig. 101.9). Though clearly of the same fabric, decoration, and general style, Hayes' shape, with four handles, is different from any found at Fabrika, confirming the considerable variation in forms. Other parallels for fabric and surface treatment, if not form, include the rouletted jugs of Kalenderhane Camii in Istanbul, also dated to the 16th century (Sabuncu, in Striker and Kuban 1975: 317, fig. 20: 1),[5] as well as those from Limassol (Hayes 1992: 311).

Sixteenth-century dates are in accord with the distribution of jugs at Fabrika, mainly in deposits that have Middle and Late Phase material together, but also in two deposits where the context is securely dated to the Late Phase. These jugs may prove to date, at least in Fabrika, more to a transition between the Middle and Late Phases than to the Late period itself. This possibility is supported by the absence of rouletted jugs in stratigraphic association with North African imports of the same, as well as with jugs bearing Kornos-style decoration, both of which are securely Ottoman in date. Their Levantine origin cannot be taken as an indication that their import post-dates the

Ottoman conquest, since throughout the period of hostilities between Europe and the Ottoman Empire, trade with the Levantine ports never stopped (Amouric et al. 1999: 172).

The North African jugs are highly distinctive by their well levigated, bluish-gray (less often light-grayish-white) fabric and nearly eggshell-thin walls. They are wheelmade with a smooth and well-finished surface and decorated with fine, seemingly casually made single or multiple incisions, often without any obvious pattern. Probably because of their fine walls, these jugs only survive in very fragmented form;[6] there is a scatter of them all through the site, but only one specimen preserves a neck and shoulder (fig. 6.9: 3) with an edge of a strainer. Elaborately patterned strainers are a regular feature of these jugs, but their fragmented state at Fabrika prevented their recognition.

These vessels are known throughout the Mediterranean, notably from shipwrecks (Raban 1971; Amouric et al. 1999: 174–75), and like the jugs with rouletted decoration above, they reflect a wide variety of shapes (Hayes 1992: 300 no. 34; Amouric et al. 1999: 175, fig. 338; von Wartburg 2001: 382–84, figs. 8 and 10). They come from centers of manufacture in North Africa and Egypt, and their production continued from the 17th century to the 19th (Amouric et al. 1999: 174–75).

The association of the North African jugs with datable fine wares at Fabrika leans towards a date in the first half of the Late Phase, and it is noteworthy that the North African jugs have not been recovered with jugs of Kornos-style decorations, which are found only in 18th- and 19th-century deposits. Nonetheless, North-African jugs have been found in three deposits with other kinds of 18th- and 19th-century pottery. One should also note that the best parallels for the jugs of this type found in Kouklia are 18th-century ones (von Wartburg 2001: 382).

Only one sherd of the third type of imported jug (fig. 6.9: 4) was found so far at Fabrika, and that in a context with no datable finds but in association with Cypriot jugs with a long neck. This sherd also reflects an easily identifiable ware with thin walls, gray fabric, white slip, and a flowing decoration that is incised through the slip, showing as a gray design. The full shape, with a spout on the shoulder, is known from 18–19th-century contexts in Akko (Edna J. Stern, personal communication).

The fourth type of import are glazed casseroles thrown on the fast wheel (fig. 6.7: 6–7). The preserved handles are thin, vertical, with a distinct twist, and a sharp dimple on their upper face. Some have a very micaceous surface, and one has an oval stamp, carrying the manufacturer's name. All these characteristics identify the casseroles most likely as products of Siphnos dating to the 18th to 20th centuries (Vroom 2005: 192–93). The casseroles from Siphnos were well-known for their quality and were widely distributed across the Aegean (Vroom 2005: 193; Matson 1972: 221). Ionas and Matson report that local imitations were not of comparable quality, and Ionas adds that those made in Cyprus were handmade (Ionas 2000: 69–70; Matson 1972: 221). Casseroles at Fabrika were found only in topsoil context, probably do not pre-date the 19th century, and are, strictly speaking, outside of the Ottoman period (Britain gained control of Cyprus in 1878). They should, however, be mentioned, because their import may well have started earlier, even if not necessarily to Paphos.

The appearance of these casseroles is particularly interesting because the trade mechanism was most likely a small-scale regional one, rather than part of an international large-scale trade, as was the case with the North African jugs. Even in recent times, small fishing boats (caïque) visit the small harbors, selling and buying local products (Matson 1972: 213, 220–21). In its distribution mechanism, the import of the Siphnian casseroles illustrates ways in which Ottoman Cyprus was incorporated into both Aegean and Levantine regional exchange networks, much as the island was in the Crusader period.

The dividing lines between local manufacture and imports for the Ottoman period are not as clear-cut as they are for the 13th-century Frankish period, when local production was uniform in fabric, form, and decoration. So while these four fabrics are undoubtedly foreign, there are other jugs in the Fabrika assemblage which seem foreign to the site but may represent production at another site in Cyprus rather than imports (fig. 6.9: 5).

Conclusions

The evidence from Fabrika indicates that the period of the 16th century onwards (the Late Phase of coarse ware) can be subdivided ceramically. In the early part of the Late Phase, which is a transition from the Middle Phase, trade of coarse ware with the Levant resumed, with a targeted import of jugs with rouletted decoration. Later, imports from North Africa began to arrive, possibly with some overlap between the two wares. Import of the jugs ceased completely probably no later than the 18th century, although fine wares continued to arrive in considerable quantities. During the 18th or 19th centuries, when import of jugs from the Levant and North Africa ceased, a trade in casseroles from Siphnos began. Distributed throughout the Aegean by small boats (Matson 1972: 220), these products represent a regional trade system, similar to the one that prevailed during the Lusignan period with the Crusader Levant. So far, the sub-division of the period depends mainly on imports, but the fact that the decorative motif of interconnected arches (a Kornos motif) does not seem to predate the 18th century promises one way surface treatment can be used to distinguish earlier from later Ottoman-era products.

Increased diversity in coarse ware is apparent in Cyprus during the Ottoman period. The process had, however, started prior to the conquest and cannot be correlated directly with political change. This is not surprising in a corpus of material culture that is part of the fundamental activities of everyday life. Nevertheless, an influence of the new culture is apparent in the development of the forms and in the function of the individual vessels, as well as in the assemblages as a whole.

Some socio-economic explanations for the change in the composition of the assemblages, namely the increase in popularity of jugs, and particularly jugs with a long neck, can be offered, albeit tentatively. The reason for their initial popularity and for their subsequent increase may follow from very different circumstances. The introduction of the long-necked jug may be related to the introduction of coffee, which led to the new and revolutionary invention of the 16th century, the coffee houses, and to the somewhat later introduction of tobacco, which became intimately connected with coffee and coffee houses (Baram 1999: 141). Coffee was introduced from Yemen to the Ottoman Empire in the 15th century, and coffee houses became popular both in urban centers and in the country by the second quarter of the 16th century. Tobacco made its first appearance in the late 16th century and became widespread in the 17th (Simpson 2002: 167–69). Both coffee and tobacco may have been introduced to Cyprus before the Ottoman conquest. In Saraçhane, Hayes suggests that the initial introduction of the Ottoman shapes may have predated the conquest, although they only become predominant after 1453 (Hayes 1992: 233). Coffee drinking and smoking had an element of secular ritual, in which aesthetics played an important part (Simpson 2002: 170). It is possible that the jugs were part of the same culture, functioning as a more elegant utilitarian ware than typical coarse wares. In this way they were serving vessels appropriate for leisure.[7] The reduction in quantities of jugs with long necks in 18th- and 19th-century contexts cannot yet be satisfactorily explained. One possibility is that glass decanters, which are the preferred vessels today, were already coming into more common use, but further research is needed before firm conclusions can be drawn. It is perhaps worth adding that although the study of the tobacco pipes has not yet been completed, they exhibit a very wide range of sub-types and manufacturing centers.

Coffee houses cannot, however, be responsible for the initial popularity of the new type of jug in the 15th century and the investment in their decoration. This, I would suggest, stems from another reason. The economic crisis of the 15th century may have resulted in more coarse ware being used as table ware so that households that could previously afford glazed jugs, glass, or metal, now used decorated coarse ware jugs.

Another possible factor is the adoption of the fast wheel for manufacture of coarse ware of reddish-brown fabric. This change in manufacturing technique cannot be positively tied to the increased popularity of jugs, but it is suggested, since, at least at Fabrika, the largest part of the vessels manufactured on the wheel are jugs. Wheel manufacture does not replace, but rather coexists with, hand-forming, and the two should represent two production modes. There is a dynamic interaction between these two local industries in decorative motifs and morphological features, and both are influenced by imports. The most obvious influence of imports on the local industry is in the increase in manufacture of jugs with a spout on the shoulder, which is a typical Mamluk/Ottoman shape. The adoption of the shape into the local industry is, however, an adaptation of a concept and not a straightforward imitation. This is probably the reason that another typical feature of the Ottoman jugs with long neck, the strainer neck, is missing from the jugs manufactured in the reddish-brown fabric. Strainer necks are a common feature of North African jugs and of jugs with a spout on the shoulder found in Mamluk and Ottoman assemblages in the Levant, as at Akko (Edna J. Stern, personal communication). The function of the strainer would be to strain liquid that is decanted into the jug, as opposed to a strainer on a spout, whose purpose is to strain the liquid which is poured. So far in the assemblages at Fabrika, strainer necks are found only on North African jugs or jugs of unknown origin. The lack of interest in producing strainer necks with jugs that have spouts on the shoulder may indicate that their common use in Cyprus varied somewhat from that in the Levant, and the potters incorporated features selectively, while continuing to follow their traditional aesthetics.

Notes

1 [Editor's note] The Ottoman state had a rich bureaucratic tradition and kept detailed tax registers and legal records for most of their provinces. Contemporary written records relevant to anthropological and archaeological study of landscape and local society do exist, but as is also the case for the Arab provinces, these records have either not been identified in the archives or the published studies of the source material are unknown outside specialists' circles. For Ottoman Cyprus, one should note Hadjianastasis' dissertation on 17th-century *Shari'a* court registers (2004), as well as the following published works on Ottoman inscriptions and documents: Theocharides 1993; Theocharides and Andreev 1996; Sarinay 2000 (the editor is grateful to Prof. Michael Given at the University of Glasgow for these references and to Prof. Hadjianastasis for information regarding his research).

2 A full description of these phases and the data supporting them can be found in Gabrieli 2004 and 2006.

3 In this report, the "Middle Phase" refers to the period of the disappearance of features of 13th- and 14th-century coarse wares until the introduction of the wheel in roughly the 15th to 16th centuries. The "Early Phase" predates this and can be attributed to the 13th to 14th or early 15th centuries. The "Late Phase" corresponds to the Ottoman period in Cyprus from the late 16th until the middle of the 19th centuries.

4 I am grateful to the excavator, Dr. Eustathios Raptou from the Department of Antiquities, for allowing me to publish this material.

5 The photograph and description in Sabuncu's article would not necessarily have identified the vessel as a parallel; however, I feel secure in using it as an additional support for a date in the 16th century on the basis of Hayes' identification.

6 I am grateful to Dr. von Wartburg for drawing my attention to this ware and published examples of it.

7 For a collection of studies on the history of coffee drinking and its many socio-political functions, see Tuchscherer 2001.

Bibliography

Abd Rabu, O.

2000   Khirbit Beirzeit Research and Excavation Project 1996: The Pottery. *Journal of Palestinian Archaeology* 1.1: 13–24.

Abu Jaber, R.

1989   *Pioneers Over Jordan: the Frontier of Settlement in Transjordan, 1850–1914.* London: I.B. Tauris.

Abu Sha'r, H.

1995   *Irbid wa jiwaruha.* Beirut: al-Mu'assah al-'Arabiyyah li-l-Dirasat wa a-Nashr.

Algaze, G.

1989   A New Frontier: First Results of the Tigris-Euphrates Archaeological Reconnaissance Project, 1988. *Journal of Near Eastern Studies* 48.4: 241–81.

'Ali, N.

2005   *The Development of Pottery Technology from the Late 6th to the 5th Millennium B.C. in Northern Jordan: Ethnographic and Archaeological Studies: Abu Hamid as a Key Site.* BAR International Series 1422. Oxford: Archaeopress.

Allen, S.H.

1994   Trojan Grey Ware at Tel Miqne-Ekron. *Bulletin of the American Schools of Oriental Resarch* 293: 39–51

Amiry, S., and Tamari, V.

1989   *The Palestinian Village Home.* London: British Museum Publications.

Amouric, H.; Richez, F; and Vallauri, L.

1999   *Vingt mille pots sous les mers. Le commerce de la céramique en Provence et Languedoc du Xe au XIX siècle.* Aix-en-Provence: Edisud.

Armstrong, P., and Günsenin, N.

1995   Glazed Pottery Production at Ganos. *Anatolia Antiqua* 3: 179–201.

Aslanapa, O.

1971   Turkish Ceramic Art. *Archaeology* 24: 201–19.

Atil, E.

1987   *The Age of Sultan Suleyman the Magnificent.* Washington, DC: National Gallery of Art.

Avissar, M.

1996   The Clay Tobacco Pipes. Pp. 198–201 in *Yoqne'am I: The Late Period,* eds. A. Ben-Tor, M. Avissar, and Y. Portugali. Qedem Reports 3. Jerusalem: The Institute of Archaeology of the Hebrew University.

2005   *Tel Yoqne'am: Excavations on the Acropolis.* Israel Antiquities Authority Reports 25. Jerusalem: Israel Antiquities Authority.

2006   The Pottery Finds in *El-Qubab,* ed. M. Ein Gedy. *'Atiqot* 51: 58*–61* (Hebrew).

Avissar M., and Stern, E. J.

2005   *Pottery of the Crusader, Ayyubid, and Mamluk Periods in Israel.* Israel Antiquities Authority Reports 26. Jerusalem: Israel Antiquities Authority.

Avni, U., and Magness, J.

1998   Early Islamic Settlement in the Southern
        Negev. *Bulletin of the American Schools of
        Oriental Research* 310: 39–57.

Badè, W. F.

1931   *Excavations at Tell en-Nasbeh, 1926 and 1927.*
        Washington, DC: Smithsonian Institution.

al-Bakhit, M. A.

1989a   *Nahiyat Beni Kinana (Shamal al-Urdunn)
        fi al-qarn al-'ashr al-hijri, al-sadis 'ashr
        al-miladi.* Amman: University of Jordan.
        (Turkish with Arabic summary)

1989b   *Tapu Defteri No. 275: Detailed Register of the
        Private-Khass of the Governor of the Province
        of Damascus 958 A.H./A.D. 1551–2.* Amman:
        University of Jordan. (Turkish with Arabic
        summary).

al-Bakhit, M. A., and Hmoud, N. R.

1989a   *The Detailed Defter of al-Lajjun. Tapu
        Defter No. 181. 1005 A.H./1596 A.D.* Amman:
        University of Jordan (Turkish with Arabic
        Summary).

1989b   *The Detailed Defter of Liwa' 'Ajlun (The
        District of Ajlun) Tapu Defteri No. 970,
        Istanbul.* Amman: University of Jordan
        (Turkish with Arabic summary).

1991   *The Detailed Defter of Liwa' 'Ajlun (The
        District of Ajlun) Tapu Defteri No. 185,
        Ankara 1005 A.H./A.D. 1596.* Amman:
        University of Jordan (Turkish with Arabic
        summary).

Bakirtzis, Ch.

1980   Didymoteichon: Un centre de céramique
        post-byzantine. *Balkan Studies* 21: 147–53;
        figs. 1–30; pls. 1–7.

Baram, U.

1995   Notes on the Preliminary Typologies of
        Production and Chronology for the Clay
        Tobacco Pipes of Cyprus. *Report of the
        Department of Antiquities of Cyprus*: 299–
        309.

1999   Clay Tobacco Pipes and Coffee Cup Sherds
        in the Archaeology of the Middle East:
        Artifacts of Social Tensions from the
        Ottoman Past. *International Journal of
        Historical Archaeology* 3.3: 137–51.

Baram, U., and Carroll, L. (eds.)

2000   *A Historical Archaeology of the Ottoman
        Empire: Breaking New Grounds.* New York:
        Kluwer Academic and Plenum.

Barbé, H.

2006   Horbat Shamshit. *Hadashot Arkheologiyot
        Online* 118: http://www.hadashot-esi.org.il/
        report_detail_eng.asp?id=445&mag_id=111.

Barclay, J. T.

1858   *The City of the Great King: Or, Jerusalem as
        it was, as it is, and as it is to be.* Philadelphia,
        PA: Challen.

Bats, M.

1988   *Vaisselle et alimentation à Olbia de Provence
        (v. 350–v. 50 av. J.-C.): Modèles culturels
        et catégories céramiques.* Suppléments à
        la Revue Archéologique de Narbonnaise
        18. Paris: Centre National de Recherche
        Scientifique.

Baumgarten, M. von

1704   *Peregrinatio in Aegyptum, Arabiam,
        Palaestinam et Syriam.* Pp. 489–91 in the
        first English edition, vol. 1, ed. M. Christoph
        Donauer. London: Kaufmann.

Ben- Tor, A., and Rosenthal, R.

1978   The First Season of Excavations at Tell
        Yoqne'am, 1977: Preliminary Report. *Israel
        Exploration Journal* 28: 57–82.

Ben-Tor, A.; Avissar, M.: and Portugali, Y. (eds.)

1996   *Yoqne'am I: The Late Period.* Qedem Reports
        3. Jerusalem: The Institute of Archaeology
        of the Hebrew University.

Berlin, A.

1997   The Plain Wares. Pp. 1–244 in *Tel Anafa II, I: The Hellenistic and Roman Pottery*, ed. S. C. Herbert. Journal of Roman Archaeology Supplementary Series 10.2. Portsmouth, RI: Journal of Roman Archaeology.

Blakely, J. A.; Toombs, L. E.; and O'Connell, K. G.

1980   *The Joint Archaeological Expedition to Tell el-Hesi.* Cambridge, MA: American Schools of Oriental Research.

Boas, A. J.

2000   Pottery and Small Finds from the Late Ottoman Village and the Early Zionist Settlement. Pp. 547–80 in *Ramat Hanadiv Excavations: Final Report of the 1984–1998 Seasons,* ed. Y. Hirschfeld. Jerusalem: Israel Exploration Society.

Bonar, H.

1857   *The Desert of Sinai: Notes of a Spring-Journey from Cairo to Beersheba.* London: Adamant.

Brown, R. M.

1988   Summary Report of the 1986 Excavations. Late Islamic Shobak. *Annual of the Department of Antiquities of Jordan* 32: 225–45.

1989   Excavations in the 14th Century A.D. Mamluk Palace at Kerak. *Annual of the Department of Antiquities of Jordan* 33: 287–304.

1991   Ceramics of the Kerak Plateau. Pp. 232–46 in *Archaeological Survey of the Kerak Plateau,* ed. J.M. Miller. Atlanta, GA: Scholars.

1992   Late Islamic Ceramic Production and Distribution in the Southern Levant: A Socio-Economic and Political Interpretation. Unpublished Ph.D. Dissertation, State University of New York at Binghamton.

2006   Late Islamic Ceramic Sequences from el-Lejjun: Stratigraphic and Historical Contexts. Pp. 373–92 in *The Roman Frontier in Central Jordan. Final Report on the Limes Arabicus Project, 1980–1989, Vol. 2,* ed. S. Thomas

Parker. Washington, DC: Dumbarton Oaks Research Library and Collection.

Burckhardt, J. L.

1822   *Travels in Syria and the Holy Land.* London: Murray.

Carroll, L.

2008   Sowing the Seeds of Modernity on the Ottoman Frontier: Agricultural Investment and the Formation of Large Farms in Nineteenth-Century Transjordan. *Archaeologies* 4.2: 233–49.

n.d.   Northern Jordan Survey Project: 2006 Season Field Report on the Survey of Sahm Village. Unpublished field supervisor's report. NJP Project Archives, Grand Valley State University, MI.

Carroll, L.; Fenner, A.; and LaBianca, Ø. S.

2006   The Ottoman *Qasr* at Hisban: Architecture, Reform and New Social Relations. *Near Eastern Archaeology* 69.3–4: 1–6.

Cobham, C. D.

1908   *Excerpta Cypria: Materials for a History of Cyprus.* Cambridge: Cambridge University.

Cohen, A., and Lewis, B.

1978   *Population and Revenue in the Towns of Palestine in the Sixteenth Century.* Princeton, NJ: Princeton University.

Coleman, H. R.

1881   *Light from the East.* Whitefish, MT: Kessinger.

Conder, C., and Kitchener, H.

1881   *The Survey of Western Palestine. Memoirs of the Topography, Orography, Hydrology and Archaeology,* 3 vols. (1881–83). London: Palestine Exploration Fund.

Crowfoot, G. M.

1932   Pots, Ancient and Modern. *Palestine Exploration Fund Quarterly Statement, October 1932*: 179–87, pls I–III.

Cushion, J. P.

1996   *Handbook of Pottery and Porcelain Marks.* London: Faber and Faber.

Dabagh, M.

1964   *Biladna Filastin.* Beirut: Dar el-Tali'ah.

Dalman, G.

1964   *Arbeit und Sitte in Palästina.* Hildesheim: Olms.

Dionyssiou, G.

1994   The Ottoman Administration of Cyprus and the Tanzimat Reforms. *Epeteris* 20: 591–600.

Eakins, J. K.

1993   *Tell el-Hesi: The Muslim Cemetery in Fields V and VI/IX (Stratum II).* The Joint Archaeological Expedition to Tell el-Hesi 5. Winona Lake, IN: Eisenbrauns.

Edelstein, G., and Avissar, M.

1997   A Sounding in Old Acre. *'Atiqot* 31: 129–36

Ein Gedy, M.

2006   El-Qubab. *'Atiqot* 51: 58*–67* (Hebrew, English summary p. 239).

Einsler, L.

1914   Das Töpferhandwerk bei den Bauernfrauen von Ramallah und Umgegend. *Zeitschrift des Deutschen Palästina-Vereins* 37: 249–60, Pls. XLV–XLVII.

Fischbach, M. R.

2000   *State, Society and Land in Jordan.* Leiden: Brill.

Flourentzos, P.

1994   *A Hoard of Medieval Antiquities from Nicosia.* Nicosia: Cyprus Department of Antiquities.

François, V.

1995   Byzantine ou Ottoman? Une céramique peinte à l'engobe découverte en Méditerranée orientale. *Anatolia Antiqua* 3: 203–17.

1997   *Bibliographie analytique sur la céramique à glaçure: Un nouvel outil de travail.* Paris: DeBoccard.

2001   Elements pour l'histoire ottomane d'Aphrodias: La vaisselle de terre. *Anatolia Antiqua* 9: 147–90.

2002   Production et consommation de vaisselle á Damas, à l'époque ottomane. *Bulletin d'Études Orientales* 54: 157–74.

2004   Réalités des échanges en Méditeranée orientale du XIIe au XVIIIe siècles: L'apport de la céramique. *Dumbarton Oaks Papers* 58: 241–49.

2005   *Tabak, ibrik, fincan* et autres pots d'époque ottomane au Bilâd al-Châm. *Turcica* 37: 281–308.

Franken, H. J., and Kalsbeek, J.

1975   *Potters of a Medieval Village in the Jordan Valley: Excavations at Tell Deir 'Alla – A Medieval Tell, Tell Abu Gourdan, Jordan.* North-Holland Ceramic Studies in Archaeology 3. New York: North-Holland.

Gabrieli, R. S.

2004   Under the Surface: Decoration and Shape in the Coarse Ware of Medieval and Post-Medieval Cyprus. *Mediterranean Archaeology* 17: 287–98.

2006   Silent Witnesses: The Evidence of Domestic Wares of the 13th–19th Centuries in Paphos, Cyprus, for Local Economy and Social Organisation. Unpublished PhD dissertation, The University of Sydney.

Garnsey, P.

1999   *Food and Society in Classical Antiquity.* Cambridge: Cambridge University.

Gatt, G.

1885   Industrielles aus Gaza. *Zeitschrift des Deutschen Palästina-Vereins* 8: 69–79.

Gazioglu, A. C.

1990   *The Turks in Cyprus: a Province of the Ottoman Empire (1571–1878).* London: Rustem and Brothers.

Ghawanmeh, Y.

1986a *Madinat Irbid fi al-'Asr al-Islamii.* Irbid:
       Yarmouk University.

1986b *Al-Masajid al-Islamiyya al-Qadima fi
       Mintaqat 'Ajlun.* Irbid: Yarmouk University.

Gibson, S.; Ibbs, B.; and Kloner, A.

1991   The Sataf Project of Landscape Archaeology
       in the Judean Hills: A Preliminary Report
       on Four Seasons of Survey and Excavation
       (1987–89). *Levant* 23: 29–54.

Giudice, F. G., et al.

1993   Paphos, Garrison's Camp, Campagna 1989.
       *Report of the Department of Antiquities of
       Cyprus:* 279–312.

1996   Paphos, Garrison's Camp, Campagna 1991.
       *Report of the Department of Antiquities of
       Cyprus:* 171–267.

Giudice, F. G, and Giudice, E.

2004   Paphos, Garrison's Camp. IXa Campagna.
       *Report of the Department of Antiquities of
       Cyprus:* 271–314.

Given, M., and Gregory, T. E.

2003   Medieval to Modern Landscapes. Pp.
       284–294 in *Medieval to Modern Landscapes.
       The Sydney Cyprus Survey Project: Social
       Approaches to Regional Archaeological
       Survey,* eds. M. Given and A. B. Knapp.
       Monumenta Archaeologica 21. Los Angeles,
       CA: Cotsen Institute.

Goody, J.

1984   *Cooking, Cuisine and Class: A Study
       in Comparative Sociology.* Cambridge:
       Cambridge University.

Graf, B.

2001   Türkische Tabakpfeifen "*Chibouk*" aus
       Kouklia. *Report of the Department of
       Antiquities of Cyprus:* 390–96.

Graham-Brown, S.

1980   *Palestinians and Their Society 1880–1946, a
       Photographic Essay.* London: Quarter.

Grant, E.

1931–39 *Beth Shemesh (Palestine).* Haverford,
         PA: Haverford College.

Gregory, T. E.

1987   Canadian Palaepaphos Survey Project:
       Second Preliminary Report of the Ceramic
       Finds 1982–1983, with L.W. Sørensen, et
       al. *Report of the Department of Antiquities
       Cyprus:* 259–78.

1993   Byzantine and Medieval Pottery. Pp. 157–76
       in *The Land of the Paphian Aphrodite,* Vol. 2:
       *The Canadian Palaepaphos Survey Project:
       Artifact and Ecofactual Studies,* eds. L.
       W. Sørensen, and D.W. Rupp. Göteborg:
       Åströms.

Grey, A. D.

1994   The Pottery of the Later Periods from Tel
       Jezreel: An Interim Report. *Levant* 26:
       51–62.

Grivaud, G.

1990   *Excerpta Cypria Nova.* Vol. I: *Voyageurs oc-
       cidentaux à Chypre au XVE siècle.* Sources et
       études de l'histoire de Chypre XV. Nicosia:
       Centre des Recherches Scientifiques.

Hadjianastasis, M.

2004   Bishops, Ağas and Dragomans: A Social
       and Economic History of Ottoman Cyprus,
       1640–1704. Unpublished Ph.D. Dissertation,
       University of Birmingham.

al-Hamawi, Yaqut ibn 'Abdallah (d. 1229)

1955   *Mu'jam al- Buldan.* Beirut: Dar al-Kitab al-
       'Arabi.

Hanfmann, G. M. A.

1964   The Sixth Campaign at Sardis (1963).
       *Bulletin of the American Schools of Oriental
       Research* 174: 3–58.

Hayes, J. W.

1992   *Excavations at Saraçhane in Istanbul.* Vol.
       2: *The Pottery.* Princeton, NJ: Princeton
       University.

1995   A Late Byzantine and Early Ottoman Assemblage from the Lower City in Troia. *Studia Troica* 5: 197–210.

Heyd, U.

1976   *Dahir al-ʿUmar: Ruler of the Galilee in the 18th Century.* Jerusalem: Reuben Mass.

Hildyard, R.

1999   *European Ceramics.* Philadelphia, PA: University of Pennsylvania.

Hodges, R., and.Patterson, H.

1986   San Vincenzo al Volturno and the Origins of the Medieval Pottery Industry in Italy. Pp. 13–26 in *La Ceramica Medievale nel Mediterraneo Occidentale.* Coloquio internacional de Cerámica medieval en el Mediterráneo Occidental. Faenza: University of Siena.

Holzweg, L.

n.d.   Petrography and Stylistic Analysis of the Middle Islamic Wares in the Oklahoma State University Ceramic Study Collection: A Provenance Study. Unpublished senior thesis and project report. Northern Jordan Project Archives, Missouri State University.

Honey, W. B.

1946   *Dresden China: An Introduction to the Study of Meissen Porcelain.* London: Faber and Faber.

Hütteroth, W., and Abdulfattah, K.

1977   *Historical Geography of Palestine: Transjordan and Southern Syria in the Late 16th Century.* Erlangen: Palm and Elke.

Ibn al-Athir, ʿIzz al-Din (d. 1233)

1983   *Al-Kamil fi al-Tarikh.* Beirut: Dar al-Kitab al-ʿArabi.

İnalçık, H.

1978   *The Ottoman Empire: Conquest, Organization, and Economy* London: Variorum Reprints.

İnalçık, H., and Quataert, D. (eds.)

1997   *An Economic and Social History of the Ottoman Empire.* Vol. 2: *1600–1914.* Cambridge: Cambridge University.

Ionas, I.

2000   *Traditional Pottery and Potters in Cyprus. The Disappearance of an Ancient Craft Industry in the 19th and 20th Centuries.* Birmingham Byzantine and Ottoman Monographs 6. Hampshire: Ashgate.

Israel, Y.

1994   Survey of Pottery Workshops, Nahal Lakhish–Nahal Besor. *Excavations and Surveys in Israel* 13: 106–7.

Jennings, R. C.

1993   *Christians and Muslims in Ottoman Cyprus and the Mediterranean World, 1571–1640.* New York University Studies in Near Eastern Civilization 18. New York: New York University.

Johns, J.

1998   The Rise of Middle Islamic Hand-Made Geometrically-Painted Ware in Bilad al-Sham (11th–13th Centuries A.D.). Pp. 65–93 in *Colloque internationale d'archéologie islamique: IFAO, Le Caire, 3–7 février 1993,* ed. R.-P. Gayraud. Textes arabes et études islamiques 36. Cairo: Institut Français d'Archéologie Orientale.

Joudah, A. H.

1987   *Revolt in Palestine in the Eighteenth Century: The Era of Shaykh Zahir al-ʿUmar.* Princeton, NJ: Kingston.

Kaimio, M.; Tiedeseura, S; and Hällström, G.

1963   *Commentationes Humanorum Litterarum.* Helsinki: Societas Scientiarum Fennica.

Kalter, J.; Pavaloi, M.; and Zerrnickel, M.

1992   *The Arts and Crafts of Syria. Collection Antoine Touma and Linden-Museum Stuttgart.* London: Thames and Hudson.

Kareem, J. M. H.

2000   *The Settlement Patterns in the Jordan Valley in the Mid- to Late Islamic Period.* BAR International Series 877. Oxford: Archaeopress.

Kempinski, A.

1988   *Excavations at Kabri. Reprint of the English Preliminary Reports of 1987–1991 Seasons.* Tel Aviv: Tel Aviv University.

Khalidi, W. (ed.)

1992   *All that Remains: The Palestinian Villages Occupied and Depopulated by Israel in 1948.* Washington, DC: Institute for Palestinian Studies.

Khammash, A.

1986   *Notes on Village Architecture in Jordan.* Lafayette, LA. University Art Museum, University of Southwestern Louisiana.

Kletter, R.

2005   Zikhron Ya'aqov. *Hadashot Arkheologiyot Online* 117: http://www.hadashot-esi.org.il/report_detail_eng.asp?search=&id=251&mag_id=110.

Kogan-Zehavi, E.

2006   Nes Ziyyona. *Hadashot Arkheologyot Online* 118: http://www.hadashot-esi.org.il/report_detail_eng.asp?id=320&mag_id=111.

Kramer, C.

1985   Ceramic Ethnoarchaeology. *Annual Review of Anthropology* 14: 77–102.

LaBianca, Ø. S.

1990   *Sedentarization and Nomadization: Food System Cycles at Hesban and Vicinity in Transjordan.* Hesban 1. Berrien Springs, MI: Andrews University.

De La Boullaey-Le Gouz, F.

1653   *Les voyages et observations de sieur de la Boullaye-Le Gouz, gentilhomme angevin.* Paris.

Lancaster, W., and Lancaster, F.

1993   Graves and Funerary Monuments of the Ahl al-Gabal, Jordan. *Arabian Archaeology and Epigraphy* 4: 151–69.

Landgraf, J.

1980   Keisan's Byzantine Pottery. Pp. 51–99 in *Tell Keisan (1971–1976)*, eds. J. Briend and J. B. Humbert. Paris: Gabalda.

Lazar, D.

1999   A Mamluk and Ottoman Settlement at Giv'at Dani in the Ayalon Valley. *'Atiqot* 38: 127*–38* (Hebrew), 231–32 (English summary).

Le Strange, G.

1965   *Palestine Under the Moslems: A Description of Syria and the Holy Land from A.D. 650 to 1500.* Beirut: Khayats.

Lévi-Strauss, C.

1965   Le triangle culinaire. *L'Arc* 26: 19–29.

London, G.

1989   On Fig Leaves, Itinerant Potters, and Pottery Production Locations in Cyprus. Pp. 65–80 in *Cross-craft and Cross-cultural Interactions in Ceramics. Ceramics and Civilization*, Vol. 4, eds. P. E. McGovern, M. D. Notis, and W. D. Kingery. Westerville, OH: The American Ceramic Society.

Longacre, W. A.; Xia, J; and Yang, T.

2000   I Want to Buy a Black Pot. *Journal of Archaeological Method and Theory* 7.4: 273–93.

Lucke, B.; al-Saad, Z; Schmidt, M; Bäumler, R; Lorenz, S. O.; Udluft, P; Heussner, K.-U.; and Walker, B. J.

2009   Soils and Land Use in the Decapolis Region (Northern Jordan): Implications for Landscape Development and the Impact of Climate Change. *Zeitschrift des Deutschen Palästina-Vereins* 124.2: in press.

al-Maqrizi, Taqi al-Din Ahmad ibn ʿAli (d. 1442)

1924   *Al-Mawaʾiz wa -l-iʿtibar fi dhikr al-khitat wa-l-athar*, ed. G. Wiet. Cairo: Institute Français d'Archéologie Orientale.

Mason, R. B., and Milwright, M.

1998   Petrography of Middle Islamic Ceramics from Kerak, Jordan. *Levant* 30: 175–90.

Matson, F. R.

1972   Ceramic Studies. Pp. 200–24 in *The Minnesota Messenia Expedition: Reconstructing a Bronze Age Regional Environment*, eds. W. A. McDonald and G. R. Rapp. Minneapolis, MN: University of Minnesota.

1974   The Archaeological Present: Near Eastern Village Potters at Work. *American Journal of Archaeology* 78.4: 345–47.

Mayerson, P.

1985   The Wine and Vineyards of Gaza in the Byzantine Period. *Bulletin of the American Schools of Oriental Research* 257: 75–80.

McCarthy, J.

2001   *The Ottoman Peoples and the End of Empire.* New York: Oxford University.

McGovern, P. E.

2003   *Ancient Wine: The Search for the Origins of Viniculture.* Princeton, NJ: Princeton University.

McGovern, P. E.; Bourriau, J.; Harbottle, G.; and Allen, S. J.

1994   The Archaeological Origin and Significance of the Dolphin Vase as Determined by Neutron Activation Analysis. *Bulletin of the American Schools of Oriental Research* 296: 31–43.

McQuitty, A.

2001   The Ottoman Period. Pp. 561–93 in *The Archaeology of Jordan*, eds. B. McDonald, R. Adams, and P. Bienkowski. Sheffield: Sheffield Academic.

McQuitty, A., and Falkner, R.

1993   The Faris Project: Preliminary Report on the 1989, 1990 and 1991 Seasons. *Levant* 25: 37–61.

Megaw, A. H. S.

1937–39   Three Medieval Pit-groups from Nicosia. *Report of the Department of Antiquities of Cyprus*: 145–68.

1971   Excavations at ʿSaranda Kolones,ʾ Paphos. Preliminary Report on the 1966–67 and 1970–71 Seasons. *Report of the Department of Antiquities of Cyprus*: 117–46.

1972   Supplementary Excavations on a Castle Site at Paphos, Cyprus, 1970–1971. *Dumbarton Oaks Papers* 26: 322–44.

Megaw, A. H. S., and Rosser, J.

2001   A Watchtower Before Pafos Castle. *Report of the Department of Antiquities of Cyprus*: 319–34.

Mershen, B.

1985   Recent Hand-made Pottery from North Jordan. *Levant* 33: 75–87.

1992   Settlement History and Village Space in Late Ottoman Northern Jordan. *Studies in the History and Archaeology of Jordan* 4: 409–16.

Metcalf, D. M. (ed.)

2002   *Lusignan Cyprus and Its Coinage,* by J. R. Stewart. Nicosia: Bank of Cyprus Cultural Foundation.

Milwright, M.

1999   Trade and Patronage in Middle Islamic Jordan: The Ceramics of Kerak Castle. Unpublished Ph.D. Dissertation, University of Oxford.

2000   Pottery of Bilad al-Sham in the Ottoman Period: A Review of the Published Archaeological Evidence. *Levant* 32: 189–208.

2008   *The Fortress of the Raven: Karak in the Middle Islamic Period (1100–1650).* Leiden: Brill.

Mintz, S. W., and du Bois, C. M.

2002   The Anthropology of Food and Eating. *Annual Review of Anthropology* 31: 99–119.

Mundy, M.

1992   Shareholders and the State: Representing the Village in the Late 19th Century Land Registers of the Southern Hawran. Pp. 217–38 in *The Syrian Land in the 18th and 19th Century: The Common and the Specific in the Historical Experience*, ed. T. Philipp. Stuttgart: Steiner.

1996   *Qada' 'Ajlun in the Late Nineteenth Century: Interpreting a Region from the Ottoman Land Registers. Levant* 28: 77–95.

Mundy, M., and Smith, R. S.

2007   *Governing Property, Making the Modern State: Law, Administration and Production in Ottoman Syria.* New York: I.B. Tauris.

Murphy, T.

n.d.   Final Results of Thin Section Petrographic Analysis. Unpublished Project Report of 2006. Northern Jordan Project Archives, Grand Valley State University, MI.

al-Nabulusi, A. G. I.

1986   *Al-Haqiqah wa al-Majaz fi al-Rihlah ila Bilad al-Sham wa-Misr wa-al-Hijaz.* Cairo: Al-Ha'yah al-Misriyah al-'Ammah lil-Kitab.

Nashef, Kh. and Abd Rabu, O.

2000   Khirbet Birzeit Research and Excavation Project 1998: Second Season Excavation. *Journal of Palestinian Archaeology* 1.1: 4–12.

Negev, A.

1993   Elusa. Pp. 378–82 in *The New Encyclopedia of Archaeological Excavations in the Holy Land*, Vol. 1, ed. E. Stern. Jerusalem: The Israel Exploration Society & Carta.

Olenik, Y.

1983   *Rashia of the Potters: A Catalogue of an Exhibition of Pottery of Rashia el-Fukhar.* Tel Aviv: Eretz Israel Museum (in Hebrew).

Oleson, J. P., and 'Amr, K.

1993   The Humeima Excavation Project: Preliminary Report of the 1991–1992 Seasons. *Annual of the Department of Antiquities of Jordan* 37: 461–502.

Pamuk, O.

2004   *Istanbul: Memories and the City.* New York: Vintage International.

Parker, T.

1998   The Pottery from the 1977 Season. Pp. 205–218 in *Umm el-Jimal: A Frontier Town and its Landscape in Northern Jordan*, Vol. I: *Fieldwork 1972–1981*, by B. de Vries. Journal of Roman Archaeology Supplementary Series 6. Portsmouth, RI: Journal of Roman Archaeology.

Peacock, D. P. S.

1982   *Pottery in the Roman World: An Ethnoarchaeological Approach.* Longman Archaeology Series. London: Longman.

Peake, F.

1958   *A History of Jordan and its Tribes.* Coral Gables, FL: University of Miami.

Petersen, A.

2005   *The Towns of Palestine under Muslim Rule AD 600–1600.* BAR International Series 1381. Oxford: Archaeopress.

2007   The Ottoman Hajj Route in Jordan: Motivation and Ideology. Pp. 31–50 in *Exercising Power in the Age of the Sultanates: Bilad al-Sham and Iran*, eds. B. J. Walker and J.-F. Salles. Bulletin d' Études Orientales Supplement 67. Damascus: Institut Français d'Études Arabes.

Philipp, T.

2004   Bilad al-Ŝam in the Modern Period:
       Integration into the Ottoman Empire and
       New Relations with Europe. *Arabica* 51.4:
       401–18.

Pitcher, D. E.

1972   *An Historical Geography of the Ottoman
       Empire from the Earliest Times to the End
       of the Sixteenth Century.* Leiden: Brill.

Prag. K. (ed.)

2008   *Excavations by K.M. Kenyon in Jerusalem
       1961–1967.* Vol. V: *Discoveries in Hellenistic
       to Ottoman Jerusalem Centenary Volume:
       Kathleen M. Kenyon 1906–1978.* Levant
       Supplementary Series 6. Oxford: Oxbow.

Pringle, D.

1986   *The Red Tower (al-Burj al-Ahmar). Settlement
       in the Plain of Sharon at the Time of the
       Crusaders and Mamluks A.D. 1099–1516.*
       British Schools of Archaeology in Jerusalem
       Monograph Series 1. London: The British
       School of Archaeology in Jerusalem.

Prokopiou, E.

1997   Λεμεσοσ Οδοσ Ζικ Ζακ. Εκθεση αποτελε-
       σματων σωστικησ ανασκαφικησ ερευνασ
       1993. *Report of the Department of Antiquities
       of Cyprus:* 285–323.

Quataert, D.

2000a *The Ottoman Empire, 1700–1922.* Cambridge:
       Cambridge University.

2000b *Consumption Studies and the History of the
       Ottoman Empire, 1550–1922: An Introduction.*
       Albany, NY: State University of New York.

Raban, A.

1971   The Shipwreck off Sharm-el-Sheikh.
       Archaeology 24: 146–55.

Rafeq, A.

1980   *Gaza: Architectural. Social and Economic
       Study from the Shari'a Court Documents.*
       Amman: The Third International Conference

on the History of Bilad esh Sham. (In
Arabic).

Raptou, E.

2006   The Built Tomb in Icarus Street, Kato
       Paphos. *Report of the Department of
       Antiquities of Cyprus:* 317–42.

Rapuano, Y.

2000   *Pottery from the First and Second Seasons of
       the New Excavations at Emmaus Nicopolis.*
       Http://www.hi-rez.co.il/emmaus/site_
       research/rapuano/emmauspot.html.

Rautman, M.

1998   Handmade Pottery and Social Change: The
       View from Late Roman Cyprus. *Journal of
       Mediterranean Archaeology* 11.1: 81–104.

Redford, S., and Blackman, M. J.

1997   Luster and Fritware Production and
       Distribution in Medieval Syria. *Journal of
       Field Archaeology* 24.2: 233–47.

Robinson. E., and Smith, E.

1856   *Biblical Researches in Palestine.* London:
       Crocker and Brewster.

Robinson, R.

1983   Clay Tobacco Pipes from the Kerameikos.
       *Mitteilungen des Deutschen Archäologischen
       Instituts* 98: 265–85, Pls. 52–56.

1985   Tobacco Pipes of Corinth and of the
       Athenian Agora. *Hesperia* 54: 149–203, Pls.
       33–64.

Rogan, E. L.

1999   *Frontiers of the State in the Late Ottoman
       Empire. Transjordan, 1850–1921.* Cambridge:
       Cambridge University.

Rosen S. A., and Goodfriend, G. A.

1993   An Early Date for Gaza Ware from the
       Northern Negev. *Palestine Exploration
       Quarterly* 125: 143–48.

Russell, M. B.

1989 Hesban During the Arab Period: A.D. 635 to the Present. Pp. 25–35 in *Hesban 3: Historical Foundations*, eds. L. T. Geraty and G. L. Running. Berrien Springs, MI: Andrews University.

Rye, O. S.

1976 Traditional Palestinian Potters. *National Geographic Society Research Reports* 17: 769–76.

Salem, H. J.

1986 Pottery Ethnoarchaeology: A Case Study. M.A. Thesis, The University of Arizona, Tucson.

1999 Implications of Cultural Traditions: The Case of the Palestinian Traditional Pottery. Pp. 66–83 in *Archaeology, History and Culture in Palestine and the Near East, Essays in Memory of Albert Glock*, ed. T. Kapitan. Atlanta, GA: Scholars.

2006 Cultural Transmission and Change in Traditional Palestinian Pottery Production. *Leiden Journal of Pottery Studies* 22: 51–63.

Saller, S. J,

1946 Discoveries at St.John's 'Ein Karim 1941–1942. *Studium Biblicum Franciscanum* 3. Jerusalem: Franciscan.

Sarinay, Y. (ed.)

2000 *Osmanlı İdaresinde Kıbrıs (Nüfusu-Arazi Dağılımı ve Türk Vakıflar.* Osmanlı Arşivi Daire Başkanlığı 43. Ankara: Başbakanlık Devlet Arşivleri Genel Müdürlüğü.

Schaefer, J.

1989 Archaeological Remains from the Medieval Islamic Occupation of the Northwest Negev Desert. *Bulletin of the American Schools of Oriental Research* 274: 33–60.

Schick, R.

1998 The Archaeology of Palestine/Jordan in the Early Ottoman Period. *ARAM Periodical* 10: 563–75.

Schölch, A.

1993 *Palestine in Transformation 1856–1882: Studies in Social, Economic and Political Development*, trans. W. C. Young and M. C. Gerrity. Washington, DC: Institute for Palestine Studies.

Segal, O.

2006 Tirat Karmel. *Hadashot Arkheologiyot Online* 118. Http://www.hadashot-esi.org.il/report_detail_eng.asp?id=353&mag_id=111 and http://www.hadashot-esi.org.il/report_detail_eng.asp?id=442&mag_id=111.

Shami, S.

1987 Umm Qeis – A Northern Jordanian Village in Context. *Studies in the History and Archaeology of Jordan* 3: 211–13.

1989 Settlement and Resettlement in Umm Qeis: Spatial Organization and Social Dynamics in a Jordanian Village. Pp. 451–76 in *Dwellings, Settlements, and Tradition: Cross-Cultural Perspectives*, eds. J.-P. Bourdier and N. al-Sayyad. Berkeley, CA: University Press of America.

Shaqirat, A. S.

1988 *Al-Masjid al-Zaydani fi Tubna*. Amman: Shaqirat.

1992 *Tarikh Idarat al-Uthmaniyyah fi Sharq al-Urdunn 1864–1918*. Amman: Dirasat Tarikhiyyah Urdunniyah.

Shryock, A.

1997 *Nationalism and the Genealogical Imagination: Oral History and Textual Authority in Tribal Jordan*. Berkeley, CA: University of California.

Simpson, St. J.

1997 A Late Islamic Ceramic Group from Hatara Saghir. *Mesopotamia* 32: 87–129.

2000 The Clay Pipes. Pp. 147–171 in *Belmont Castle: The Excavation of a Crusader Stronghold in the Kingdom of Jerusalem*, eds. R. P. Harper and D. Pringle. Oxford: Oxford University.

2002   Ottoman Pipes from Zir'in (Tell Jezreel). *Levant* 34: 159–72.

Smith, R. H.

1973   *Pella of the Decapolis*. Vol. 1: *The 1967 Season of the College of Wooster Expedition to Pella.* Sydney: The College of Wooster.

1989   *Pella of the Decapolis*. Vol. 2: *Final Report on the College of Wooster Excavations in Area IX, the Civic Complex, 1979–1985.* Sydney: The College of Wooster.

Smith, W.; Abbot, E.; and Hackett, H.

1888   *Dr. William Smith's Dictionary of the Bible: Comprising its Antiquities, Biography, Geography.* Boston, MA: Houghton Mifflin.

Solecki, R. S.

1957   The 1956 Season at Shanidar. *Sumer* 13: 165–71.

Stark, M.

2003   Current Issues in Ceramic Ethnoarchaeology. *Journal of Archaeological Research* 11.3: 193–242.

Stern, E. J.

1997   Excavation of the Courthouse Site at 'Akko: The Pottery of the Crusader and Ottoman Periods. *'Atiqot* 31: 35–70, Color Pls. I–IV.

Striker, C. L., and Kuban, Y. D.

1975   Work at Kalenderhane Camii in Istanbul: Fifth Preliminary Report (1970–1974). *Dumbarton Oaks Papers* 29: 307–18.

Taha, H.; Pol, A.; and van der Kooij, G.

2006   *A Hoard of Silver Coins at Qabatiyah, Palestine.* Ramallah: Department of Antiquities and Cultural Heritage.

Tekkök-Biçken, B.

2000   Pottery Production in the Troad: Ancient and Modern Akköy. *Near Eastern Archaeology* 63.2: 94–101.

Theocharides, I. P.

1993   *Οθωμανικα εγραφα 1572–1839.* Nicosia: Kykko Monastery Research Centre.

Theocharides, I. P., and Andreev, S.

1996   *Τραγώδιασ 1821 συνεχεια Οθωμανικι πηγη για την Κυπρο.* Nicosia: Kykko Monastery Research Centre.

Toombs, L. E.

1985   *Tell el Hesi: Modern Military Trenching and Muslim Cemetery in Field L, Strata I–II.* The Joint Archaeological Expedition to Tell el-Hesi 2. Waterloo, ON: Wilfred Laurier University.

Tuchscherer, M. (ed.)

2001   *Le commerce du café avant l'ère des plantations coloniales: Espaces, réseaux, sociétés (XVe–XIXe siècle).* Cahiers des Annales Islamologiques 20. Cairo: Institut Français d'Archéologie Orientale.

Tushingham, A. D.

1985   *Excavations in Jerusalem 1961–1967*, Vol. I. Toronto: Royal Ontario Museum.

Ustinova Y., and Nahshoni P.

1994   Salvage Excavations in Ramot Nof, Be'er Sheva. *'Atiqot* 25: 157–77.

de Vaux R., and Stève, A. M.

1950   *Fouilles à Qaryet el-'Enab, Abu Gosh, Palestine.* Paris: Gabalda.

von Wartburg, M.-L.

1997   Medieval Glazed Pottery from the Sanctuary of Aphrodite at Palaipaphos (site TA). A Preliminary Survey. *Report of the Department of Antiquities of Cyprus*: 184–94.

2001   Types of Imported Table Ware at Kouklia in the Ottoman Period. *Report of the Department of Antiquities of Cyprus*: 361–89.

2003   Cypriot Contacts with East and West as Reflected in Medieval Glazed Pottery from the Paphos Region. Pp. 153–66 in *VIIe*

Congrés International sur la Céramique Médiévale en Méditerranée. Thessaloniki, 11–16 Octobre 1999, ed. Ch. Bakirtzis. Athens: Ministère de la Culture.

Vroom, J.

2000   Byzantine Garlic and Turkish Delight. *Archaeological Dialogues* 7.2: 199–216.

2003   *After Antiquity. Ceramics and Society in the Aegean from the 7th to the 20th Century A.D.* Leiden: Leiden University.

2005   *Byzantine to Modern Pottery in the Aegean: 7th to 20th Century. An Introduction and Field Guide.* Utrecht: Parnassus.

Vyhmeister, W. K.

1989   Hesban in the Literary Sources Since 1806. Pp. 65–72 in *Hesban 3: Historical Foundations*, eds. L. T. Geraty and L. G. Running. Berrien Springs, MI: Andrews University.

Walker, B. J.

1999   Militarization to Nomadization: The Middle and Late Islamic Periods. *Near Eastern Archaeology* 62.4: 202–32.

2001   The Late Ottoman Cemetery in Field L, Tall Hisban. *Bulletin of the American Schools of Oriental Research* 322: 47–65.

2003   The Byzantine and Medieval Pottery. Polis-Pyrgos Archaeological Project: Fifth Preliminary Report on the 1999 Survey Season in Northwestern Cyprus, ed. Dariusz Maliszewski et al., *Thetis* 10: 7–38.

2004   Mamluk Investment in the Transjordan: A 'Boom and Bust' Economy. *Mamluk Studies Review* 8.2: 119–47.

2005   The Northern Jordan Survey 2003 – Agriculture in Late Islamic Malka and Hubras Villages: A Preliminary Report of the First Season. *Bulletin of the American Schools of Oriental Research* 339: 1–44, 67–111.

2007a   The Politics of Land Management in Medieval Islam: The Village of Malka in Northern Jordan. *Studies in the History and Archaeology of Jordan* 9: 253–61.

2007b   Sowing the Seeds of Rural Decline? Agriculture as an Economic Barometer for Late Mamluk Jordan. *Mamluk Studies Review* 11.1: 173–99.

2007c   Regional Markets and their Impact on Agriculture in Mamluk and Ottoman Transjordan. Pp. 117–25 in *On the Fringe of Society: Archaeological and Ethnoarchaeological Perspectives on Pastoral and Agricultural Societies*, eds. E. van der Steen and B. Saidel. BAR International Series 1657. Oxford: Archaeopress.

2007d   Rural Sufism as Channels of Charity in Nineteenth-Century Jordan. Pp. 217–34 in *Between Missionaries and Dervishes: Interpreting Welfare and Relief in the Middle East,* eds. N. Naguib and I. M. Okkenhaug. Social, Economic and Political Studies of the Middle East and Asia 103. Leiden: Brill.

Walker, B. J., and Kenney, E.

2006   Rural Islam in Late Medieval Jordan: NJP 2006 – the Mosques Project. *Newsletter of the American Center of Oriental Research* 18.2: 1–4.

Walker, B. J.; Kenney, E.; Carroll, L.; Holzweg, L.; Boulogne, S.; and Lucke, B.

2007   The Northern Jordan Project 2006: Village Life in Mamluk and Ottoman Hubras and Sahm: A Preliminary Report. *Annual of the Department of Antiquities of Jordan* 52: 429–70.

Walker, B. J., and LaBianca, Ø. S.

2003   The Islamic *Qusur* of Tall Hisban: Preliminary Report on the 1998 and 2001 Seasons. *Annual of the Department of Antiquities of Jordan* 47: 443–71.

2004   Tall Hisban, 2004 – An Investigation in Medieval Rural History. *Newsletter of the American Center of Oriental Research* 16.2: 1–3.

Wightman, G. J.

1989   *The Damascus Gate, Jerusalem. Excavations by C.-M. Bennet and J. B. Hennessy at the*

Damascus Gate, Jerusalem 1964–66. BAR International Series 519. Oxford: British Archaeological Reports.

Wilson, C. W.
1880   *Picturesque Palestine.* London: Virtue and Company.

Wright, K. I.
2000   The Social Origins of Cooking and Dining in Early Villages of Western Asia. *Proceedings of the Prehistoric Society* 66: 89–121.

Ze'evi, D.
1996   *An Ottoman Century: The District of Jerusalem in the 1600s.* Albany, NY: State University of New York.

Zevelon, U.
1978   The Pottery of Rashia el-Fukhar. Pp.190–97 in *Hermon and its Slopes*, eds. S. Applebaum et al. Jerusalem: Section for Homeland Studies of the Kibbutz Movement (Hebrew).

Ziadeh, Gh.
1995   Ottoman Ceramics from Ti'innik, Palestine. *Levant* 27: 209–45.
2000   The Archaeology of Ottoman Ti'innik. Pp. 79–91 in *A Historical Archeology of the Ottoman Empire: Breaking New Ground*, eds. U. Baram and L. Carroll. New York: Kluwer Academic and Plenum.

Contributors

ABU KHALAF, MARWAN

al-Quds University/Institute of Islamic Archaeology (Jerusalem/Ramallah)
marwanak@yahoo.com

AVISSAR, MIRIAM

Israeli Antiquities Authority (Jerusalem)
avissar@israntique.org.il

DE VRIES, BERT

Calvin College (Grand Rapids, Michigan),
Department of History
DVBR@calvin.edu

GABRIELI, RUTH SMADAR

Hebrew University (Jerusalem)
Lady Davis Fellow
smadar.gabrieli@arts.usyd.edu.au

LABIANCA, ØYSTEIN S.

Andrews University (Berrien Springs, Michigan),
Department of Behavioral Sciences/
Institute of Archaeology
labianca@andrews.edu

SALEM, HAMED

Birzeit University (Birzeit),
Department of Archaeology
hsalem@birzeit.edu

WALKER, BETHANY J.

Missouri State University (Springfield, Missouri),
Department of History
BethanyWalker@MissouriState.edu

Index

Illustrations

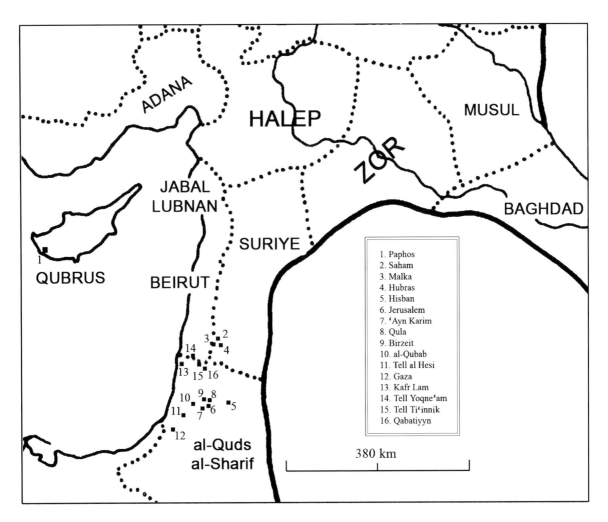

FIG. 1.1   *Administrative map of the 16th-century Levant with sites mentioned in the book.*

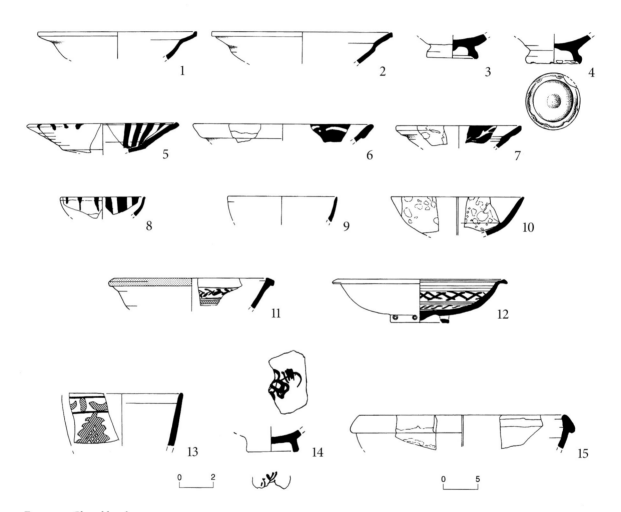

FIG. 2.1   *Glazed bowls.*

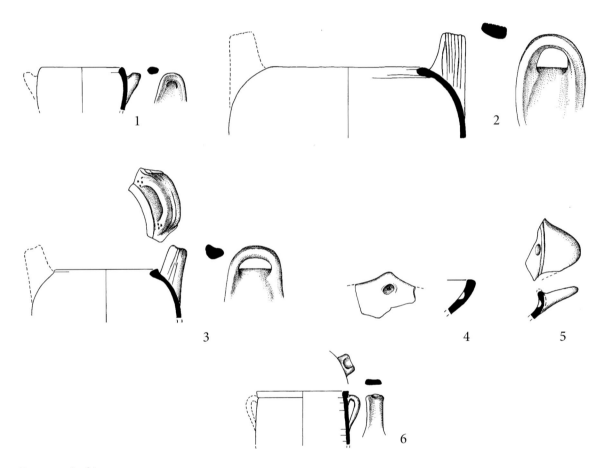

FIG. 2.2 *Cooking pots.*

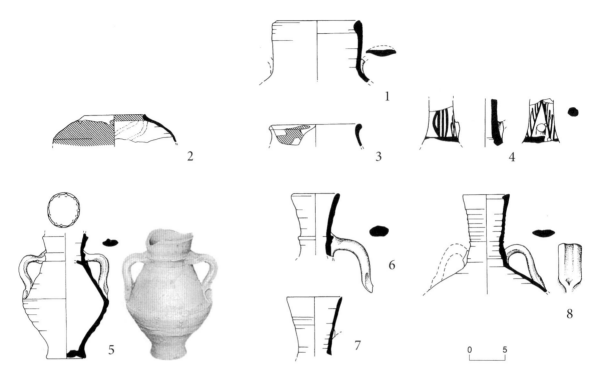

FIG. 2.3 *Jars and jugs.*

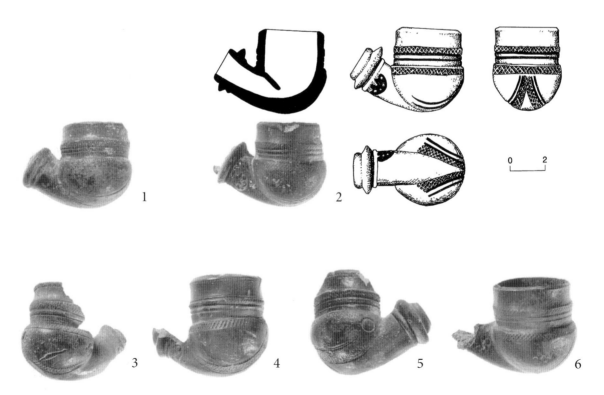

FIG. 2.4 *Tobacco pipes.*

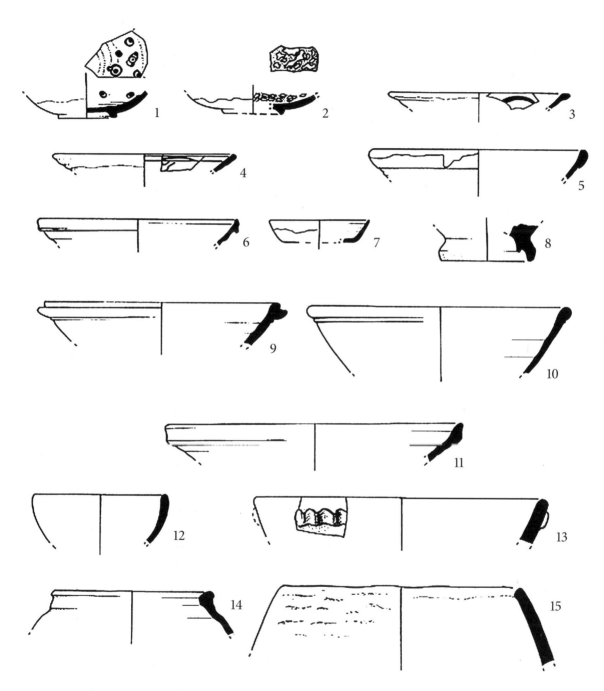

FIG. 2.5 *Bowls and craters.*

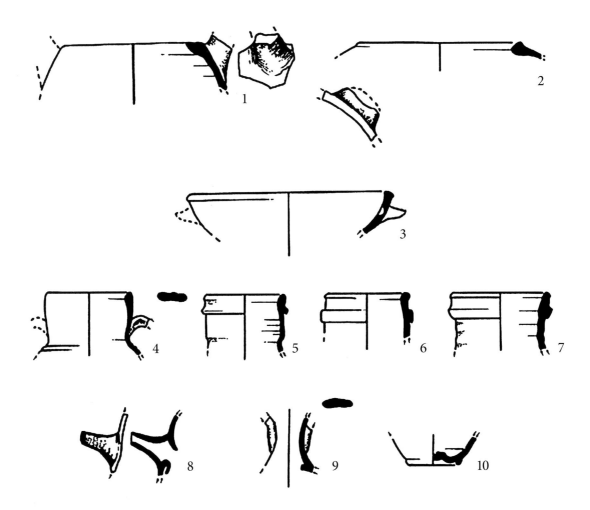

FIG. 2.6 *Cooking vessels, jugs and jars.*

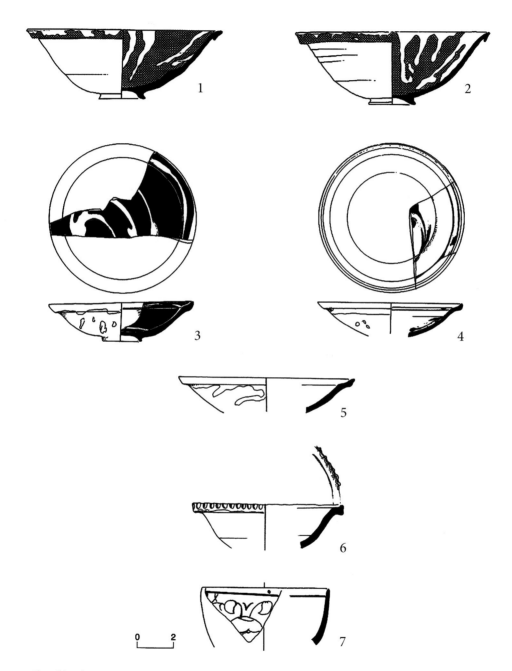

FIG. 2.7 *Glazed bowls.*

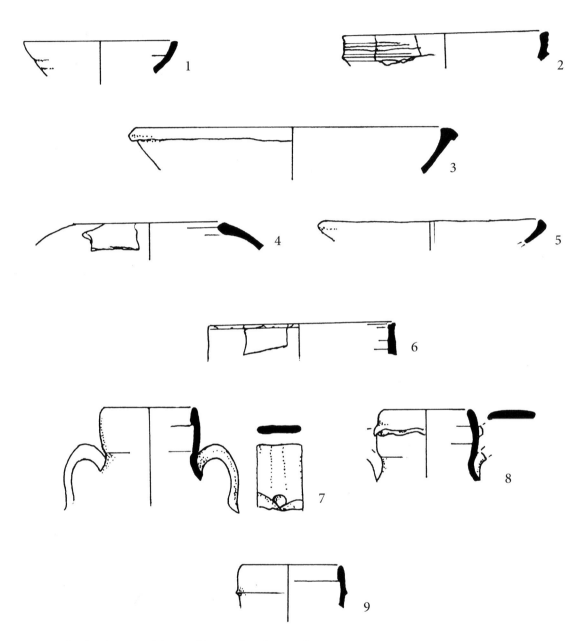

FIG. 2.8   *Plain bowls in Gaza-Ware, cooking vessels and storage jars.*

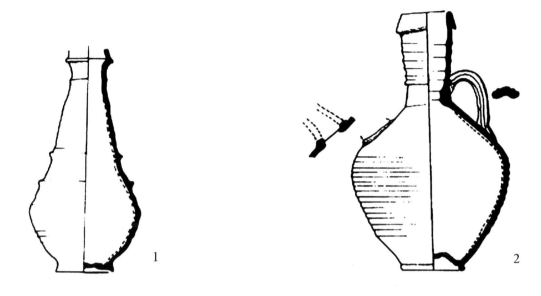

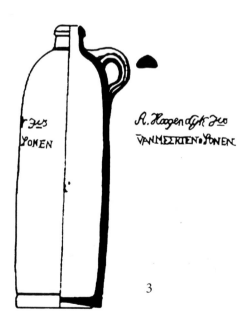

FIG. 2.9 *Various closed containers.*

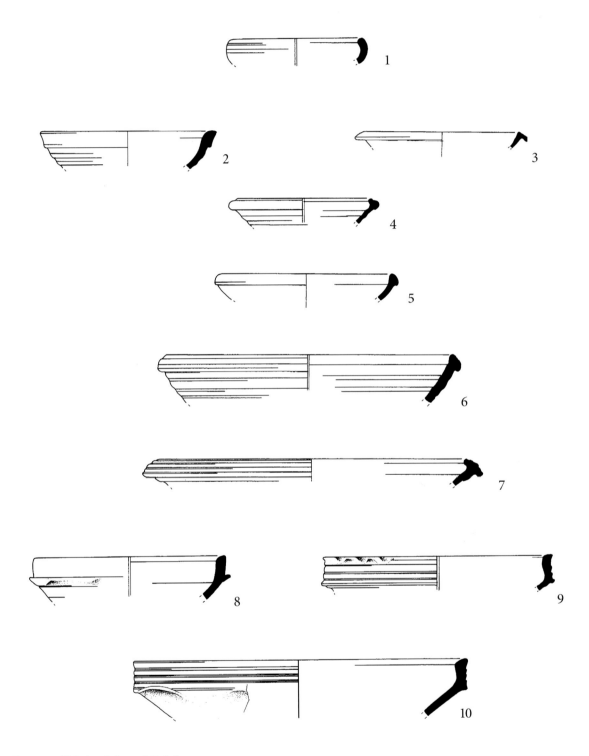

FIG. 2.10 *Plain bowls from al-Qubab.*

Qula

al-Qubab

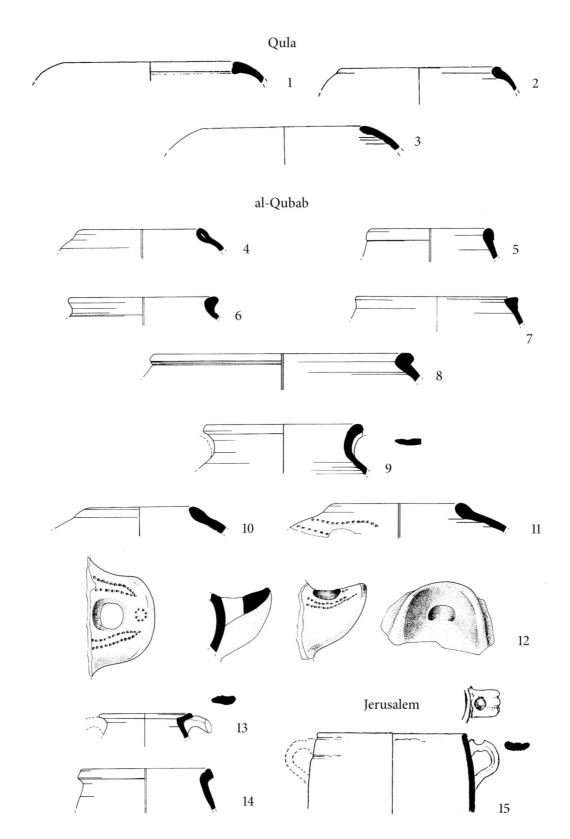

Jerusalem

FIG. 2.11 *Craters and cooking pots.*

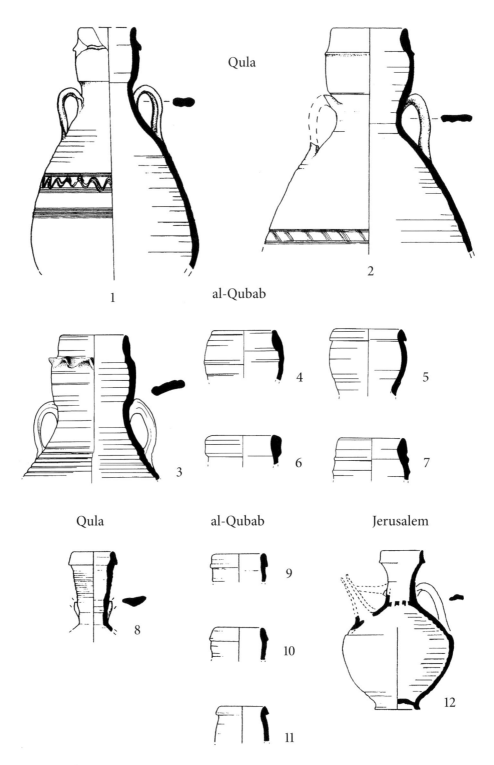

FIG. 2.12 *Storage jars and jugs.*

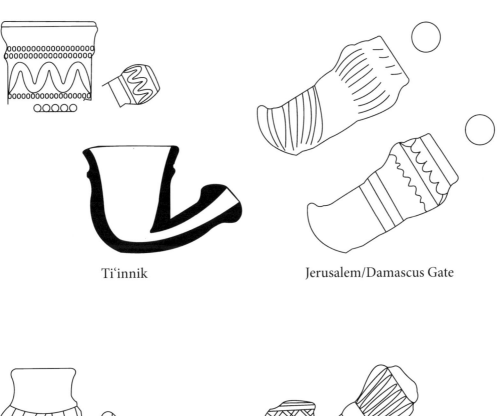

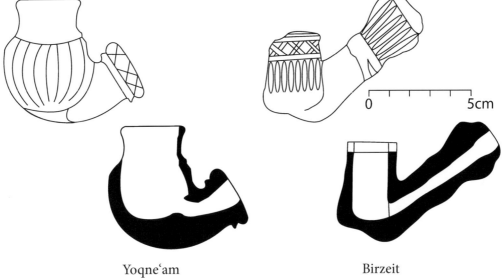

FIG. 3.1   *Tobacco pipes from Ti'innik, Jerusalem/Damascus Gate, Yoqne'am, and Birzeit.*

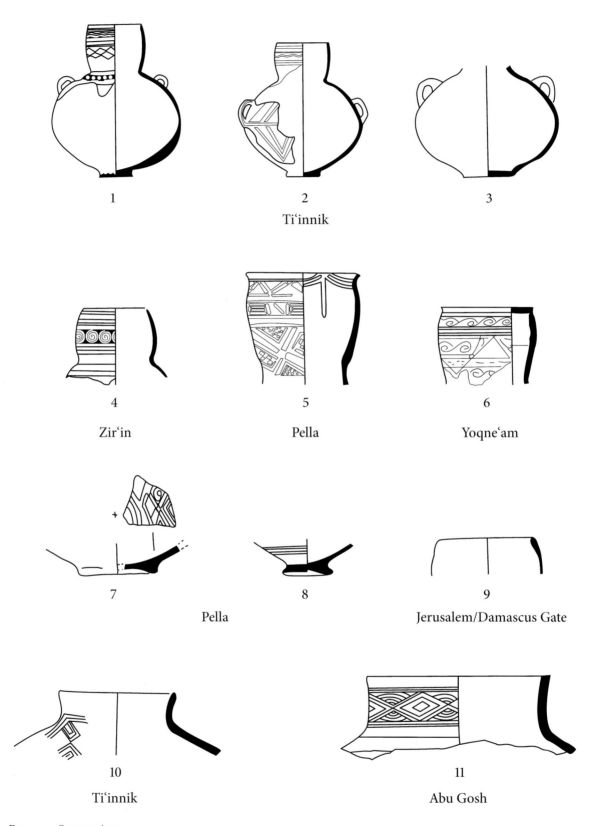

1   2   3

Ti'innik

4   5   6

Zir'in   Pella   Yoqne'am

7   8   9

Pella   Jerusalem/Damascus Gate

10   11

Ti'innik   Abu Gosh

FIG. 3.2   *Ottoman jars.*

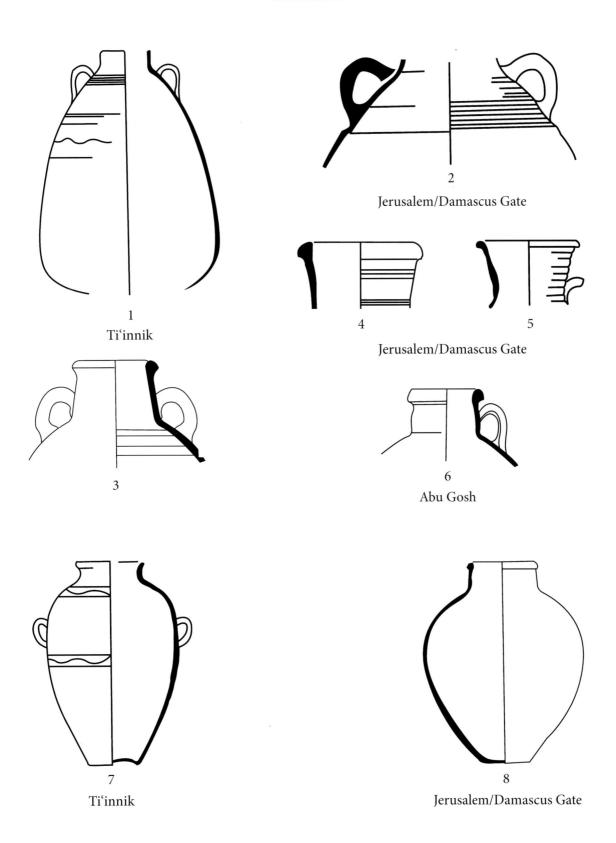

1
Ti'innik

2
Jerusalem/Damascus Gate

4   5
Jerusalem/Damascus Gate

3

6
Abu Gosh

7
Ti'innik

8
Jerusalem/Damascus Gate

FIG. 3.3   *Ottoman jars.*

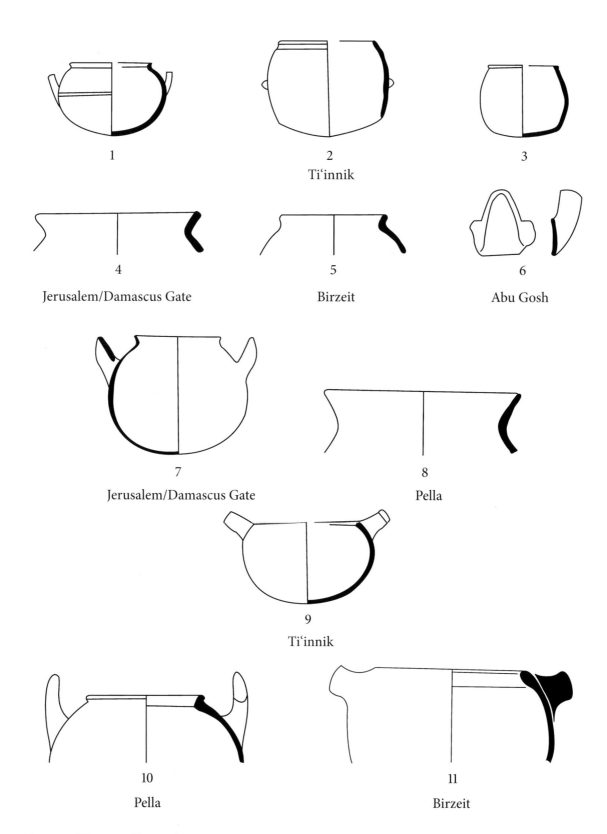

1

2

Ti'innik

3

4

Jerusalem/Damascus Gate

5

Birzeit

6

Abu Gosh

7

Jerusalem/Damascus Gate

8

Pella

9

Ti'innik

10

Pella

11

Birzeit

FIG. 3.4   *Ottoman cooking vessels.*

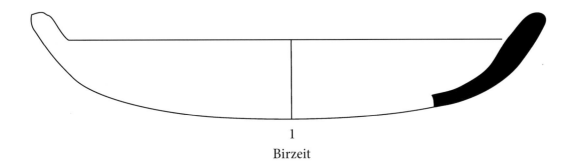

1
Birzeit

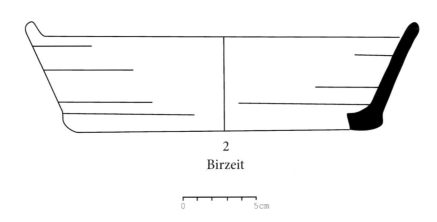

2
Birzeit

0   5 cm

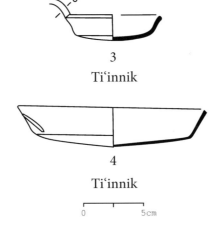

3
Ti'innik

4
Ti'innik

0   5 cm

FIG. 3.5 *Ottoman cooking vessels.*

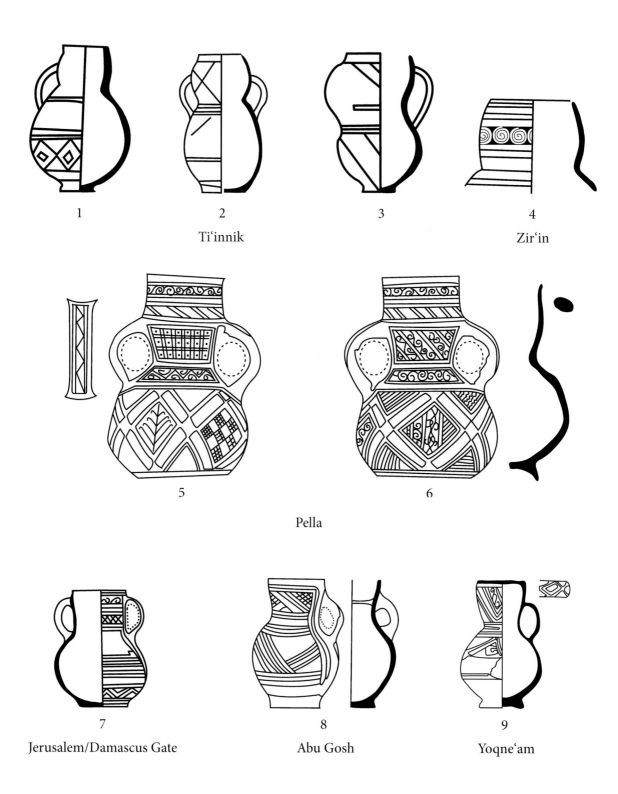

FIG. 3.6   *Ottoman jugs.*

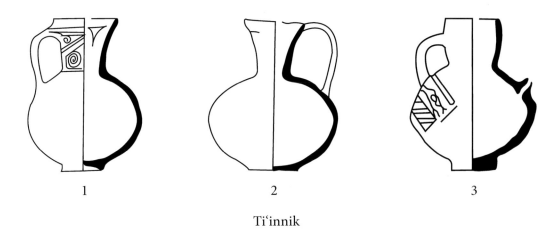

1   2   3

Ti'innik

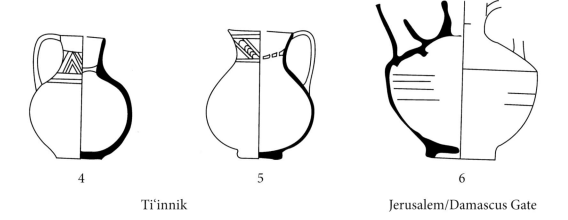

4   5   6

Ti'innik   Jerusalem/Damascus Gate

FIG. 3.7   *Ottoman jugs.*

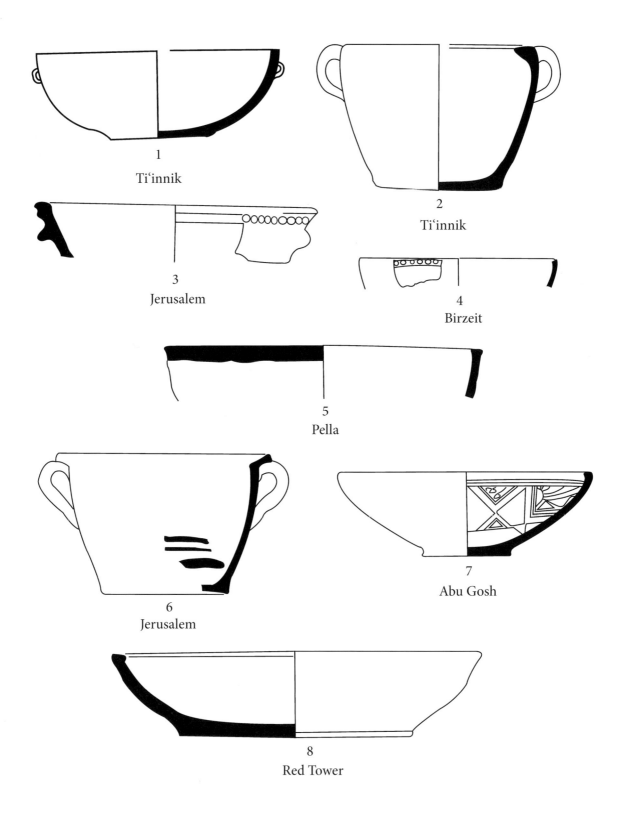

1
Ti'innik

2
Ti'innik

3
Jerusalem

4
Birzeit

5
Pella

6
Jerusalem

7
Abu Gosh

8
Red Tower

FIG. 3.8 *Ottoman basins or craters and bowls.*

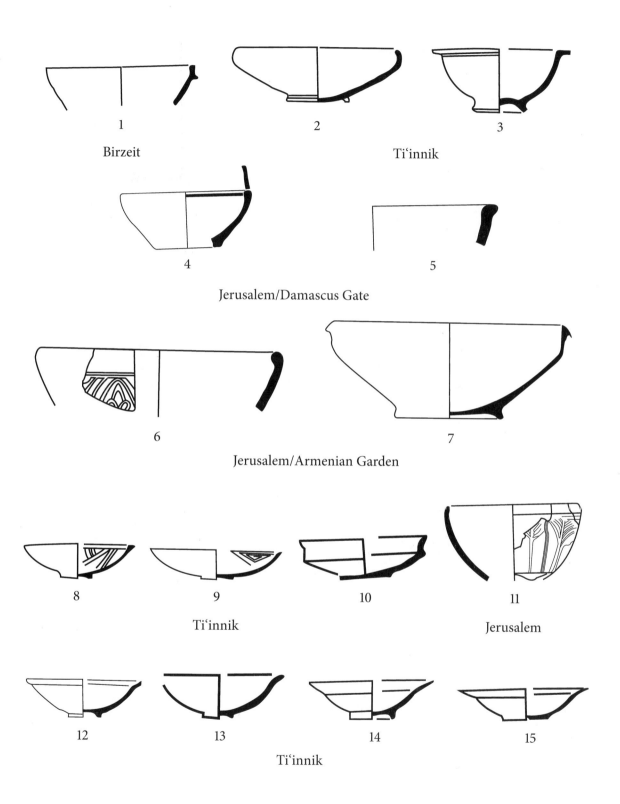

Birzeit

Ti'innik

Jerusalem/Damascus Gate

Jerusalem/Armenian Garden

Ti'innik

Jerusalem

Ti'innik

FIG. 3.9 *Ottoman bowls and dishes.*

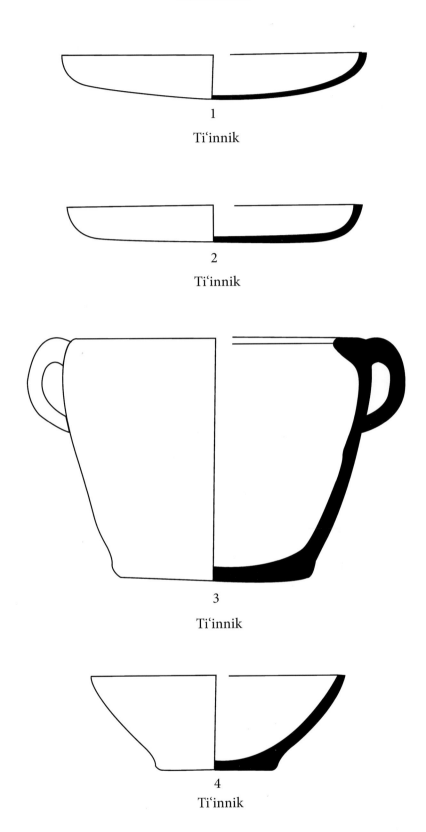

1

Ti'innik

2

Ti'innik

3

Ti'innik

4

Ti'innik

FIG. 3.10 *Ottoman basins or craters, bowls, and trays.*

FIG. 4.1 *General map of historic Palestine showing the locations mentioned in the text.*

FIG. 4.2 – REFERENCES

1   Jar from Tell Ti'innik. Black, pear-shaped, with loop handles and occasional combing (Ziadeh 1995: fig. 10.6).

2   Jar from Tell Jemmeh (Schaefer 1989: fig. 8.5).

3   Qabatiyah small jar with a "bag-shaped body, high wide neck, with a triangular rim two loop handles and flat base; ribbing at the upper part of the body; organic temper quartz sand, lime grits" (Taha et al. 2006: fig. 9).

4   Jar from Birzeit ethnographic collection, collected from an abandoned house in Old Birzeit Village.

5   Oval-shaped jar from a house abandoned in the late 1970s in Birzeit Village.

6   Storage jar from Tell Qaymun (Yoqne'am). Very well fired, light grayish brown on surface with white grits (lime?); appears to have wide neck with a flat handle (Avissar 2005: fig. 2.26.2).

7   Jar from Tirat Karmel (Segal 2006: fig. 9.11).

8   Jug or *ibriq* from Khirbat Shimshit (Barbé 2006: fig. 7.1).

9   Jar from Khirbat al-Saharij (Kogan-Zehavi 2006: fig. 8.19).

10   Jar from Emmaus (Rapuano 2000: Dr.15:10).

11   Amphora from Tell Jemmeh (Schaefer 1989: fig. 7.12).

12   Cooking pot from Tell Jemmeh, calcite-tempered (Schaefer 1989: fig. 8.4).

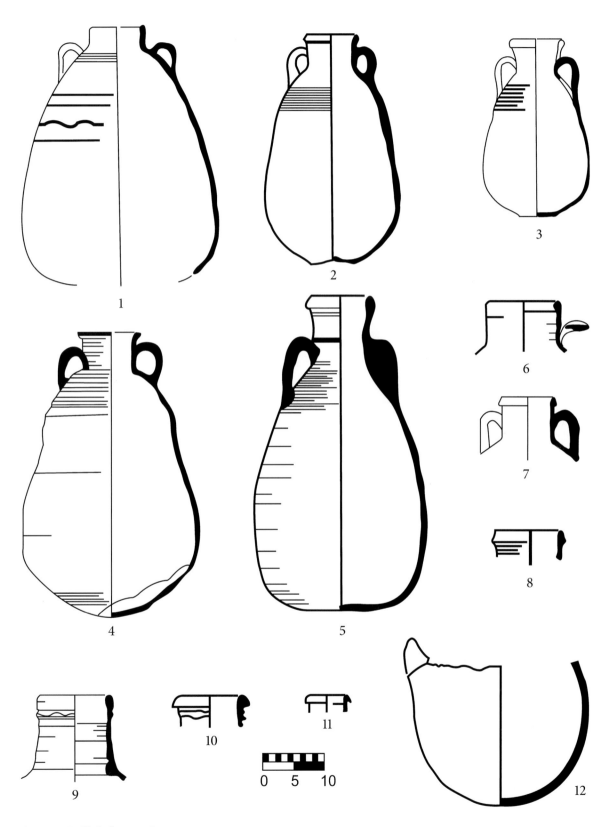

FIG. 4.2 *Published pottery jars.*

FIG. 4.3 – REFERENCES

1   Jug from Kerak, Jordan with filter in neck, thin walls, finely incised lines and pin pricks, medium hard fabric firing grey green (5 Y 6/2), impure sand, and feldspars and quartz inclusions (Mason and Milwright 1998: 177, fig. 2.8, A 3065).

2   Tell Ti'innik *ibriq* (jug) with ovoid body, a small concave base, narrow neck, triangular rim, a handle attached to shoulder, and no evidence of combing (Ziadeh 1995: 237, fig. 13.9).

3   Jug from Zamarin (Kletter 2005: fig. 10:4).

4   Jug from Tirat Karmel (Segal 2006: fig. 9.13).

5   Water jug (*ibriq?*) from Tell Qaymun (Yoqne'am) with a long neck and rounded rim, dark gray surface, and light gray fabric (Avissar 2005: fig. 2.26.9).

6   Rim of *ibriq* from Lod (Lazar 1999: fig. 8.8).

7   *Ibriq* from Tell Hesi (Toombs 1985: pl. 88).

8   Jug or *ibriq* from Tell Jemmeh (Schaefer 1989: fig. 8:4).

9   Jug from Sataf with black core and fine white grits (lime?) (Gibson et al. 1991: 46, fig. 23.2.).

10   Spout of *ibriq* from Lod (Lazar 1999: fig. 8.7).

11   Spout of *ibriq* from Tirat Karmel (Segal 2006: fig. 9.12).

12   Bowl from Tirat Karmel (Segal 2006: fig. 9.10).

13   Bowl from Tirat Karmel (Segal 2006: fig. 9.8).

14   Bowl from Lod (Lazar 1999: fig. 8.2).

15   Bowl from Lod (Lazar 1999: fig. 8.1).

16   Bowl from Tell Jemmeh (Schaefer 1989: fig. 7:10).

17   Bowl from Tell Jemmeh (Schaefer 1989: fig. 7:12).

18   Bowl or Crater (*kwar*) from Tirat Karmel (Segal 2006: fig. 9.11).

19   Bowl from Lod (Lazar 1999: fig. 8.65).

20   Bowl or crater (*kwar*) from Lod (Lazar 1999: fig. 8.6).

21   Crater (*kwar*) from Tell Jemmeh (Schaefer 1989: fig. 8).

22   Crater sherds from Tell Jemmeh (Schaefer 1989: fig. 8:7).

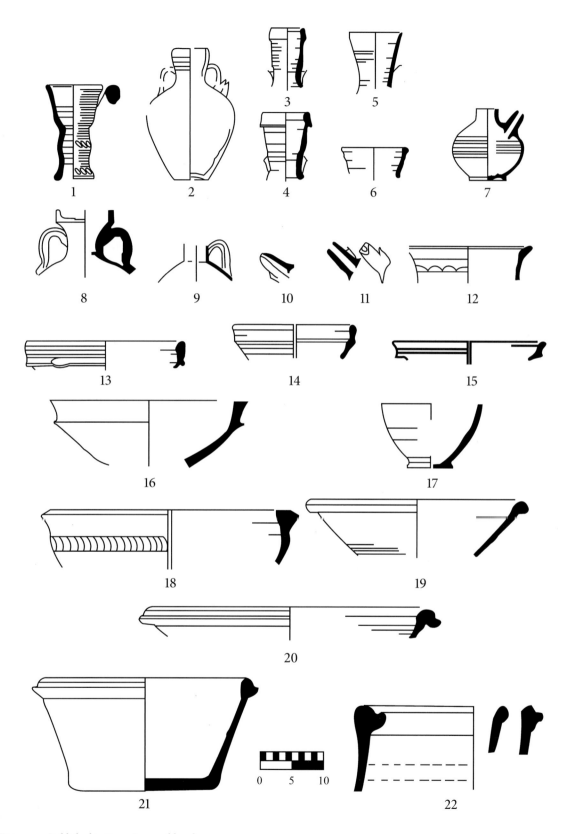

FIG. 4.3 *Published pottery: Jugs and bowls.*

FIG. 4.4 – REFERENCES

1   *Jarra* (jar) for water or olive oil; profiled rim with two handles at the shoulder, oval body, round base, regular ribbing; also occurs with narrow neck; used by women to carry water or to store oil.

2   *Zir,* or water jar

3   *Asaliye*, a small water jar usually carried by young girls.

4   *Ibriq* (water jug, pitcher); a typical form occurs with spout, two handles, a high neck, oval body and shallow ring base; ribbings may cover all the body or only the upper parts. It is either used for water or as a drinking or washing vessel, but not for both.

5   Small common jar, usually with low neck.

6   *Baqlula* (jug) with a wide neck and oval body, two loop handles attached either to rim or shoulder, a ring base; shallow ribbing on central zones of the body.

7   *Mahlibiah* and *Tus*. A form with elongated shape, two handles at the shoulder, a wide opening with profile rim, and a narrow ring base; used for water, yoghurt, and milk.

8   *Baqlula* (jug) with a wide neck and oval body, one loop handle, and a ring base; shallow ribbings on central zones of the body.

9   *Qidreh* (cooking pot) with two long loop handles, grooved rim to receive a lid, and a very wide flattened base; very shallow ribbing over the whole body.

10 A flower pot, made like a *tabakha* (cooking pot), with two handles attached from rim to the lower part of the shoulder, rounded body, very wide ring base with a hole in the middle, and shallow ribbing.

11 *Zibayya* (also flower pot form); a large bowl with wide profiled rim, plastic knob decoration below rim, rounded walls, and very shallow ribbing.

12 *Zidya* (*mushan* form); small bowl with thickened rim and rounded walls, ribbing on major zones of the body, and ring base.

13 *Zibdiya* with very thick walls, flat thickened base and rounded rims, wide ribbing on inside and outside; a common form in Gaza for making salads in.

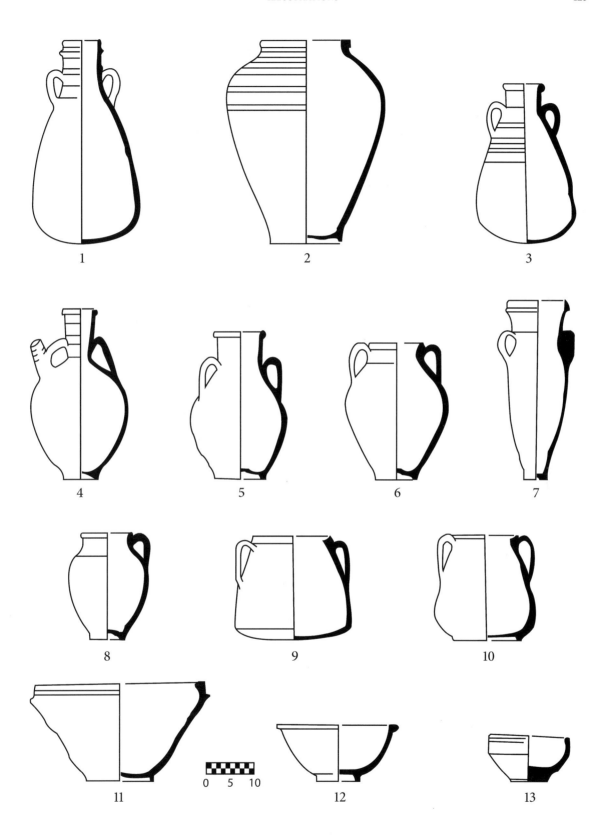

FIG. 4.4 *Drawings of traditional pottery from Gaza in the Birzeit University collection.*

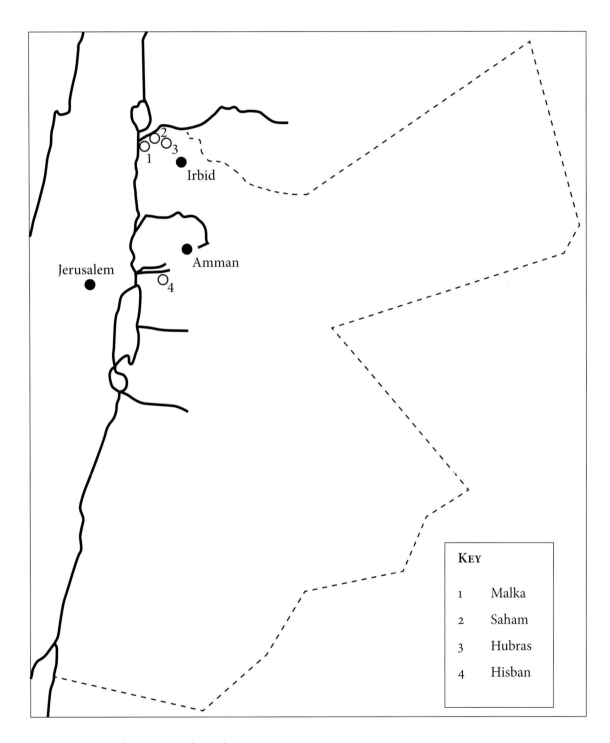

FIG. 5.1 *Map of Jordanian sites in the catalogue.*

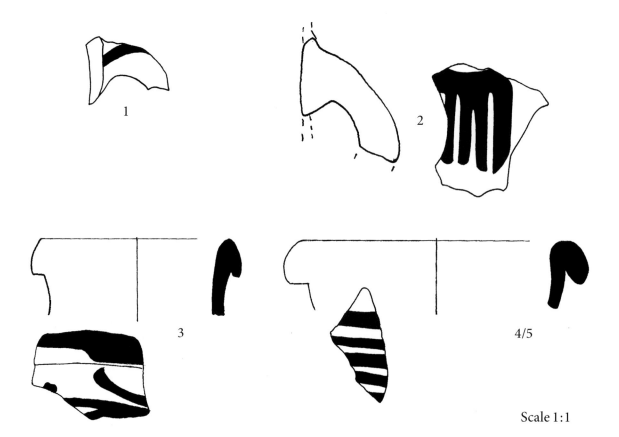

Scale 1:1

NO	REGISTRATION	WARE	FORM	FABRIC	SURFACE	PUBLISHED PARALLELS	DATE
1	HF06-B3-17.23-P50	Rashaya al-Fakhkhar	jug	A	purple-painted lines	(Tibnah) Khammash 1986: 69, lower	Late Ottoman–Mandate
2	HM06-A3-4.6-P153.2	Rashaya al-Fakhkhar	jug	A	spotted yellow glaze, purple painted lines	(Yoqne'am) Avissar 2005: 77, fig. 2.26.6	19th c.
3	SW06-01-02-P72	Rashaya al-Fakhkhar	jar	A	brown painted lines, zigzags of dark green glaze	(sites in Israel) Zevelon 1978: 196, #11	Late Ottoman–Mandate
4	HM06-A6-12.8-P352	Rashaya al-Fakhkhar	jar	B	dark brown paint (rim)	(sites in Israel) Zevelon 1978: 195, nos. 5 and 6	Late Ottoman–Mandate
5	HM06-A6-12.10-P353	Rashaya al-Fakhkhar	jar	B	ribbed and painted body fragment of same vessel as #4		Late Ottoman–Mandate

FIG. 5.2 *Rashaya al-Fakhkhar Ware.*

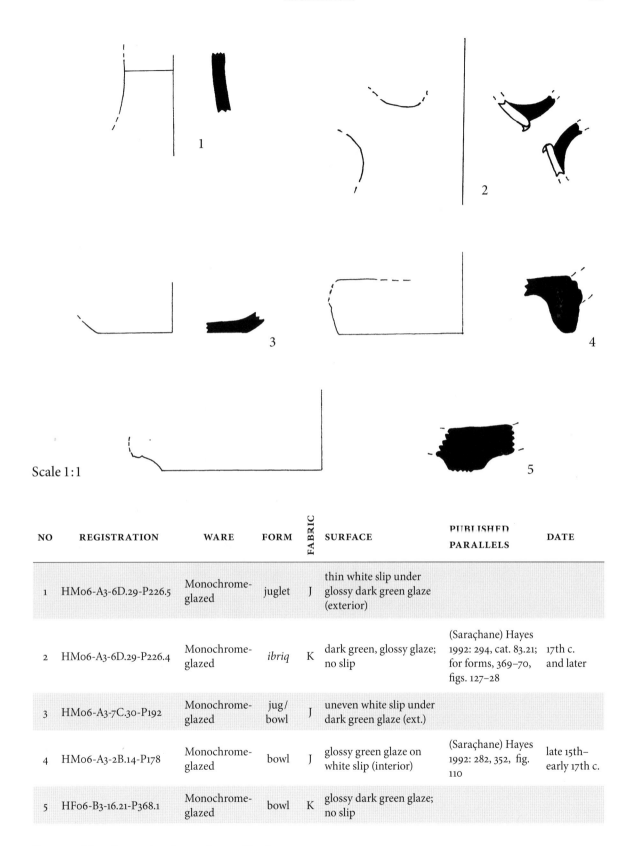

NO	REGISTRATION	WARE	FORM	FABRIC	SURFACE	PUBLISHED PARALLELS	DATE
1	HM06-A3-6D.29-P226.5	Monochrome-glazed	juglet	J	thin white slip under glossy dark green glaze (exterior)		
2	HM06-A3-6D.29-P226.4	Monochrome-glazed	*ibriq*	K	dark green, glossy glaze; no slip	(Saraçhane) Hayes 1992: 294, cat. 83.21; for forms, 369–70, figs. 127–28	17th c. and later
3	HM06-A3-7C.30-P192	Monochrome-glazed	jug/bowl	J	uneven white slip under dark green glaze (ext.)		
4	HM06-A3-2B.14-P178	Monochrome-glazed	bowl	J	glossy green glaze on white slip (interior)	(Saraçhane) Hayes 1992: 282, 352, fig. 110	late 15th–early 17th c.
5	HF06-B3-16.21-P368.1	Monochrome-glazed	bowl	K	glossy dark green glaze; no slip		

FIG. 5.3 *Monochrome-glazed wares: jugs and bowls.*

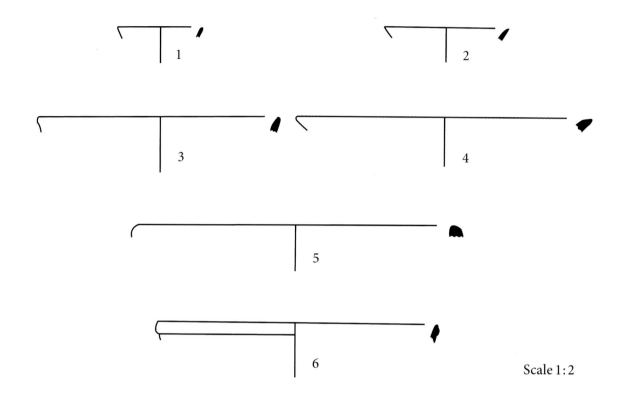

Scale 1 : 2

NO	REGISTRATION	WARE	FORM	FABRIC	SURFACE	PUBLISHED PARALLELS	DATE
1	HM06-A3-1B.13-P176	Monochrome-glazed	cup	J	green glaze over white slip (int. and ext.)		
2	HM06-A3-3.22-P206	Monochrome-glazed	cup	J	glossy green glaze over uneven white slip (int. and over rim)		
3	HF06-B3-11.12-P301	Monochrome-glazed	bowl	J	dark green glaze over white slip (int. and over rim)		
4	HF06-B4-12.12-P356.2	Monochrome-glazed	bowl	J	dark green glaze over white slip		16th c.?
5	HM06-A3-8C.31-P189	Monochrome-glazed	bowl	K	dark green glaze (no slip)		
6	HF06-B3-1.1-P386.4	Monochrome-glazed	bowl	J	bright yellow glaze over white slip		

FIG. 5.4 *Monochrome-glazed wares: cups and bowls.*

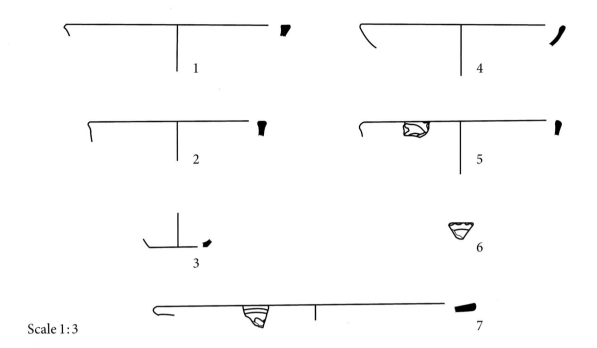

Scale 1 : 3

NO	REGISTRATION	WARE	FORM	FABRIC	SURFACE	PUBLISHED PARALLELS	DATE
1	HF06-B1-17.20-P253	Monochrome-glazed	bowl	J	spotted yellow glaze (int. and over rim)	(Jerusalem, 13–15th c.), Avissar and Stern 2005: 15, fig. 5.7	late 15th–early 16th c.
2	SW06-01-01-P56	Monochrome-glazed	bowl	J	spotted green glaze (int. and over rim)	(Jerusalem, 13–15th c.), Avissar and Stern 2005: 15, fig. 5.7	late 15th–early 16th c.
3	HF06-B3-6.20-P351.3	Monochrome-glazed	bowl/jar	J	spotted yellow-green glaze over white slip (int.)		
4	HF06-B1-3.3-P347.3	Monochrome-glazed	bowl	J	pale yellow glaze over white slip (int. and over rim); green stains as streaks	(Saraçhane), Hayes 1992: 283, 353; fig. 111	late 16th c.
5	HM06-A3-7.10-P161	Slip-painted	bowl	J	spotted yellow-green glaze over white slip-painted "tongues" in int.; green stains		
6	HF06-B3-16.21-P368.3	Sgraffito	dish	K	olive green glaze (no slip; int.); deep sgraffito straight and wavy lines (int.)	(as above)	16th–17th c.; possibly fr. the Troad
7	HM06-A3-Balk3.19-P234.3	Sgraffito	dish	K	dark green glaze (no slip; int. and over rim); deep sgraffito straight and wavy lines (int.)	(Saraçhane, c. 1500–1650, Ware E2): Hayes 1992: 274–845; (Kouklia, mid 16th–mid 17th c.): von Wartburg 2001: 370	16th–17th c.; possibly fr. the Troad

FIG. 5.5 *Miscellaneous glazed wares.*

NO	REGISTRATION	WARE	FORM	FABRIC	SURFACE	PUBLISHED PARALLELS	DATE
1	SW06-03-03-P19	HMGP	jar	F	red-painted zigzags over a pale brown slip (possible Sinjil Ware)	(Shobak, "Ottoman"), Brown 1989: 241, fig. 14.47	19th c. (floor deposit of a house built in 1880s)
2	HF06-B3-5.7-P238	HM	bowl/jar	G	surfaces smoothed		
3	SV06-03-03-P18	HM	store jar	F	slightly burnished ext.; evidence of burning		

Scale 1:1.33

FIG. 5.6 *Handmade wares.*

NO	REGISTRATION	WARE	FORM	FABRIC	SURFACE	PUBLISHED PARALLELS	DATE
1	KM03.1812.41	Gaza Ware	krater	L1		(Giv'at Dani, "Ottoman"), Lazar 1999: fig. 8.2	
2	KM03.1812.55	Gaza Ware	krater	L1			
3	KM03.123.3	Gaza Ware	krater	L1			
4	KM03.121.26	Gaza Ware	krater	L1			
5	KM03.124.31	Gaza Ware	krater	L1		(Giv'at Dani, "Ottoman"), Lazar 1999: fig. 8.5	
6	KM03.123.4	Gaza Ware	krater	L1	traces of dark green glaze in rim (fired with glazed wares)	(Ramat Hanadiv), Boas 2000: pl. 2.1-4	19th c.
7	KM03.1812.43	Gaza Ware	krater	L1			
8	KM03.1812.38	Gaza Ware	krater	L1			
9	KM03.1115.31	Gaza Ware	krater	L1		(Giv'at Dani, "Ottoman"), Lazar 1999: fig. 8.4; (Kerak Plateau, "Ottoman"), Brown 1991: cat. 481, pp. 270, 279	

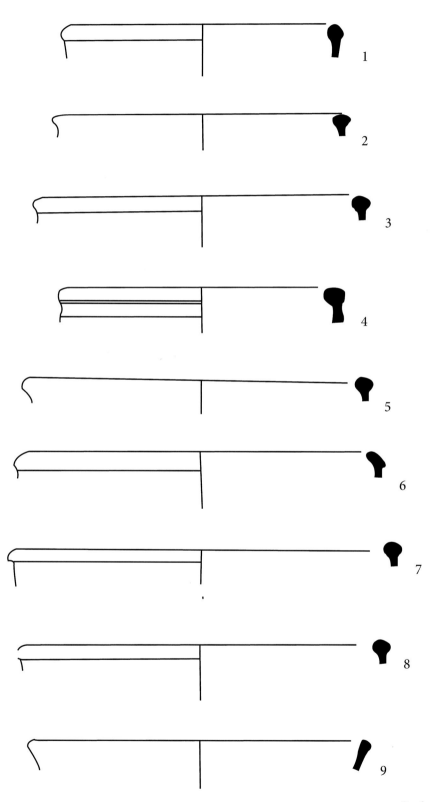

Scale 1 : 4.19

FIG. 5.7 *Gaza Ware: craters.*

NO	REGISTRATION	WARE	FORM	FABRIC	SURFACE	PUBLISHED PARALLELS	DATE
1	HF06-B2-3.4-P381	Gaza Ware derivative	basin	M	deeply combed design (ext.)		Late Ottoman/ Mandate
2	HF06-B2-3.4-P382	Gaza Ware derivative	basin	M	(possibly same vessel as #1)		Late Ottoman/ Mandate
3	HM06-A3-4D.25-P217	Gaza Ware derivative	basin	M	deeply combed lines (ext.)		Late Ottoman/ Mandate
4	SW06-03-4.5-P88	Gaza Ware derivative	large jar/ basin	M	incised wave (ext.)		Late Ottoman/ Mandate
5	HF06-B4-10.10-P259	Gaza Ware derivative	large jar	M	trace of black glaze and incised wave (ext.)	(Umm al-Jimal, "Late Ott/ Man," for glaze and ware, Parker 1998: 216; fig. 158.62	Late Ottoman/ Mandate
6	SW06-03-4B-P122.3	Gaza Ware derivative	jar (handle)	M			Late Ottoman/ Mandate
7	SW06-03-4B-P122.4	Gaza Ware derivative	jar (handle)	M	possible thumb-impression at base of handle	(Sataf, "Ottoman"), Gibson et al 1991: 46, fig. 23.5	Late Ottoman/ Mandate

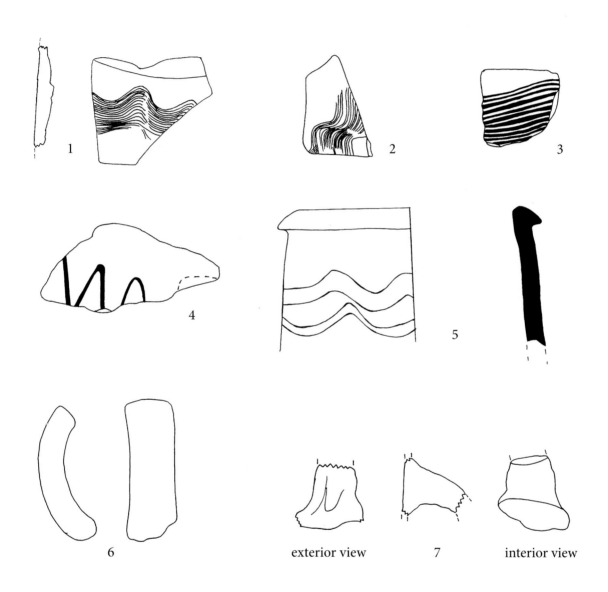

1   2   3

4   5

6   exterior view   7   interior view

Scale 1:1.33

FIG. 5.8   *Gaza Ware derivatives.*

1: R2   2: R4

3: R5

NO	REGISTRATION	WARE	FORM	FABRIC	SURFACE	PUBLISHED PARALLELS	DATE
1	HN06-A3-Balk3.20-R2	*chibouk*	pipe, shank end	R	impressed circles	(Saraçhane), Hayes 1992: 393; (Greece), Robinson 1985: pl. 46	18th c.
2	HM06-A3-8.11-R4	*chibouk*	pipe, bowl	L	vertical incisions	(Tell Jezreel), Simpson 2002: 163, fig. 3.19	second half 19th c.
3	HF06-B4-11.11-R5	*chibouk*	pipe, bowl	M	impressed ferns in vertical columns	(Greece), Robinson 1985: 190, C. 115–6, pl. 58; 177, C.32	18th/19th c.

FIG. 5.9   Chibouks *(tobacco pipes), NJP.*

1: R6

2: R10

3: R11

NO	REGISTRATION	WARE	FORM	FABRIC	SURFACE	PUBLISHED PARALLELS	DATE
1	HM06-A3-1B.13-R6	*chibouk*	pipe, rounded bowl	O	impressed woven pattern	(Greece), Robinson 1985: 185, C82, pl. 55	19th c.
2	HF06-B4-7.7-R10	*chibouk*	pipe, bowl	Q	impressed circles	(Saraçhane), Hayes 1992: 393; (Greece), Robinson 1985: 168	17th/18th c. (Turkish)
3	HM06-A3-6D.29-R11	*chibouk*	pipe, gourd-shaped bowl	P	burnished	(Yoqne'am), Avissar 2005: 84, fig. 4.1	18th c.

FIG. 5.10 Chibouks *(tobacco pipes), NJP.*

1: R12

2: R31

NO	REGISTRATION	WARE	FORM	FABRIC	SURFACE	PUBLISHED PARALLELS	DATE
1	HM06-B4-2.12-R12	*chibouk*	pipe, shank end	P	wreath, rayed dots, and scallops	(Kerameikos), Robinson 1983: 276, #23, pl. 53	early 19th c.
2	HF06-B5-5.1-R31	*chibouk*	pipe, shank	O	triangular notches at end	(Saraçhane, for fabric), Hayes 1992: 383; (Greece, for forms), Robinson 1985: 182, C63 and 187, C95, pl. 56	18th– early 19th c.

FIG. 5.11 Chibouks *(tobacco pipes)*, NJP.

1: R35

2: R37

3: R42

NO	REGISTRATION	WARE	FORM	FABRIC	SURFACE	PUBLISHED PARALLELS	DATE
1	HF06-B2-5.4-R35	*chibouk*	pipe, shank and bowl end	L	heavily burnished		early 19th c.
2	HM06-A3-7.10-R37	*chibouk*	pipe, bowl rim	P		(Saraçhane, for fabric), Hayes 1992: 393	18th c.?
3	HM06-A3-Balk3.20-R42	*chibouk*	pipe, rim of a disk-based bowl	O	red-slipped and burnished	(Tell Jezreel), Simpson 2002: 165; (Greece), Robinson 1985: 188, C104, pl. 57	Mid–late 19th c.

FIG. 5.12 Chibouks *(tobacco pipes)*, NJP.

NO	REGISTRATION	WARE	FORM	FABRIC	SURFACE	PUBLISHED PARALLELS	DATE
1	HM06-A3-9C.32-P193	Stoneware (Sponge Ware)	plate	N	white enamel glaze with overglaze-painted dark pink sponge-applied pattern (int.)		19th c. (Europe)
2	HM06-A3-Balk3.19-P234.1	Stoneware	jar	N	white enamel glaze (int.); uneven sky blue enamel glaze (ext.)		18th c. (Europe)
3	HM06-A3-6D.29-P224	Stoneware (Staffordshire Creamware)	jar/ pitcher	N	white enamel glaze (int.); cobalt blue enamel glaze (ext.)	(Staffordshire "Little Blue," 18th c.), Hildyard 1999: 75, lower right	18th c. (British)
4	HF06-B4-7.7-P403	Stoneware (Staffordshire Blue-and-White)	cup	N	blue and white floral design painted on white enamel glaze (int.)		18th c. (British)

FIG. 5.13 *European stonewares.*

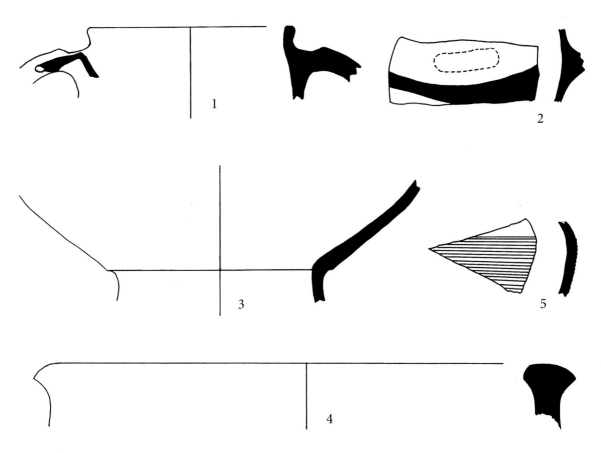

Scale 2:1

NO	REGISTRATION	WARE	FORM	FABRIC	SURFACE	PUBLISHED PARALLELS	DATE
1	C108.8.7	Rashaya al-Fukhar	jar	C	reddish brown painted line along side of handle; tripod scar and trace of glaze (fired with glazed vessels)		first half 20th c.
2	M7.20.13	20th-Century Painted Ware	jar	D	reddish brown painted lines		first half 20th c.
3	M7.20.9	20th-Century Painted Ware	store jar	D	reddish brown painted lines		first half 20th c.
4	M7.2.1	Gaza Ware	basin	L1		(Malka), Walker 2005: 96, fig. 18	19th c.
5	O8.8.9	Gaza Ware derivative	jar/basin	M	coarsely ribbed and combed (ext.)		

FIG. 5.14 *Miscellaneous wares, turn of the 20th century.*

NO	REGISTRATION	WARE	FORM	FABRIC	SURFACE	PUBLISHED PARALLELS	DATE
1	M6.14.1	*chibouk*	pipe, shank	L1	crescent stamp	(Belmont Castle, 18th c.), Simpson 2000: 154, fig. 13.3.43; (Yoqne'am, second half 18th c.), Avissar 2005: 85, fig. 4.2.13–17	18th c.
2	O5.25.2	*chibouk*	pipe, shank	O	red-slipped and burnished	(Tell Jezreel), Simpson 2002: 161, fig. 1.5; (Belmont Castle), Simpson 2000: 148, fig. 13.1.4, 9; (Yoqne'am), Avissar 1996: 199, cat.6	18th–early 19th c.; likely Palestinian (Jerusalem)
3	O9.5.1	*chibouk*	pipe, bowl	O	incised lines and limited rouletting	(Tell Jezreel), Simpson 2002: 161, fig. 1.5; (Belmont Castle), Simpson 2000: 154, fig. 13.3.64; (Yoqne'am), Avissar 1996: 199, cat. 6	18th–early 19th c.; likely Palestinian (Jerusalem)
4	H01.AN.09	*chibouk*	pipe, shank end	O	incised register of vertical lines with circular finials, burnished	(Belmont Castle), Simpson 2000: 156, fig. 13.4.94	19th c.; possibly Syrian or Palestinian
5	H01.AN.03	*chibouk*	pipe, shank end	O	register of vertical, six-sided angular petals	(Belmont Castle), Simpson 2000: 156, fig. 13.4.98	late 19th c.; possibly Syrian or Palestinian

FIG. 5.15 Chibouks *(tobacco pipes), Hisban.*

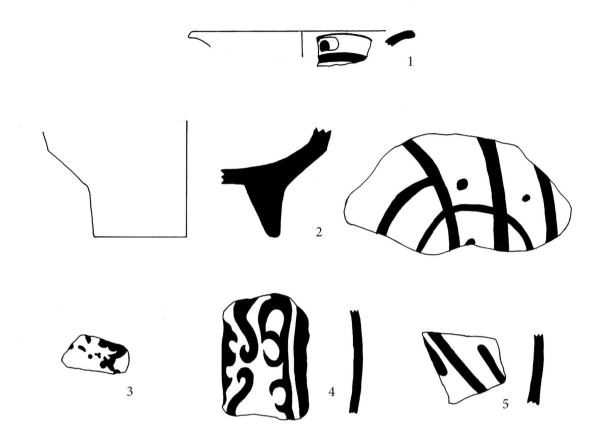

NO	REGISTRATION	WARE	FORM	FABRIC	SURFACE	PUBLISHED PARALLELS	DATE
1	C107.10.4	Iznik or Iznik derivative	bowl	E	blue and red pained under turquoise glaze	(Saraçhane, late 15th c., for form), Hayes 1992: 257, fig. 97.4	16th c.; Iznik or Syria
2	M7.O.A.1	Iznik derivative	large bowl	E	abstract lines and circles in underglaze blue		16th–17th c.; possibly Syria
3	O8.8.1	Iznik derivative	jar?	E	polychrome (red, yellow, and blue) underglaze-painted dots and florals		16th–17th c.; possibly Syria
4	O5.14.2	Iznik derivative	dish/ large bowl	E	blue-painted tendrils and dots (int.); wavy lines (ext.)		
5	O10.8.2	Iznik derivative	dish	E	blue-painted lines and dots (int.)		

FIG. 5.16 *Iznik Ware and derivatives.*

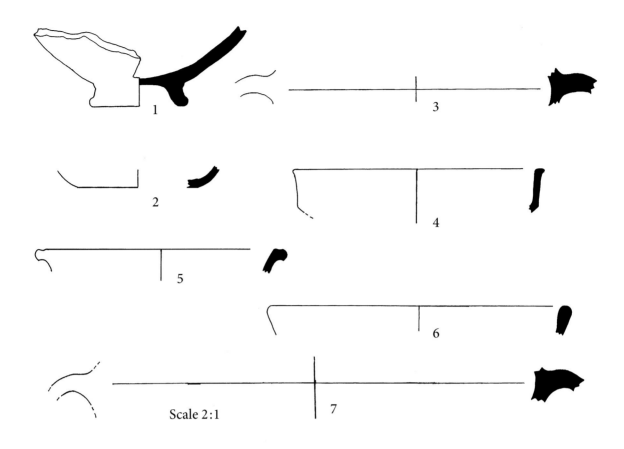

Scale 2:1

NO	REGISTR.	WARE	FORM	FABRIC	SURFACE	PUBLISHED PARALLELS	DATE
1	Q1.32.1	Monochrome-glazed	bowl	K	green glaze (no slip)	(Saraçhane, 15th to 16th c., for form), Hayes 1992: 355, fig. 113.73.51	Early Ottoman
2	Q4.0.1	Monochrome-glazed	bowl	J	mustard yellow glaze over thin white slip (int. and ext.)		
3	C106.8.1	Monochrome-glazed	large jar	K	mustard yellow glaze, no slip (int.)		
4	O5.1.4	Monochrome-glazed	bowl	K	clear or green glaze (no slip)		
5	C102.54.1	Monochrome-glazed	bowl	K	mustard yellow glaze, no slip (int.)		
6	C108.4.1	Monochrome-glazed	bowl	J	uneven pink slip under glossy olive glaze (int. and ext.)		
7	C107.4.2	Monochrome-glazed	large jar	K	mustard yellow glaze, no slip (int.)		

FIG. 5.17 *Monochrome-glazed wares.*

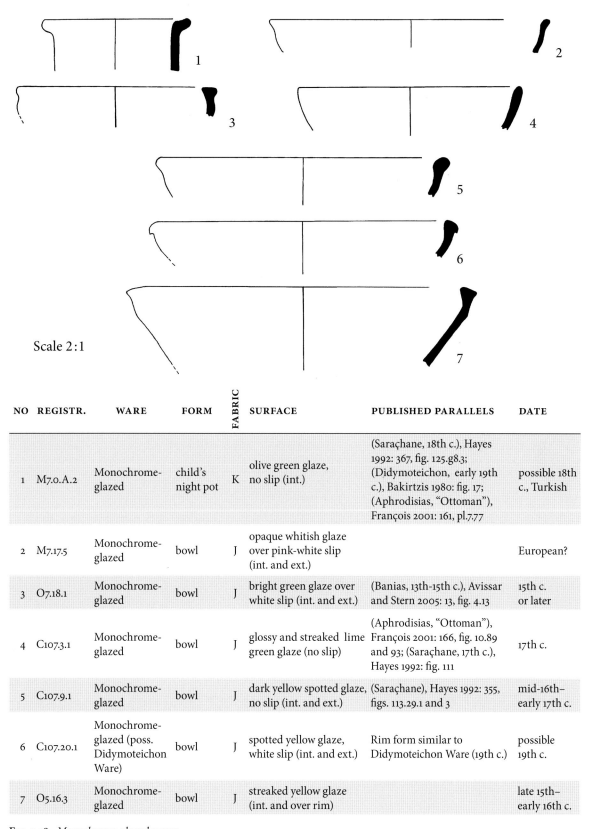

Scale 2:1

NO	REGISTR.	WARE	FORM	FABRIC	SURFACE	PUBLISHED PARALLELS	DATE
1	M7.0.A.2	Monochrome-glazed	child's night pot	K	olive green glaze, no slip (int.)	(Saraçhane, 18th c.), Hayes 1992: 367, fig. 125.g8.3; (Didymoteichon, early 19th c.), Bakirtzis 1980: fig. 17; (Aphrodisias, "Ottoman"), François 2001: 161, pl.7.77	possible 18th c., Turkish
2	M7.17.5	Monochrome-glazed	bowl	J	opaque whitish glaze over pink-white slip (int. and ext.)		European?
3	O7.18.1	Monochrome-glazed	bowl	J	bright green glaze over white slip (int. and ext.)	(Banias, 13th-15th c.), Avissar and Stern 2005: 13, fig. 4.13	15th c. or later
4	C107.3.1	Monochrome-glazed	bowl	J	glossy and streaked lime green glaze (no slip)	(Aphrodisias, "Ottoman"), François 2001: 166, fig. 10.89 and 93; (Saraçhane, 17th c.), Hayes 1992: fig. 111	17th c.
5	C107.9.1	Monochrome-glazed	bowl	J	dark yellow spotted glaze, no slip (int. and ext.)	(Saraçhane), Hayes 1992: 355, figs. 113.29.1 and 3	mid-16th–early 17th c.
6	C107.20.1	Monochrome-glazed (poss. Didymoteichon Ware)	bowl	J	spotted yellow glaze, white slip (int. and ext.)	Rim form similar to Didymoteichon Ware (19th c.)	possible 19th c.
7	O5.16.3	Monochrome-glazed	bowl	J	streaked yellow glaze (int. and over rim)		late 15th–early 16th c.

FIG. 5.18 *Monochrome-glazed wares.*

NO	REGISTR.	WARE	FORM	FABRIC	SURFACE	PUBLISHED PARALLELS	DATE
1	L1.2.1	Slip-painted	dish	I	slip-painted lines under dark, glossy green glaze	(Iznik, mid-15th c., for ware), Hayes 1992: 238; (Saraçhane, 16th c., for form), Hayes 1992: 349, fig. 107.7.1–3; (Yoqne'am, "Ottoman"), Avissar 2005: 75; (Iznik, 14th c. on, for design), Aslanapa 1971: 214	15th–16th c., Turkish import
2	O8.2.1	Slip-painted (related to Didymoteichon Ware?)	bowl	I	yellow glaze over thickly applied and wide slip-painted lines	(Aphrodisias, 15th–16th c.), François 2001: 168, pl. 12.12, 124, 126; (Yoqne'am, "Ottoman"), Avissar 2005: 75, fig. 2.25; (Saraçhane, late 19th c.), Hayes 1992: 386, fig. 144.17; (Acre, 18th–19th c.), Edelstein and Avissar 1997: 131, fig. 1.8	19th c.
3	O5.4.1	Slip-painted	bowl		slip-painted floral arabesque under a pale yellow glaze	(Iznik), Aslanapa 1971: 214	15th–16th c.; likely Iznik import
4	O7.10.3	Slip-painted	bowl	I	green glaze over slip-painted dotted medallion	(Iznik), Aslanapa 1971: 214	15th c.; possible Iznik import
5	Q1.12.1	Slip-painted (possible Didymoteichon Ware)	bowl	I	yellow glaze over wide, slip-painted lines	Rim form as in Didymoteichon Ware (12th–19th c.), François 1995	19th c.; poss. Thrace
6	O8.8.4	Slip-painted	bowl	H	green glaze over wide, slip-painted criss-crossed design	(Troy, for form), Hayes 1995: 77, fig. 4.58	15th c.; likely Anatolia
7	O6.10.1	Slip-painted	bowl	H	dark green glaze over white-painted lines	(Aphrodisias), François 2001: 168, pl. 12: 123–24, 126, 129	16th c.; Turkish import
8	O10.3.1	Slip-painted	bowl	H	(as #4)	(as above, #4)	16th c.; Turkish import

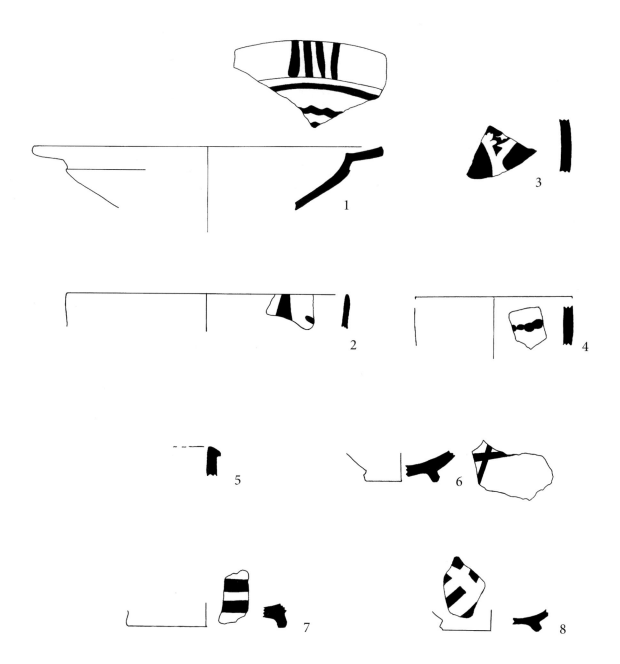

Scale 2:1

FIG. 5.19 *Slip-painted wares: dishes and bowls.*

NO	REGISTR.	WARE	FORM	FABRIC	SURFACE	PUBLISHED PARALLELS	DATE
1	O8.6.1	HMGP	juglet	F	yellow-pink slip, red-painted designs (recalls Mamluk geometric patterns)		Ottoman
2	C107.10.1	HMGP	jug	F	coarse red-painted triangles and dots		Late Ottoman–Mandate
3	M7.6.2	HMGP	large jar	F	self-slip and vertical red-brown painted stripes		Late Ottoman–Mandate
4	O5.1.3	HMGP (possible Sinjil Ware)	jar	F	red-painted crossed lines on pale yellow-pink slip	(Dhra' al-Khan, post-16th c.), Kareem 2000: 181, fig. 47; (Sinjil, early 20th c.), Amiry and Tamari 1989: 45, lower left	Late Ottoman
5	O5.1.2	HMGP (possible Sinjil Ware)	jar	F	(as above)	(as above)	Late Ottoman
6	O6.12.2	HMGP	bowl	F	red-painted design (int.)		
7	C106.4.1	HMGP	large bowl	F	trace of red-painted wavy line on rim		Late Ottoman–Mandate
8	M7.20.1	HMGP	basin	F	trace of wavy red-painted line on rim		
9	Q4.6.1	HMGP	basin	F	thumb-impressed rope molding, pink slip, burnished int., red paint on rim	(Kufranja and Satana, early 20th c.), Mershen 1985: 82, figs. 2 and 86, fig. 18; (Sinjil, 1930s), Crowfoot 1932: pl. 1, fig. 5; (Sataf, "Ottoman"), Gibson et al. 1991: 44, fig. 21.3; (Shobak Castle, "Ottoman"), Brown 1988: 241, fig. 14.54	late 19th–early 20th c.
10	C106.8.2	HMGP	basin	F	(as above), red-painted wavy line on rim	(as above)	late 19th–early 20th c.

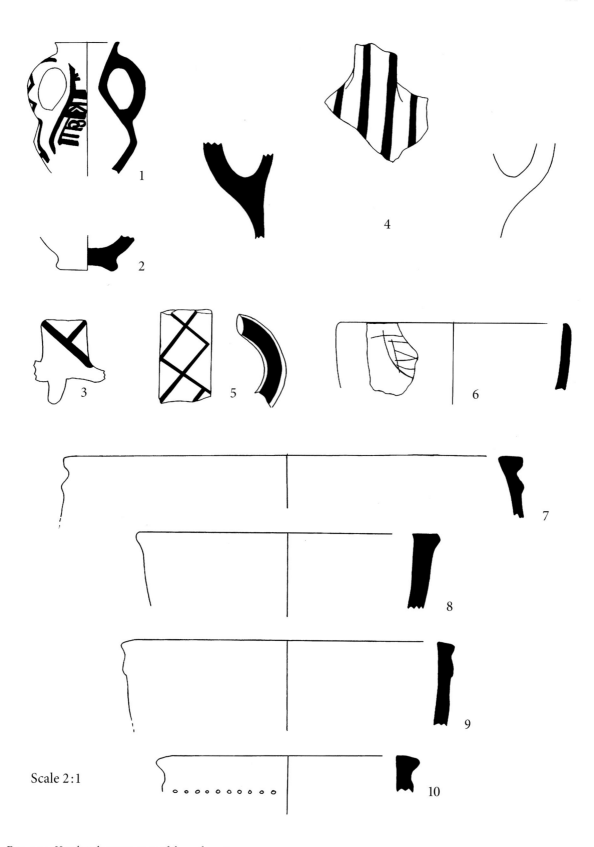

Scale 2:1

FIG. 5.20 *Handmade wares, turn of the 20th century.*

NO	REGISTR.	WARE	FORM	FABRIC	SURFACE	PUBLISHED PARALLELS	DATE
1	M4.119.1	Handmade	jar/ cook pot	G	white slip		
2	O7.5.1	Handmade	water jar	F		(Umm Qeis, 1940s), Parker 1998: 216, fig. 158.67	Mandate
3	O8.5.1	Handmade	cook pot	F		(Sinjil, 1930s), Crowfoot 1932: pl. III, fig. 10)	Late Ottoman–Mandate
4	O10.7.1	Handmade	basin	F	wreath-shaped appliqué	Milwright 1999: 105, no.5	likely late Mamluk–early Ottoman
5	O5.1.1	Handmade	bowl	F		(Umm al-Jimal, pre-1920), Parker 1998: 216, fig. 158.67	Late Ottoman–Mandate
6	O10.2.2	Handmade	bowl	F	pale slip (ext.), formed over a cloth mold (textile impressions inside)	(Sataf, "Ottoman"), Gibson et al. 1991: 44, figs. 21.2 and 9	
7	O6.2.1	Handmade	cook pot/ basin	F	thumb-impressed rope molding (ext.); slight burnishing (int.)	(Sataf, "Ottoman," for form), Gibson et al. 1991: 44, fig. 21.3	
8	M7.25.1	Handmade	basin	F	plaster-like slip (ext.); burnished int.		Late Ottoman–Mandate
9	O7.9.1	Handmade	basin	G			Late Ottoman–Mandate

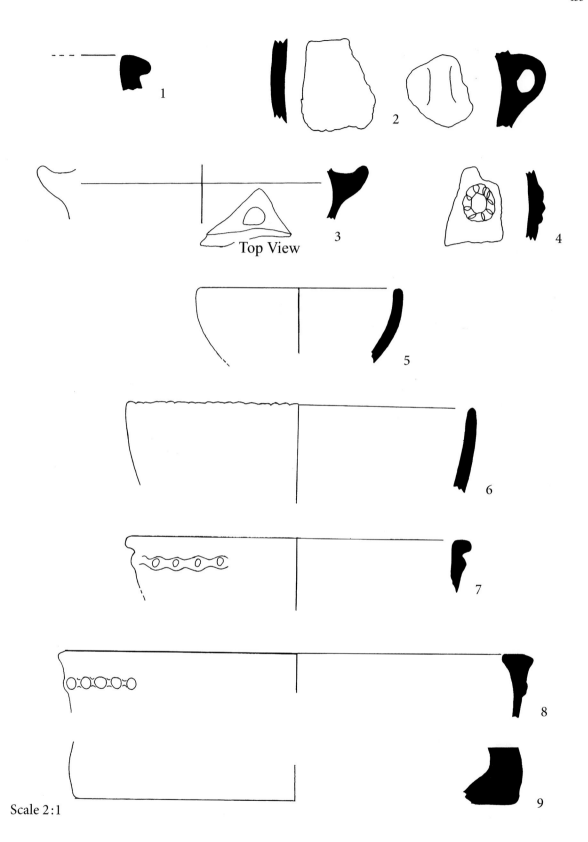

Top View

Scale 2:1

FIG. 5.21 *Handmade wares, late Ottoman to mid-20th century.*

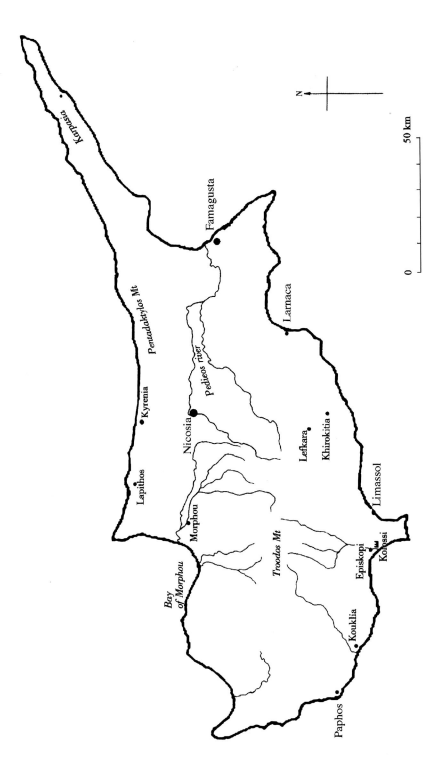

FIG. 6.1   *Map of Cyprus with the location of Paphos and other sites mentioned in the text.*

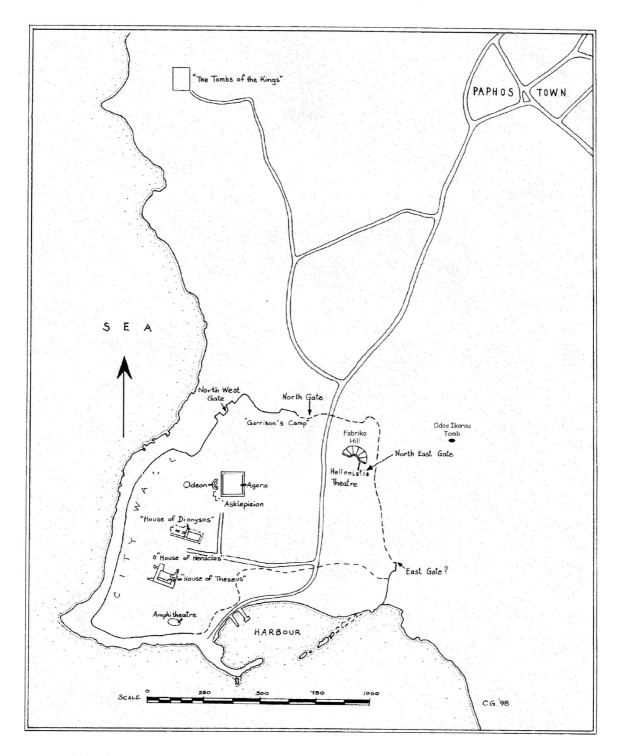

FIG. 6.2   *Plan of Paphos with the location of Fabrika and other sites mentioned in the text.*

FIG. 6.3   *Paphos, Fabrika. Walls of the Venetian/Ottoman period.*

FIG. 6.4 →   *Common shapes of the coarse wares of the medieval and post-medieval periods.*

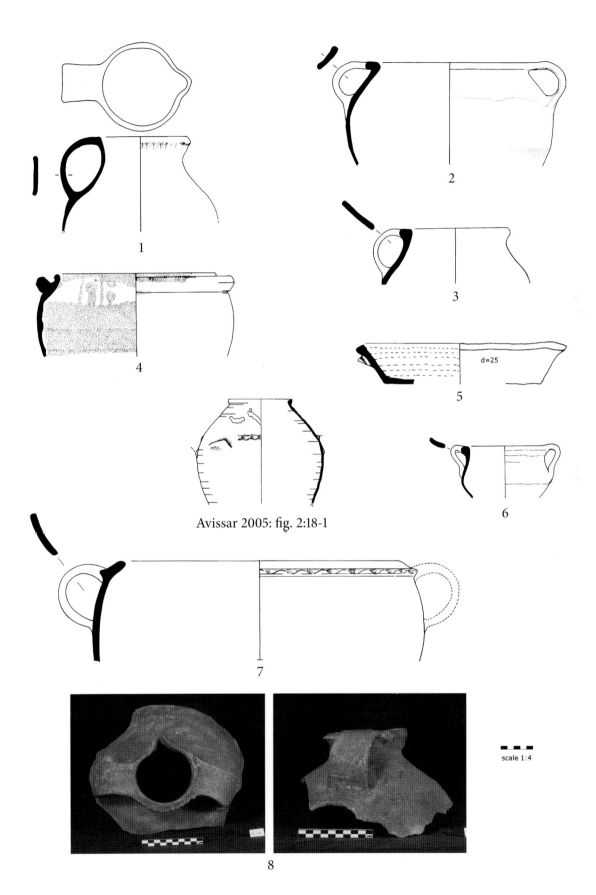

Avissar 2005: fig. 2:18-1

scale 1:4

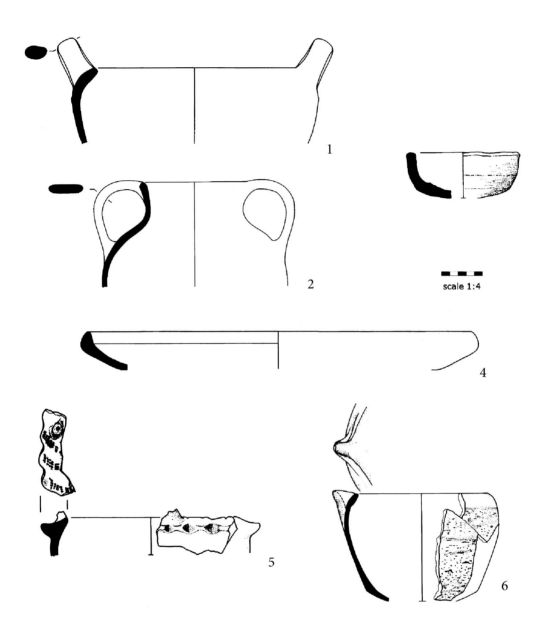

FIG. 6.5 *Common shapes of the coarse wares of the medieval and post-medieval periods.*

Fig. 6.6 *Common shapes of the coarse wares of the medieval and post-medieval periods.*

scale 1:4

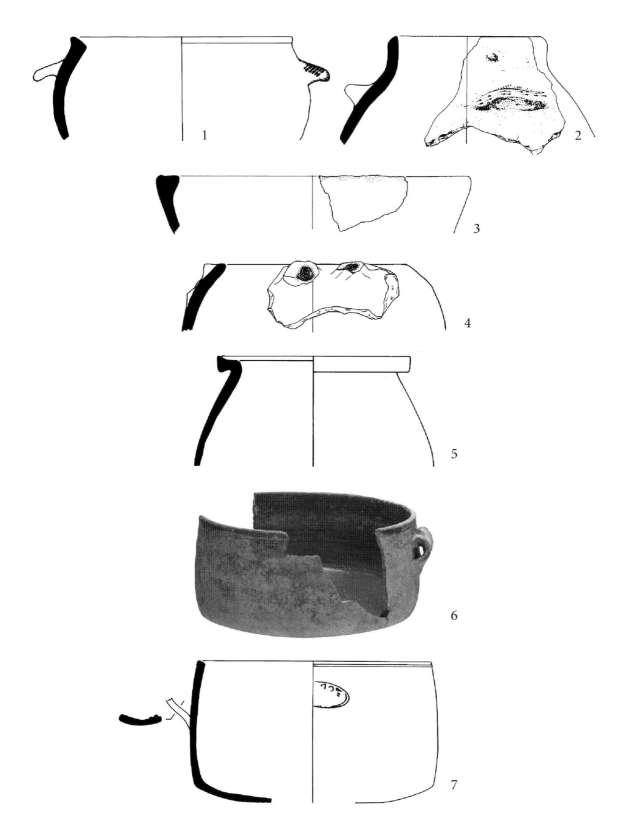

FIG. 6.7   *Common shapes of the coarse wares of the medieval and post-medieval periods.*

FIG. 6.8   *Modern kiln in Phini.*

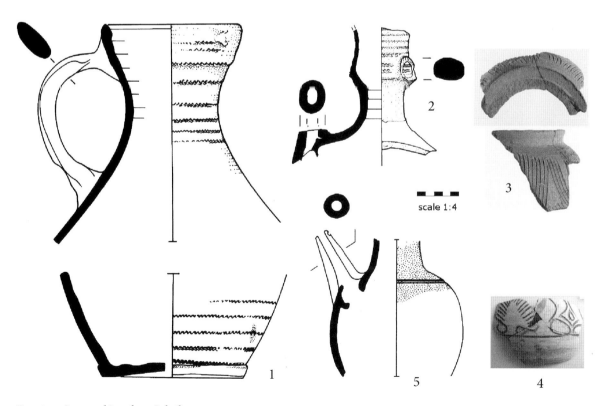

FIG. 6.9   *Imported jugs from Fabrika.*

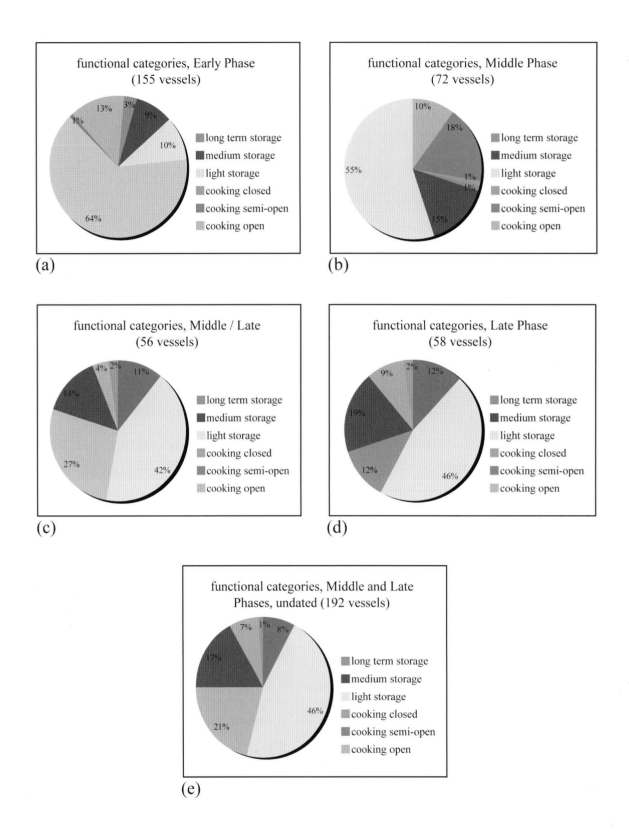

FIG. 6.10 *Proportional representation of the functional categories in the three chronological phases at Fabrika.*